NEW UNDERSTANDINGS OF HUMAN BEHAVIOR

Non-Freudian Readings from Professional Journals, 1960-1968

NEW UNDERSTANDINGS

Non-Freudian Readings from

Edited, with Commentary, Introduction and Conclusion

OF HUMAN BEHAVIOR

Professional Journals, 1960-1968

by HAROLD D. WERNER, ACSW

ASSOCIATION PRESS / NEW YORK

NEW UNDERSTANDINGS OF HUMAN BEHAVIOR
Non-Freudian Readings from Professional Journals, 1960-1968

Copyright © 1970 by
Association Press
291 Broadway, New York N.Y. 10007

Standard Book Number: 8096-1723-4

Library of Congress Catalog Card Number: 69-18848

PRINTED IN THE UNITED STATES OF AMERICA

For Hilda, Sophie, April and Ken

Psychology is something like a ship drifting in a storm. It needs to anchor to a solid base. Psychological theory might be anchored to the physical world, to physiological processes, to the sociocultural environment, to individual conscious experience. Perhaps the ship would be more secure with several anchors.

—PAUL THOMAS YOUNG, PH.D., D.SC.*

Emeritus Professor of Psychology
The University of Illinois, Urbana

* Paul Thomas Young, *Motivation and Emotion: A Survey of the Determinants of Human and Animal Activity* (New York: John Wiley, 1961), p. 599.

Contents

"The Neurology of Behavior: Its Application to Human Violence." *Vernon H. Mark, M.D.*

"A Study of Political Assassinations."
G. Wilse Robinson, M.D.

"Toward a Theory of Hypnosis: Posthypnotic Behavior."
Theodore X. Barber, Ph.D.

"The Dream Process." *Montague Ullman, M.D.*

"A Critique of Freud's Theory of Infantile Sexuality."
Paul Chodoff, M.D.

"The Social Meaning of the Oedipus Myth." *Frances Atkins*

Introduction

Dr. Robert Coles [1] states that in the mid-1920's Sigmund Freud's work was "ignored and despised all over the world—except in this country, where puritanical revulsion had given way rather quietly to a surprisingly eager embrace." If we are interested in the reason for this eager embrace, it may be helpful to note Nathan Edward Cohen's [2] comment that "the impact of World War I and the conservative social climate of the period after it was conducive to a refocusing of attention on the individual and on methods for dealing with his personal problems, and away from the broader societal factors." It is a matter of history now that, at the end of World War I, the prevailing mood in the United States was that our society was the best of all possible worlds. There was fierce intolerance of social criticism. With this in mind, one could build a good case for the notion that Freudian theory found a ready acceptance here partly because of its premise that emotional disturbance stems from intra-psychic conflict rather than from society's shortcomings.

Whatever the reason or reasons, the fact remains that psychoanalytic explanations of the nature of man, the origins of his behavior, and the causes of his emotional difficulties dominated the American scene for the next thirty years. While Pavlov's conditioned reflex, Watson's behaviorism, and the views of Adler and Rank had some impact during this span of time, Freudian psychology became the Establishment. Starting with the East Coast and gradually moving westward, the conviction took hold that the psychoanalytic interpretation of man and his behavior was the definitive one.

In the thirties and forties, Horney, Fromm, Sullivan and others developed their own variations of psychoanalysis. They emphasized man's need to satisfy culturally-determined rather than instinctual drives. They stressed the ego rather than the id and superego. They focused on the present situation rather than early experiences. They were more interested in the individual's striving for total fulfillment than in his sex drive. However, these neo-Freudians still kept some ties with Freud through their acceptance and utilization of his concept of the unconscious. This concept of the unconscious as the primary source of behavior, motivation and emotions is the essential core of Freudian doctrine, and it was not fundamentally challenged on a large scale until a dozen years ago.

This book is a collection of readings from professional journal articles which take the view that the determinants of behavior, motivation and emotions are in consciousness, or that human beings can be understood without recourse to a concept of the unconscious. These articles, published from 1960 to 1968, are part of the great outpouring of books and papers which began in the mid-1950's and continues today to provide a variety of new approaches to the understanding of man. Since Freud came upon the American scene, no period of time has produced the volume of non-psychoanalytic writing which has been published in the last decade. I have supplied brief introductions and commentaries on the readings to help place them in proper perspective.

At this point, the reader is entitled to some explanation of the word "new" as it appears in the name of this volume. The word "new" was felt to be an appropriate description of the material which follows because these writings depart from the Establishment. Therefore, they are "new" in the sense that they invite us to look at man from points of view different from those proposed by the Establishment. Actually, some of these writings are revivals or restatements of previously established psychological theories, while others present recent extensions and elaborations of already known concepts. On the other hand, some offer interpretations of human behavior which are largely original. I have taken the liberty of classifying all of them as "new" to point up the fact that their publication in the sixties makes them part of the fresh current that is running through American psychological thought. Regardless of whether these ideas had their beginnings in 1955 or 1915, their iteration or reiteration at this time makes them part of the new ideological climate.

These readings are intended for students preparing for psychology, social work, pastoral counseling, school guidance, teaching, medicine, psychiatry and nursing. They are also intended for professionals in these fields and for the college-educated or self-educated layman with a special interest in human psychology. For all categories of readers, the aim of the book is to introduce them to the growing body of non-Freudian ideas about the nature of man, his behavior, and his emotional disturbances. For the most part, the psychoses have been omitted.

The material is grouped according to subject matter. Each chapter contains readings that deal with a particular topic. The Table of Contents lists under each chapter heading the titles and authors of all the journal articles from which excerpts have been drawn and used in that chapter. The complete reference appears in the text.

The reader will observe that the texts of journal articles do not appear until Chapter 2. I came to the conclusion that new concepts about the nature of man could be presented more concisely and in greater variety through brief summaries of recent books. Accordingly, Chapter 1 ("The Nature of Man") sketches the main ideas in seven non-Freudian books published since 1956, and then attempts to synthesize them into a unified view.

The final chapter ("Practical Applications of Our New Understandings") takes up the use of ideas which emerge from this book in the counseling and treatment of people who seek professional help for personal problems. The focus is on individual treatment techniques for the sake of simplicity and clarity. However, these new theoretical concepts can also be applied in group processes. I have confined the discussion to psychological helping techniques, while recognizing fully the supreme importance in human behavior of physiological factors such as general health, constitutional endowment, brain damage, and aberrations of chemistry. We obviously cannot forget that behavior results from the functioning of a brain and nervous system, and that sometimes behavior can be modified through the intervention of medication or other medical therapies. However, since physiological treatment is outside the competence of the editor as a social worker, it will not be discussed here and the reader is referred elsewhere for information about it. At the same time, it is a basic assumption of this book that the physiology of an individual plays a part in every behavioral situation.

I wish to express my deep appreciation to the following authors for permission to reproduce, in whole or in part, the professional journal articles which appear in this volume: Gustav Ichheiser, Ph.D.; Demetrios Papageorgis, Ph.D.; Leon Salzman, M.D.; Richard C. LaBarba, Ph.D.; Irving Markowitz, M.D.; Richard E. Gordon, M.D., Ph.D.; Marcia B. Singer, and Katherine K. Gordon; Ronald Leifer, M.D.; Aaron T. Beck, M.D.; Kurt A. Adler, M.D.; Herbert H. Krauss, Ph.D.; Theodore R. Sarbin, Ph.D.; Harold M. Mosak, Ph.D.; William M. Easson, M.B., Ch.B., and Richard M. Steinhilber, M.D.; Nathan Blackman, M.D., James M. A. Weiss, M.D., and Joseph W. Lamberti, M.D.; Vernon H. Mark, M.D.; G. Wilse Robinson, M.D.; Theodore X. Barber, Ph.D.; Montague Ullman, M.D.; Paul Chodoff, M.D.; Frances Atkins.

Mrs. Lee G. Robbins was most gracious in giving me permission to reprint portions of articles published in *Psychotherapy* by her late husband, Bernard S. Robbins, M.D.

Frederick C. Thorne, Ph.D., gave his approval in the dual

role of author and editor of the *Journal of Clinical Psychology*.

Heinz L. Ansbacher, Ph.D., was exceedingly helpful in his double role, giving various permissions as author and editor of the *Journal of Individual Psychology*. In the latter capacity, he generously consented to the use of nine articles from that journal.

John H. Talbott, M.D., editor of the *Journal of the American Medical Association*, gave his kind permission for the use of seven articles from the *Archives of General Psychiatry*, which is published by the Association.

Richard L. Sigerson, editor and publisher of *Medical Opinion & Review*, approved the reprinting of the two articles by Doctors Markowitz and Mark.

Torrence J. Collier, Jr., M.D., M.P.H., granted permission for reproducing a section of an advertisement by Schering Corporation, for which he is director of medical liaison.

Dr. Ansbacher's article in *Social Casework* was used by permission of its editor, Elinor P. Zaki.

Evelyn S. Myers, managing editor, granted permission on behalf of the *American Journal of Psychiatry* to reprint two articles, and was most helpful in other ways. The article by Dr. Robinson is Copyright 1965, the American Psychiatric Association.

Stanley Lesse, M.D., editor of the *American Journal of Psychotherapy*, authorized the use of Dr. Ullman's article on dreams.

I am grateful to these book publishers for permission to quote passages from their books: W.B. Saunders Company, Philadelphia; Oxford University Press, London; and Basic Books, Inc., New York. Lawrence C. Kolb, M.D., author of the first of these volumes, *Noyes' Modern Clinical Psychiatry*, extended his personal approval as well, which I acknowledge with appreciation.

The *Saturday Review* kindly agreed to the Charles Frankel quotation from their copyrighted article which appears in Chapter 6.

I am indebted to Donald G. Livingston, Ph.D., corporate director, organization development, Curtiss-Wright Corporation, for his valuable comment on occupational stresses which became part of Chapter 8; to Leonard Cammer, M.D., who brought to my attention one of the two articles by him on conditioning theory which are summarized in Chapter 7; and to Paul Thomas Young, Ph.D., D.Sc., who has allowed me to use the meaningful words which appear at the head of this book.

I record with gratitude the kindnesses of Robert M. Milford, serials librarian, and the staff of the periodical department, Friendship Library, Fairleigh Dickinson University, Florham-Madison Campus, Madison, New Jersey.

Finally, my thanks are due to Miss Julia Bolcar and Mrs. Claire Mueller, secretaries par excellence.

The readings in Chapters 2 through 7 are verbatim reproductions of the original texts of journal articles in all respects except the following: references and footnotes are omitted, as are subheadings with two exceptions. However, most articles are not reproduced in their entirety. This is indicated in each case in the reading itself and by the page numbers given in the footnote.

It is suggested that the entire book be read first in sequence. Although the individual readings can be studied separately and in any order, the book as a whole has an overall plan and internal continuity, with each chapter presenting premises and material which prepare the reader for subsequent chapters.

REFERENCES

1. *New York Times* Book Review (October 8, 1967), p. 8.
2. Nathan Cohen, *Social Work in the American Tradition* (New York: Holt, Rinehart and Winston, 1958), p. 129.

NEW UNDERSTANDINGS OF HUMAN BEHAVIOR

Non-Freudian Readings from Professional Journals, 1960-1968

1

The Nature of Man

Freud and the Human Psyche

Sigmund Freud believed each human being was born with selfish, aggressive impulses toward his fellows. As he saw it, cooperation with others develops only when one represses his primary urges under the pressure of society, thus distorting what he really is. Freud contended that all individuals had to pass through a situation in which they struggled with their sexual attraction to the opposite parent and their wish to replace the parent of the same sex. He became convinced that sexual libido was the main dynamic force in human behavior. Neurosis in his view was always a defense against one's sexual drives. Most aspects of an individual's behavior were seen as manifestations or sublimations of the sex urge.

Freud believed that, as Brenner puts it, "the majority of mental functioning goes on without consciousness and that consciousness is an unusual rather than a usual quality or attribute of mental functioning." [1] The core of his theoretical system is the concept of an unconscious which serves as a repository for instinctual drives, primitive urges, painful conflicts, and feelings of guilt. Freud asserted that society's disapproval of man's inborn sexual and aggressive urges forces us to repress them, that is, push them down into our unconscious. There, they continue to exist and control our behavior without our knowledge. Likewise, all sorts of unpleasant experiences, feelings of being bad or unworthy, and hard-to-resolve conflicts between opposing wishes also are pushed down into the unconscious because we find them too painful to think about. In many cases, Freud saw these conflicts or guilt feelings as unconscious from their very beginning.

He divided the human psyche into three sections—the id (instincts and urges repressed into the unconscious); the ego (the totality of man's conscious awareness); and the superego (the censor or sense of conscience derived from society). In his view, individuals generally did not develop problems in living and emotional disturbances from external circumstances. Rather, they developed problems in living as a result of losing control of socially unacceptable instincts or urges, or they became emotionally disturbed because of anxiety or guilt breaking through from repressed sexual material in the unconscious. According to Freud, this repressed sexual material was often the remains of an unresolved sexual attraction to the parent of opposite gender (Oedipus or Electra complex). He saw the human psyche as an energy system and seemed to concentrate his main attention on how psychic energy was exchanged and distributed among the id, superego, and ego.

Freud believed that the determinants of human behavior were man's biological drives and the ways he coped with them. Behavior depended on a person's ability to control these drives or feel comfortable about them. The characteristics of the particular environment where each man lived were of no special significance. An act of behavior was the result of a specific inner drive or conflict and the balance, at the moment, among the forces of his id, superego, and ego.

In this chapter, we shall present alternative ideas concerning the nature of man as the first step in developing new understandings of human behavior. This will be done through brief summaries of recent non-Freudian books, as explained in the Introduction. We begin with the views of Alfred Adler.

Alder, the "Original Non-Freudian"

The ideas of Alfred Adler form a well-established conceptual system that originated decades ago. In the twenties and thirties, Adler's ideas were very popular in many parts of Europe and also won some recognition in the United States. There was a decline of interest following his death in 1937. His views have been evoking genuine interest again since the publication (1956) of *The Individual Psychology Of Alfred Adler*.[2] This volume is a systematic presentation of excerpts from his writings. Several projects are being planned to commemorate the hundredth anniversary of Adler's birth—Feburary 7, 1970.

Adler was one of the original members of the first psychoanalytic society which was founded by Freud in Vienna. He was closely associated with Freud from 1902 until 1911; then he went his own way because basic irreconcilable differences arose between them. Adler was thus the "original non-Freudian." * One area of disagreement was Freud's division of the psyche into sections, and his concept of the continual war going on between the forces of the id seeking expression and the forces of the superego attempting to inhibit or modify them. Adler saw the human personality as a unified whole never in conflict with itself; an individual developed problems primarily because his goals and life style brought him into conflict with the world around him.

Another point of difference was Freud's pessimism about the future of man. Freud saw civilization becoming increasingly complex and, in the process, forcing people to repress more and more of their inborn instincts. The result, in Freud's view, could only be further feelings of frustration, tension and guilt. Adler, on the other hand, spoke of his outlook as a "gay and optimistic science." He believed each person should work to build the kind of society he favored. Cooperation with a society *in which an individual believes* does not repress his true nature. Instead, it gives him a chance to bring it to its fullest development.

Although Adler himself first formulated the concept of the

* I am indebted to Heinz L. Ansbacher for this phrase.

aggression drive during his early association with the Vienna Psychoanalytic Society, he later abandoned it. He is reported to have said: "I enriched psychoanalysis by the aggressive drive. I gladly make them a present of it." He went on to reach a conclusion diametrically opposed to Freud's view that each man is born a savage animal to other men. Adler's final formulation was that "man is not born good or evil, but he can be trained in either direction." He asserted that people have an inborn potential for "social interest" which can be consciously developed. By "social interest" he meant a community feeling, a desire to live cooperatively with others, a sense of responsibility to society.

Adler does not see each man as "a wolf unto other men," but as an individual whose basic tendency is to strive for competence and a sense of completion. Because a child feels inferior in an adult world, he seeks to move ahead as a way of becoming stronger. Adler disagreed with Freud's idea that people want to go backward under stress because they see their infantile stage as the most desirable condition. In Adler's view, man is not essentially a mass of aggressive urges. He has a capacity for cooperative living which can be developed. As a creative being, he defines for himself what he considers to be success in life and then, on the basis of these goals, he develops a life style dedicated to its attainment. Constructive goals based on social interest will lead him to constructive behavior; antisocial or selfish goals in which social interest is absent will result in antisocial behavior. Man takes his constitutional heredity, his environment, and his experiences and under their influence—but not bound by them—he fashions his life plan and his life style in his own personal way.

Now Adler did not deny that we are born with instinctual drives or that we have primitive urges. However, he did not think that specific drives were the cause of behavior. He believed that possessing certain drives did not mean we had to act on them, either directly or indirectly. Drives and instincts can and will be controlled or deactivated if a person's goals in life require it. Adler held that a person acts in a particular way to advance a particular life plan he has developed for himself. Consequently, behavior is primarily influenced by a person's goals. Each man's opinion of himself leads him to strive for a particular kind of success and to create a total, self-consistent behavior pattern directed toward that end. We can understand each man's behavior best if we understand each man's goal, which is the unifying force in his life.

Finally, Adler's conceptual framework, which he called "Individual Psychology," led him to regard each person as unique, as different from all others. In his view, the impulses that each man displayed toward his fellows varied greatly, depending on the degree to which the potential for social interest had been cultivated in him by his parents and his society. This was in complete contrast to Freud's belief that every person's inborn impulses toward his fellows were aggressive. Adler was interested in the nuances that differentiated one man from another. Freud tended to think in terms of universal characteristics that were common to all: inborn aggression, an Oedipal or Electra conflict which everyone had to experience, and the primacy of the sex drive.

Adler denied the universality of the Oedipal or Electra conflict. While granting that children sometimes had sexual attachments to their parents, he believed that in most cases attachment to one parent and hostility toward the other were not sexually motivated; rather, they were consequences of the child's efforts to secure a more favored position for himself in terms of attention and practical advantages. Adler saw the sex drive as just one of several, and did not believe that anxiety had exclusively sexual origins or that friendships were (as Freud claimed) sublimations of unconscious sexual feelings toward others. He regarded neurosis as a life style in which certain behavior patterns safeguarded the individual from having to face things he feared. In this connection, Adler believed that each person felt threatened by something different. While it might be sexual impulses in some cases, more often it would be demands, problems and failures in everyday living. He agreed that women envied men but it was usually not penis envy. Rather, women were jealous of men's dominant role in society while resenting the inferior status allocated to themselves.

Adler saw life as the meeting of three tasks: relating to other people, work, and sexual love.

Van Kaam's Existentialism

Originating even earlier than Adler's ideas are the concepts of existentialism, which had their beginnings in religious and philosophical writings of the 19th century. Adrian Van Kaam's *The Art of Existential Counseling,* published in 1966, applies existential psychology to the practice of counseling. Van Kaam [3] states: "When I speak of existential psychology or the existential viewpoint, I am not referring to a school of psychology which I would place side by side with other schools such as behaviorism, psychoanalysis, or the psychology of Alfred Adler. Rather the existential viewpoint embraces an attitude, an orientation of attention which I find, to some degree, represented in all schools of psychology and psychiatry." Despite this qualification, his book does contain postulates about the nature of man.

For example, Van Kaam, in common with other existentialists, sees each man as unique, the source of his own world of meaning and value, understandable only in his own terms and never in terms of a standard classification or label. The essential difference between one individual and another is the degree of readiness which each has developed to be open to whatever he encounters in his environment. Man chooses his world by exercising his freedom to be open or closed to the various things which are relevant to his particular existence. The whole life of a person is built upon the decision he makes to be either open or closed to the reality of his life situation. In other words, he can face or avoid the implications of what is true in his existence, e.g., his weaknesses and limitations.

Van Kaam discusses how some people, under the impact of an unfavorable childhood, may make a decision not to be open for all of significant reality. He defines openness as the quiet, relaxed presence to whatever of pertinence may reveal itself, and states that openness has the qualities of waiting, listening and receptivity. Each man has several modes of existence: that is, he plays several different roles and functions in several different ways. Everyone wants to be somebody, a person who counts. Man, perhaps, most fears the possible discovery by others that he is unimportant or incompetent. He therefore covers up and is not open to this mode of his existence, the mode of unimportance or incompetence.

However, creativity is possible only when one can risk himself in life situations, daring to make mistakes and accepting their consequences because he feels free to be judged imperfect by others. When one is not open to a mode of his existence which is painful to face, much of that person's energy is drained off in the maintenance of defensive structures. Once he faces it, an individual is stronger by being his authentic self, whatever that may be; no matter how weak he is, he is now free from the anxiety which drained off so much energy for defense. For the existentialist, only when an individual opens himself to all of significant reality and to the many modes of his existence can he understand his authentic self—what he basically is—and fulfill his potentials and responsibilities.

As Thomas Hora [4] puts it: "Complete understanding of one's mode of being tends to bring about a shift in world view, that is, a changed attitude toward life. Change occurs the moment man can see the totality of his situation. *Change is the result of expanding consciousness.* . . . Healing occurs through a meaningful shift in the world view of an individual, brought about through genuine understanding of the structure of his existence."

A final concept offered by Van Kaam holds that each person sets up a project of existence for himself, a plan for living to which he makes a commitment. It is important to realize the discipline which our particular project of existence imposes on our daily life. If we freely act against our own commitments, we cannot live with consistency and our life will be disintegrated and disruptive.

Rank and the Human Will

Otto Rank was a contemporary of Alfred Adler and, like him, a member of Freud's original Vienna group who subsequently went his own way because of theoretical differences. His ideas about the nature of man, like Adler's, achieved their final form in the twenties and thirties. Ruth E. Smalley's recent *Theory for Social Work Practice* [5] is the first book in over a decade to restate Rank's basic concepts and apply them to a helping process.

Smalley tells us that the push toward growth and fulfillment is primary in human beings; the innate purpose in each of us is to grow. In the process, we act upon our environment and are acted upon by it. We have a continous inner necessity to find a balance between the realization of ourselves as individuals and as members of the particular society of which we are a part. In so doing, we struggle between wanting to cling and be dependent and wanting to separate and function independently. This conflict has its origins in the trauma of our birth. We fear independence and responsibility for ourselves, but we also fear domination by others.

While Freud believed that the determinants of behavior were in an "unconscious," Rank insisted on the primary importance of consciousness, of which a significant component is the will. Smalley declares that the individual pattern of any self may be understood as a balance of impulse, intellect, feeling and emotion, and will. Will is an organizing, striving, creative force, a "wanting." It is the will of an individual that may resist help offered to him regarding his problems out of fear of disorganization, change, or subjection to the will of another. At the same time, according to Rank, the will to be free engenders the guilt reaction that one should have no will of his own but thank and love those who wish to assume responsibility for him.

Rank identifies neurosis as a separation problem, a blocking of the conscious ability to endure release and separation. Individuals differ in their strength of will and in the balance of its negative and positive expression. A professional helping process best serves a client when (a) it frees him to use his will positively toward his own self-chosen ends; (b) it affords him an opportunity to develop his potential, whatever it may be; and (c) it releases his own power for choice and growth. The self of another cannot be known through intellectual assessment alone. Rankians share with the existentialists a conviction that a warm compassionate relationship is needed to enable selves to open up and become what they may be.

We can briefly add to Smalley's presentation by recalling how Otto Rank [6] in *Will Therapy* maintained that individuals are understood through their present experience where their whole reaction pattern, past and present, is apparent. People must make choices all their lives about separating from others or yielding to them, about being the same or being different. Will and consciousness are primary. We remember what we will to remember. We will unconsciousness to escape facing the present. The only reality not subject to doubt is the self—everything else is interpretation. Man's goal then should be the freedom to be himself and to accept himself.

The Behaviorist

A new approach to the treatment of emotional problems, known as "behavior therapy," has been in the process of development over the last decade by Joseph Wolpe and others. The theory of human functioning which underlies this approach derives from the much earlier work on conditioning and learning done by Pavlov in Russia and John B. Watson in the United States. Wolpe's theory culminates in some original formulations.

The behaviorist believes that most human reactions and behavior are actually habits we have learned. A habit is a consistent way of responding to a particular person, thing, event or situation. Ordinarily a habit declines and becomes extinguished when its consequences stop serving the needs of the individual or no longer avoid injury, pain or fatigue. A habit becomes neurotic when it resists extinction in the face of its unadaptiveness; that is, when it continues, although the situation no longer calls for it and it serves no realistic purpose. A major component of neurotic reactions is anxiety.

Behaviorists are greatly interested in phobias. A phobia is a fear which the person experiencing it knows is not realistic, yet he cannot tolerate the feared object or situation. A phobia is thus a persistent unadaptive habit and a form of neurosis. Since phobias and other neuroses are conditioned responses which operate through reflex pathways established in the nervous system, they cannot be overcome by reasoning. They require treatment based on the concept that neurotic reactions are physiological phenomena.

Behavior Therapy Techniques: A Guide to the Treatment of Neuroses, co-authored by Joseph Wolpe and Arnold Lazarus [7], outlines the main points of behavior theory and presents a detailed description of treatment techniques based on it, known as behavior therapy. It also discusses Wolpe's "reciprocal inhibition principle." This principle holds that if a person in the presence of something that makes him anxious can, at the same time, do something that inhibits anxiety, the feared object will become less anxiety-provoking. The classic example of Wolpe's principle was provided by an experiment in 1924 by Mary Cover Jones. She had a young child, who was very fearful of rabbits, eat while in the presence of a caged rabbit. This was repeated for several days. Each day, the cage was brought a little closer to the child, always when the child was eating. The distance was determined by how close the rabbit could be placed without causing the child to stop eating. If the child stopped, the rabbit was pulled back a bit until the child resumed eating. It was not long before the child was eating with the rabbit right next to him and petting it.

Conditioning is an important factor in the life of every individual. Conditioning is the process whereby, through deliberate training or life experiences, certain kinds of behavior connect up with certain stimuli. Thereafter, a particular stimulus will automatically trigger off a particular response in an individual every time it is present, and this reaction becomes a habit. When the conditioning (training) results in unrealistic behavior which causes an individual to suffer, the connection between a particular stimulus and a particular kind of response has to be dissolved, and a more appropriate kind of behavior connected to the stimulus in question. In the case of the child and the rabbit, the fear reaction to the animal was dissolved by having him do something anxiety-inhibiting in the presence of what he feared. The enjoyable and anxiety-inhibiting process of eating had the effect of breaking the old connection between rabbit and anxiety and forming a new connection between rabbit and pleasure.

To the Freudian contention that phobias and other neurotic behavior are merely symptoms of unconscious conflicts and not the actual problem, behaviorists answer that fear of elevators or anxiety in the presence of an employer *is* the problem. The essential thing is not to discover the origin of neurotic behavior but to alter it.

Contributions by Albert Ellis

Albert Ellis [8] has been formulating a largely new theoretical system over the last ten years as the rationale for his own approach to treatment, which he calls "rational-emotive psychotherapy." Ellis contends that we are constantly saying sentences to ourselves in which we comment on our experiences. Emotions and behavior stem from these internalized statements, from the way we think about experiences. If we judge a person or event to be dangerous to ourselves, we shall develop the emotion of fear and the behavior of avoiding that person or event. If our perception has been accurate, our emotions and behavior will be appropriate. However, if our perception has been incorrect, the emotions and behavior that develop from it will be unadaptive—that is, they will not correspond to what the situation calls for and may cause unnecessary difficulty or suffering.

Ellis sees neurosis as caused mainly by an individual's learning to blame himself too severely for the mistakes and wrongs that everyone commits just by virtue of being human. He believes that the individual originally learns this from his parents and others in his environment, but it is the individual himself who sustains and eternally perpetuates his neurosis by repeating to himself his early acquired, inaccurate judgments. Ellis teaches those who come to him for help that no one is ever to blame for anything.

Ellis holds that human emotional disturbance is essentially philosophically based. People become upset because their general outlook on life is distorted. For example, they suffer if they are not accepted by those important to them, or become hostile to persons or things they dislike. Ellis insists that no matter what the client's basic irrational philosophy of life is, nor when and how he acquired it, he is presently disturbed because he *still* believes these inaccurate views of the world and of himself. Among inaccurate perceptions, Ellis includes the notion that one *must* be accepted or loved by significant others or he is worthless, and the attitude that someone else's behavior is bad and it is terrible that he should be allowed to display it.

Reality Therapy

Another new viewpoint about the nature of man and his behavior is the one on which William Glasser [9] bases his treatment technique, reality therapy. His theory of human functioning postulates that people have two basic needs: first, to give love and receive love; second, to behave so as to feel worthwhile to others and to themselves. People who do not fulfill these needs are, in Glasser's special definition, irresponsible. Those who need professional help are the individuals who are irresponsible in this special sense. There is no mental illness, so often used to excuse their behavior. Neurosis, psychosis, schizophrenia, sociopathy, delinquency, and psychosomatic symptoms are all just different forms of irresponsibility.

Glasser believes that the concept of unconscious conflicts has served the purpose of providing a medical parallel between psychological problems and physical illness. A pain in the side is caused by appendicitis; deviant behavior is caused by unconscious conflict. In Glasser's opinion, the commitment of the Freudian to uncover the unconscious conflict hinders treatment, for it gives the person who seeks help something on which to blame his behavior other than himself. Thus, he feels no responsibility for it.

Glasser does not see people who come for help as "sick" but rather as "weak" and in need of assistance to find the strength to change. In his book, he offers the following explanation of a schizophrenic:

> Because he could not fulfill his needs in the real world, . . . the patient began to deny the existence of the real world and live in a world of his own, trying thereby to fulfill his needs. Perhaps it was a crazy world full of hallucinations and delusions; perhaps it was just a numb denial of reality and a withdrawal into a world of nothingness, a vegetative existence. . . . No matter what his behavior, it was his way of trying to fulfill his needs or denying that he had needs to fulfill.

A Rational Approach

Finally, the editor has attempted to contribute to a non-Freudian psychology by outlining a "rational approach" which regards man as fully understandable without assuming the existence of an "unconscious." [10] This "rational approach" starts with the premise that emotions and behavior are generated by the judgments we make concerning objects, events, other people and ourselves. Other formulations flow out of a central belief in the primacy of consciousness, which is the sum total of our thoughts, emotions and behavior. The problems for which people seek help are considered to stem from limitations and distortions of consciousness, which can be produced by parents, experiences, or society itself. The helping person's first aim should be to assist his client to achieve an accurate perception of himself, his world, and the relationships between them. Most people feel and act on the basis of how they think. Appropriate thinking usually produces appropriate emotions and actions, although not always.

Sometimes, emotional distress is not the result of inaccurate

thinking but of the inability to respond appropriately even
though our thinking is accurate. This implies a definition of
mental health as the ability not only to see things as they
really are but also to behave in a way consistent with this correct understanding. That individuals can perceive a situation accurately, and yet behave unrealistically, is evidenced by the
case of a person once severely bitten by a dog and now in fear
of all dogs. This person understands now that dogs in general
are not a menace; yet that one traumatic incident in the past had
such a strong conditioning effect that an automatic phobic reaction was established in the nervous system not subject to the
control of his subsequent thinking. The situation has changed—
a dog that is present does not bite—but the person cannot change
his response. In such a case, the person's behavior needs to be
reconditioned, that is, retrained.

Other definitions are offered. An emotion is described as the
feeling an individual experiences after estimating what an event
means to him and reacting with a set of involuntary physiological responses. A motive is regarded as a chosen objective based
on an individual's concept of necessity. Defined in these terms,
emotions and motives are seen as exclusively conscious phenomena, since their existence depends on the conscious activities
of thinking and evaluating. Likewise, the determinants of behavior are believed to be in consciousness, in these same thinking and evaluating activities. Even the phobic individual, whose
behavior does not correspond to his *present* thinking, established
his reaction pattern originally in response to a judgment he
made. He may later have discarded his original evaluation of a
particular thing as dangerous, but the avoidance and anxiety
continued.

This writer's "rational approach" denies the existence of a
substantive unconscious which serves as a repository for repressed material. It does accept a concept of unconsciousness as
synonymous with unawareness or ignorance. In this sense, a
person can be unconscious (i.e., unaware, ignorant) of the impression he makes on other people. In this sense, a person can
be unconscious of an idea he has forgotten or deliberately put

out of his mind. Such an idea does not exert any influence over his behavior without his knowledge: it is really ineffective until he recalls it or allows himself to resume thinking about it. Similarly, he can be unconscious of the distant origin of a current phobia.

Neurosis and anxiety are not seen as manifestations of unconscious conflict, sexual or otherwise. Neurosis is viewed as a way of living based on unrealistic fear or guilt, the individual saturated with anxiety. Anxiety, in turn, is considered a non-specific dread of imminent danger, accompanied by somatic tensions, which builds up as a person feels helpless to overcome persistent specific fears. The contents of dreams are not regarded as material from the "unconscious" in disguised form, but rather as reflections of problems or situations not mastered in our waking existence. These unmastered problems or situations continue to act as stimuli to our cortical centers during sleep, producing distorted images because parts of the brain which select, organize, and systematize are inactive when we sleep.[11]

Lastly, it is proposed that man is *not* a prisoner of unconscious forces, biologically determined or originating in childhood, which control his behavior without his knowing it. He may have strength or courage of which he is unaware, but he does know what his thoughts, feelings, and motives are. Because of his fear of revealing himself, he may hide these thoughts, feelings, and motives from those who wish to help him.

We have presented non-Freudian concepts about the nature of man which appeared in books published from 1956 to 1967. If we synthesize them into a systematic presentation, we emerge with the proposition that a person's behavior is mainly determined not by unconscious forces but by his thinking and willing. He evaluates himself, others, and the world around him; sets up goals to achieve; and behaves in ways he thinks will attain his objectives and otherwise give him maximum satisfaction. The strength of an individual's will, and the direction in which it is applied, affect the amount of effort he expends and the progress he makes toward his goals. He has the ability to control and deactivate instinctual drives which interfere with his purposes. He normally feels and acts according to the thoughts he presently holds concerning significant factors in his environment. However, when there is a very strong original association between a certain stimulus and a certain response, the same response may persist even though one's evaluation of the stimulus subsequently changes. This occurs because the reaction has become a physiological process which bypasses thinking.

People have to make choices all their lives: between dependence on others and independence; between clinging and separating; between conformity and originality; between accepting and challenging limits; between goals on the destructive and on the useful side of life; between avoiding and facing all the implications of their existence.

Emotional distress can develop in various ways. A man's goals may be destructive or antisocial, in which case the life style he evolves to reach these goals will bring pressure, rejection, or retaliation from his society. If an individual is afraid to reveal his authentic self for fear of being found imperfect by others, he erects defensive structures behind which to hide what he really is, becoming anxious and draining his emotional energy in the process. People sometimes act contrary to their chosen objectives; this not only prevents them from living with consistency, but may disintegrate and disrupt their lives. Emotional strain may be experienced in making any of the crucial choices listed in the preceding paragraph. In other cases, individuals become upset as a result of blaming themselves too severely for mistakes they commit just by virtue of being human. Some of us suffer acutely when significant people do not approve of us, or when we encounter disagreement in the world at large. Some of us become disturbed when we are unable to give love, receive love, or behave so as to feel worthwhile to others and to ourselves. There are all kinds of fears and guilt feelings, realistic and not, which prevent people from enjoying a measure of inner peace. Finally, strongly conditioned responses which a person cannot stop even though he knows they are inappropriate can cause great distress.

In this latter connection, it should be pointed out that human beings choose to live largely by conditioned responses, despite the fact that thinking and willing play the most crucial roles in shaping their existence. People cope with their daily routines by allowing habitual reactions which require no thought to take over. Repetition of any reaction pattern tends to entrench it. While this may seldom create major difficulties in routine matters, hardened patterns of inaccurate thinking or inappropriate behavior in crucial areas can lead to emotional problems.

The non-Freudian conception of man's nature views him as not born either good or evil but trainable in either direction. He is not seen as inherently aggressive; cooperation with a society in which he believes does not repress his true nature but develops it. Man is creative, possesses an innate purpose to grow, and has a basic tendency to strive for competence and a sense of completion. His sex drive is not primary, but just one of several drives. Attachments or hostilities to parents, neurosis, and anxiety do not inevitably trace back to sexuality and are more often reactions to all types of life situations. Each person is unique, differing in some ways from all other persons, and comprehensible only in his own terms. Diagnoses and labels at most can contribute only a partial understanding of an individual.

REFERENCES

1. Charles Brenner, *An Elementary Textbook of Psychoanalysis* (Garden City, N.Y.: Doubleday Anchor Books, 1957), p. 15.
2. Heinz Ansbacher, and Rowena Ansbacher, *The Individual Psychology of Alfred Adler* (New York: Basic Books, 1956).
3. Adrian Van Kaam, *The Art of Existential Counseling* (Wilkes-Barre, Pa.: Dimension Books, 1966), p. 11.

38   New Understandings of Human Behavior

4. Thomas Hora, "Existential Psychotherapy," *Current Psychiatric Therapies,* Vol. II (New York: Grune & Stratton, 1962), p. 37.
5. Ruth Smalley, *Theory for Social Work Practice* (New York: Columbia University Press, 1967).
6. Otto Rank, *Will Therapy* (New York: Alfred A. Knopf, 1936).
7. Joseph Wolpe and Arnold Lazarus, *Behavior Therapy Techniques: A Guide to the Treatment of Neuroses* (New York: Pergamon Press, 1966).
8. Albert Ellis, *Reason and Emotion in Psychotherapy* (New York: Lyle Stuart, 1962).
9. William Glasser, *Reality Therapy: A New Approach to Psychiatry* (New York: Harper & Row, 1965), p. 109.
10. Harold Werner, *A Rational Approach to Social Casework* (New York: Association Press, 1965).
11. Montague Ullman, "The Dream Process," *Psychotherapy,* Vol. 1, No. 1 (1955), pp. 30-60.

2

Consciousness, the Unconscious, and Repression

Freud, in *The Interpretation of Dreams,*[1] was very definite in his insistence upon the primacy of the unconscious in the psychic life of each individual.

In direct contrast, Robbins considered consciousness the central problem in psychiatry and in psychotherapy as a whole. Nearly sixty years after Freud published *The Interpretation of Dreams* in 1900, Robbins[2] stated:

> Although the rewards of the last half century, stimulated by the theory of an "unconscious," with its corollary instinctual and libido conceptualizations, have been enormous, an impasse has been reached (such as happens with all theories), in which further pursuit under its stimulus can be only retrogressive, that is, only further removed from reality and a correct appreciation of its nature. No longer can we explain adequately man's bizarre thinking and behavior on the basis of "unconscious motivation," "unconscious homosexuality," "unconscious incest," "unconscious envy and rivalry," "unconscious cruelty." The theory which had stood us in good stead for many years now hampers our therapeutic practice. It has outlived its

39

usefulness. It behooves us, therefore, to consider bidding adieu to it with gratitude for all that it did to inspire us to positive accomplishment and to search elsewhere for areas in which we can investigate more productively man's nature and its aberrations.

Robbins pointed out that, while man shares with all other animals an awareness of the world through sensation-perception, he possesses something unique in addition. Only man has speech and only man, through speech, can communicate his experiences to others of his kind. Only speech is capable of generalizing about external objects and their relations to one another. Because of words and language, only man can think thoughts and form concepts. His way of interacting with his environment is not just a chemico-physical one, a sensorial or even a perceptive one, but is essentially a thinking, conscious existence. It is this consciousness of man which Robbins believed would be a more productive area for studying man's nature than the "unconscious" would be. He concluded: "We can then see why the study of man's way of living as differentiated from all other living matter is the study of conscious existence, of consciousness. We can then see too the study of man's individual disturbances in living, the study of functional psychopathology, is the study of the disturbances of consciousness." [3]

Ichheiser does not regard the "unconscious" as a concept which was once useful but has now outlived its usefulness. Rather, he sees the "unconscious" as a mythology invented by Freud due to his ignorance of the true nature of consciousness. Ichheiser, like Robbins, favors a phenomenological approach to the understanding of human behavior. The phenomenological or cognitive approach holds that an individual is best understood in terms of his subjective evaluations of experiences and objects in his environment, and in terms of his goals.

On Freud's Blind Spots Concerning Some Obvious Facts

*Gustav Ichheiser, Ph.D.**

Identifying consciousness with a vague concept of perception, Freud was simply not aware of the nature nor of the immense variety of the contents, levels, dimensions, and modes of our immediate psychological experience. . . .

It is noteworthy that almost at the same time as Freud undertook his psychoanalytical revolution in claiming that the psychological reality which dominates our whole mental life consists in processes which operate below the level of consciousness, the phenomenological revolution was developing in just the opposite direction. It insisted that the basic psychological reality consists in immediately experienced subjectivity, i.e., in consciousness, in a new and redefined meaning of the term. While Freud and his followers were pointing to the unawareness of our unconscious processes, the phenomenological approach held that we were not sufficiently aware of the world of our immediate psychological experience. This new phenomenological approach has influenced European psychology and social sciences more quietly, but at least as profoundly as the psychoanalytic revolution.

The following examples will illustrate that we can be conscious of something in one way and at the same time be not conscious of it in another way. They will clarify Freud's error in calling only certain modes of consciousness conscious and declaring other modes of consciousness unconscious.

1. There are many different *modes* in which we can be conscious of the same psychological content: we can experience it immediately, in which case there is no duality of an experiencing subject and an experienced object, although retrospectively we may still know that the experience was there; we can imagine it; we can remember it; we can perceive it; we can conceptually know about it; etc.

2. If we have certain feelings about certain things, then, of

* *Journal of Individual Psychology*, Vol. 16, No. 1 (May 1960), pp. 45-46, 50.

course, we are conscious of these feelings, although in a way which is very different from the way we are conscious of, let us say, the contents of our sensory perceptions; and since our feelings are often peculiarly vague and elusive, we may have considerable difficulty in describing them correctly, i.e., in knowing them.

3. We are, of course, conscious of the innumerable symbolical meanings which permeate our perceptual experience of the external world, and we react to them. But we are mostly conscious of them in a peculiarly implicit way; we do not explicitly know what they actually are. What we call insight consists considerably in the ability to make these implicit meanings explicit. Similarly, we often understand the meaning of someone's ironical remarks and fully enjoy it, without being able to explain this meaning or why we enjoy it.

Had Freud not failed to take adequate cognizance of the variety and richness of consciousness, he might have explained much that he wanted to explore, without inventing unconscious processes. Freud's mythology of the unconscious is largely the result of his confusion and misconception regarding the nature of consciousness.

. . . Freud always assumed that human irrationality has its roots mainly in the area of the unconscious, and that the many irrationalities on the conscious level are only manifestations of the underlying unconscious mechanisms. Actually, there are plenty of irrationalities in our perceptions and judgments which have little, if anything, to do with the unconscious as conceived by Freud, but are the result of certain peculiarities and defects of our intellectual operations and of quite specific social influences. . . .

Freud did not appreciate that subjective reality may be considered in different modes of consciousness; that it is influenced by sense data, the level and type of intelligence, cultural mediation, the perspectives of social situations, as well as the objective reality. To ignore these factors in defining reality is to create serious lacunae in an understanding of the psychodynamics of personality. To assume that all distortions of social perception are due to the operation of unconscious mechanisms, or to interpret all illusions concerning motivation as rationalizations, means to misunderstand the role of genuine false perception and genuine error of judgment in human affairs.

Alfred Adler [4] said: "The unconscious is nothing other than that which we have been unable to formulate in clear concepts." Rollo May [5] wrote: "The 'unconscious,' then, is not to be thought of as a reservoir of impulses, thoughts, wishes which are culturally unacceptable; I define it rather as *those potentialities for knowing and experiencing which the individual cannot or will not actualize.*"

In the following article, Papageorgis deals with the traditional psychoanalytic concept of the unconscious by examining various Freudian ideas concerning repression. He tries to show that the traditional psychoanalytic notions of repression and the unconscious are not only unnecessary but also less appropriate to the understanding of human behavior than explanations in terms of exclusively conscious behavior.

Repression and the Unconscious: A Social-Psychological Reformulation

*Demetrios Papageorgis, Ph.D.**

This paper attempts to reconceptualize a number of human activities and behaviors that, collectively, have led Freud and many theorists since then to postulate unconscious processes and mechanisms of repression. But the same observations which have been used as evidence for the unconscious and repression can be dealt with, meaningfully and parsimoniously, without recourse to these concepts and solely on the basis of conscious and intentional functions. These functions arise and are maintained pri-

* *Journal of Individual Psychology,* Vol. 21, No. 1 (May 1965), pp. 18, 22-30.

marily through man's conscious social existence and may be traced to his learned use of language, modes of thought, and communication. The theoretical position adopted here is related to those of Adler and Szasz. . . .

Memory Losses

Under certain circumstances forgetting is believed to be evidence for repression, and the distinction between so-called "repression" and ordinary forgetting represents a major problem. The distinction is not easy, as examination of two main criteria will disclose.

1. Repression is claimed to be "motivated forgetting." This means that certain ideas, experiences, and feelings become partially or completely unavailable to recall for reasons usually hedonic in nature.

"Motivated forgetting" and "repression" are, however, not identical. The former may be based on the conscious mechanism of suppression, i.e., an aware subject intentionally avoids the unpleasant thought, so that severely weakened associations and, hence, partial or complete forgetting may result. Suppression by itself is an inadequate explanation because in most instances a person goes further and deliberately magnifies the import of extenuating details (rationalization) or enhances the role of entirely different motives (at times, reaction formation), and, in general, alters the thought itself through voluntary and intentional self-deception. The result is that in the future the event in quesion, if recalled at all, may be distorted beyond recognition. This alternative analysis does not deny the observed phenomena of human behavior that suggested the notion of repression. Instead, it emphasizes that adequate descriptions of these phenomena are possible within exclusively conscious boundaries.

A concrete example will clarify this contention: During a heated argument involving valid complaints from both sides, a husband orders his wife, whom he loves, out of the house. She storms out, drives away in the car, and meets with a fatal accident. The husband is now faced with a major readjustment in his life and with the more immediate task of his own grief and the confrontation with officials, relatives, and friends. He may feel and even openly express at least partial responsibility for his wife's death. In time, the man's own deliberations and his friends' assurances will very likely restructure his perceptions and memories. Arguments emphasizing his non-causal role in his wife's death will begin to gain ascendancy over arguments stressing his blameworthy role. Both kinds of argument are psychologically valid and will persist, though the former variety will become more prevalent and the issue of the death will lose its central importance. Despite these changes, the accident will continue to exert some effect on our hero's behavior, and the effect, to the extent that it depends on re-evaluation (distortion) of the earlier facts and implications, may appear peculiar to an observer. It would however, be detrimental to understanding to introduce in this connection notions of the unconscious and repression.

2. Repression is claimed to be distinguishable by the "completeness" of the memory loss. The major problem with this criterion is that it depends upon the ability of an outside observer to establish that a given event, now claimed to be repressed, had indeed been perceived, conceptualized, and known to the subject at an earlier time. Unfortunately, very few instances completely satisfy this requirement, and even here it is possible that the subject who claims to have forgotten may not be telling the truth or is practicing self-deception.

The usual method of ascertaining if this criterion is met, consists of either noting the appearance of a "memory" previously unavaliable (perhaps during the course of psychoanalysis), or noting the acceptance or spontaneous acknowledgement by the subject of a previously denied experience that carries the status of a "universal" within a particular theory (primal scene, castration anxiety). In neither of these instances does the observer know for a fact that the remembered item ever happened. Freud himself became wary of the trustworthiness of what some of his patients claimed were repressed memories. Also to be noted is that the majority of these instances deal with experiences presumed to have taken place during the early life of the person. It has been argued that lack of verbal labels in early life seriously limits discrimination, perception, and memory. It is also known that persuasion is facilitated when the "facts" of the case are unknown or hard to ascertain. When individuals finally admit to experiences previously "unknown" to them, it is more appropriate to view them as applying new constructions to their self-concept than as demonstrating a new awareness of a fact forgotten long ago.

This is not meant to deny the importance of early memories. It should not matter if they are incorrect or suffer from various degrees of "distortion." These are the results of misperception or of qualitative memory changes that characterize material that is repeatedly reproduced. Nor does it matter how important the recalled events were at the time they supposedly took place. Their present role is what matters as Adler has stressed.

At this point the example of the man whose wife died in the car accident will be brought back. A few years later, he repeatedly denied that he had ordered his wife to leave the house. Has he necessarily repressed a painful memory? Dismissing the possibility of an outright lie, he has most probably succeeded in a rather common form of self-deception. First, he knew (probably the moment his anger began to subside) that he never really wanted his wife to leave the house. It is quite possible, in order to relieve his guilt, that he now believes he made the statement in a manner that made obvious the fact that he did not mean it. On further thought, he did not mean the statement even at the moment he was making it! Second, he may have made such statements previously and his wife had never taken them seriously. The reader may wish to continue this game on his own. At any rate, it is possible that our hero will conclude that he never *really* made a statement that he in fact did make. Since he is also unlikely to phrase the matter in these terms, the inconsistency, after a few repetitions will be reduced and probably disappear. If this man later undergoes psychoanalysis he may be expected to (a) resist attempts to bring out the fact that he had made the statement, and perhaps (b) admit he made the statement after considerable probing, and become quite emotional about it.

This account of memory losses concentrated on two types of forgetting most often associated with repression. Other such types suggestive of retroactive inhibition or events "experienced" while the subject was intoxicated, have been left out. A later section deals more fully with self-deception.

Unavailability and Lack of Precision of Verbal Labels

Most individuals in a culture learn to name things, showing both internal consistency in applying names to objects, and agreement with the labeling used by others. These tendencies are most marked with familiar, everyday objects; less with unfamiliar objects, or those giving rise to strong affect; still less, with abstract concepts like "freedom" and "justice"; and least with feelings and emotional states. "Sadness," for example, as used by a person to describe his subjective state, does not carry the exact same meaning each time he uses it. Even less interperson agreement and communication would take place when labels of this last type are used. And not only do these labels lack a shared precision of meaning; it is also very probable that individuals vary in the frequency with which they use them and in how appropriate they consider them to be as descriptions of their own feelings as well as the feelings of others.

This brief and rather obvious analysis was meant to point out that none of the following frequent situations is evidence for unconscious or repressed impulses and feelings: (a) difficulty in communicating one's feelings to others; (b) difficulty in consistently interpreting (to himself) his own feelings; (c) difficulty in interpreting the feelings of another person; (d) disagreement between two individuals regarding the appropriateness of the labels one of them uses to describe himself; (e) convergence of the labeling operations of two interacting individuals. The interested reader should note that these situations include a considerable segment of the psychotherapeutic interaction that is thought to yield evidence for unconscious processes.

Incomplete Assimilation of Experience

Under this heading are included a number of very common phenomena of human experience. Their distinguishing characteristic is that, irrespective of the reasons or causes behind the effects, the individual, after he experiences certain events, behaves in a manner that suggests that these events have not had an effective impact upon his cognitions and/or his behavior. Events may occur that the individual is apparently unable to "take in" or assimilate at all; or, more frequently, the events do "register" but are not assimilated within at least some contexts where they would be meaningful. For example, an employee may fail to see the role his reluctance to assert himself plays in his interactions with his supervisor; and he may fail to see the connection between his present behavior and his typical reaction to past authority figures. It is granted that partially assimilated experiences significantly affect a person's psychological make-up and behavior; but it is misleading to contend that either an originally fully assimilated perception is lost to subsequent awareness (repression), or that an incompletely assimilated experience subsequently acts without the person's awareness as if it were completely assimilated (unconscious).

Characteristically, psychoanalysts trace most instances of incomplete assimilation to early childhood. Indeed, most normal instances of this type appear at that time. It is argued here that any experience that will later affect behavior has to be perceived and maintained within at least a minimum context of meaning. In addition, to the extent that an early or late experience was not included within certain contexts of meaning, its influence on subsequent behavior will appear different or less comprehensible than if it had been.

If early childhood is a period when partial or total failure of assimilation is very likely to take place, the infant and young child also perceive less, know less, understand less, and label less than the average adult. A similar but qualitatively different deficit would be expected in intellectually retarded or deteriorated persons of any age. Relevant here is the work of Piaget

as well as within the same individual in successive stages of his
large number of other factors may cause or contribute to incomplete assimilation: temporary blocks to attention, habitual
patterns of attention, and educational, physical, or cultural
handicaps.

Prevailing Cognitive Habits

In this section, the focus of interest shifts from the assimilation of single experiences to prevailing "habits" or "styles" of
thought. Differences are again expected between individuals,
as well as Jaspers' concept of "differentiation." In addition, a
development, in the manner in which relations between events
are perceived. Early stages of cognitive development (infancy,
early childhood), low intelligence, lack of education, limits of
available information, and culturally prevalent forms of reasoning are some of the factors that tend to restrict a person's reper-
tory of useful operations in the relating of events to one another.

Examples are easy to find. A person may understand incor-
rectly naturally occurring events because he may lack the necessary constructs, e.g., he may not know that coal and diamonds
can both burn. An infant may at first fail to realize the correlation between his crying and his mother's comforting arrival.
Within the confines of a family or culture a person may learn
to avoid associations between actions by authority figures and
his own anger. Thinking about an explanation for one's own
acts may be limited to only socially acceptable reasons.

This last example calls for a few further comments on rationalization. Thinking about and verbally responding with
reasons for one's actions is an acquired habit imposed on children by society. Adults begin to demand that children explain,
especially their "bad" behavior, at an early age. It does not
take very long before children recognize that apparently the
"appropriate" reasons are limited to the "good" reasons, both
because the latter are acceptable to adults and because very
often punishment may be avoided in this fashion. Conformity
to adult expectations, imitation, and identification then establish

a habitual tendency to explain actions in terms of only socially acceptable reasons.

Neither failure of a person to use a particular cognitive approach nor his subsequent use of it is evidence for repression and the unconscious. It is much simpler to view the acquisition of such styles as characteristic of the conscious "mind." It may be added that because of the particular design of man's brain and the general similarities of his social existence some cognitive styles may be more probable than others, especially within the same culture.

Self-Deception

Self-deception has already been alluded to. The notion of repression has been in part supported by the observation that people are often unable to explain their actions or give false reasons for them. In these cases recourse to unconscious motivation provides the outside observer (and, sometimes, the subject himself) with a reasonable account of the discrepancies. Two examples will suffice. A mother verbally protests her love for her children while she treats them in a manner highly suggestive of hate. A married woman accepts an invitation to visit alone with another man so that she can view his art collection.

Such instances were once regarded as outright lies but have been reinterpreted in the past sixty or so years in terms of unconscious processes. Unfortunately, and despite admonitions like those of Peters, the latter kind of interpretation is increasingly applied where it is inappropriate, and when applied in addition to other explanations is often assumed to be superior. The request that "the patient should be assumed 'insightful' until he is proved otherwise" is all too often ignored. Thus, criminals are driven by unconscious wishes for punishment, and, if other reasons for their behavior are mentioned, they are thought to be secondary. Probably the most glaring abuse of this type is found in the belief that so-called "secondary gains" in neuroses are indeed secondary. However, there is an alternative to lying and unconscious wishes, namely, self-deception or lying to one's self. Recognized as far back as Plato, this serves as a more appropriate and realistic explanation of the phenomena in question.

Since self-deception and repression describe the same observations, they are in some ways similar. Both are attempts to prevent a thought from exercising its full cognitive impact, and both fall short of this goal. The differences between the two are more crucial. Unlike repression, self-deception is, at least for a time, a conscious and intentional operation, so that the individual is at least partially aware of what he is up to. For the same reason, in self-deception the unwanted idea exerts its influence on cognition and behavior *precisely because* the individual is aware of it and is attempting to reduce its impact.

Self-deception has already been illustrated in previous sections. Another example was recently observed by the author. A 12-year-old girl was allowing a 13-year-old boy to apply suntan lotion on her body while both were near a swimming pool and in full view of several people. The parents were not present. The application of the lotion took ten minutes and can only be described as a slow "labor of love" that both participants seemed to enjoy thoroughly. Analysis in terms of repression would place the sexual component of this situation in a prominent position but below the participants' awareness. An adult would have little trouble recognizing it. In terms of self-deception, it would be assumed that both participants were privately aware of the sexual implications, yet were able to behave as they did because they, and other observers, could interpret the situation without the sexual component. They would probably have stopped from embarrassment had they been in private or if either had openly alluded to the sexual pleasure involved. Even had they been observed and scolded by their parents, their effort at self-deception would have been reinforced: the girl's mother would probably not have made a direct reference to sex, but would have cautioned of the dangers inherent even in "innocent" play. In brief, everybody, including the two participants, is aware of what is going on. Self-deception is possible because the behavior is subject to more than one interpretation, and the less controversial interpretation is more comforting and is encouraged by most observers.

Sartre would call the above examples instances of *mauvaise foi*, the literal translation of which would be "bad faith." However, it has been found that the most adequate translation of *mauvaise foi* is "self-deception," the very term with which we are concerned here. According to Kaufmann, " 'Self-deception' seems much more accurate . . . and this is also how Philip Mairet has translated the same phrase." In a chapter variously entitled "Bad Faith" or "Self-Deception" Sartre indeed criticizes Freud's notion of repression similarly to the way taken in this paper. "If we reject the language and the materialistic mythology of psychoanalysis, we perceive that the censor in order to apply its activity with discernment must know what it is repressing." Sartre also gives an example which is very similar to ours. It is that of a young woman who lets a man hold her hand, but does not notice that she lets him do so.

Self-deception has also received attention from philosophers. It creates philosophical problems only if the individual is seen as holding two logically contradictory beliefs at the same time. This would hardly seem to be the case: the beliefs (and there may be more than two) are not conceptualized in logically contradictory ways, although they may in fact be quite inconsistent in their complex ramifications. It is well-known that everyday human cognition seldom follows lines of internal consistency. Self-deception is not an activity that maintains cognitive balance. It is fluid, unstable and usually accompanied by emotional involvement.

"Psychopathology of Everyday Life" and Dreams

Temporary memory blocks, faulty recollection of ordinary events, slips of the tongue and pen, as well as dreams have, since Freud, usually been thought to reflect unconscious processes and to provide evidence for them. Space does not permit a full analysis of these phenomena, but the unconscious does not provide the only plausible description of them. Undeniably these behaviors very often provide meaningful insights into a person's psychological make-up; and, certainly, antecedent conditions for them can be found. Thus the phenomena themselves are meaningful both as additional sources of data and in that their origins can be traced. In neither context of their meaning, however, do they necessitate the postulation of an unconscious.

Errors of memory may involve either failure to recollect or the substitution of an incorrect response. These errors are sufficiently accounted for by the fact that memory shows quantitative losses and qualitative changes over time and by mechanisms like retroactive inhibition and negative transfer. Similarly, momentary errors or "slips" require no further assumptions than the momentary intrusion of a competing thought process. That the result of a "slip" is meaningful is not surprising since the majority of probable responses happen to be so.

Finally, the content of dreams can be easily derived from a variety of previously experienced events or thoughts. The peculiar organization of dreams reflects the greater freedom of association characteristic of the sleeping brain. Symbols, in dreams as well as in art and waking life in general, present no special problems. Most symbols are culturally shared and easily recognized by persons familiar with the rules of the game. They need not reside in any kind of unconscious.

Conclusion

An attempt was made to show that the traditional psychoanalytic notions of repression and the unconscious are not only unnecessary but also less appropriate to the understanding of human behavior than explanations in terms of exclusively conscious behavior. The latter has its primary origin within the social conditions of inter- and intra-person communication. Several categories of human activities were then re-examined from this point of view.

The implications of this analysis in terms of theory as well as application are: Psychoanalysis no longer provides an appropriate model for human behavior, while further support is granted to such personality theories and treatment methods as

Adler's Individual Psychology, Wolpe's behavior therapy, or Ellis' rational-emotive therapy. . . .

In the reading just concluded, Papageorgis argues that the forgetting or distorting of past events are not as well explained by the concept of repression as they are by the following: actual changes and losses of memory with the passage of time; misperception of the original event; intentional suppression and/or alteration of a painful memory to lessen the pain; lack of verbal labels for events that happened in early childhood; incomplete assimilation of an experience at the time it took place; cultural conditioning to explain one's actions in terms of only socially acceptable reasons; and self-deception.

At the beginning of this chapter, a brief quotation was given from an article by the late Dr. Bernard Robbins, and another portion of the same article was summarized. We now conclude this chapter with a reading excerpted from another article by Robbins, whose basic premise was that the study of functional psychopathology is the study of disturbances of consciousness. He contended that irrational activity is determined by an irrational consciousness, by inaccurate perceptions of self, others, and external events.

In the following reading, Robbins, like Papageorgis, challenges the concept of regression as an explanation of human behavior, but he concentrates his attention entirely on the theory of repressed emotion (with which Papageorgis does not deal). Robbins does not believe that, when an individual exhibits inappropriate emotion, it is because the appropriate emotion has been repressed into the unconscious. In his view, inappropriate emotion is the result of inaccurate perception. The individual can achieve a realistic emotional response not through recovery of the appropriate repressed emotion from the unconscious, but by altering his perception of a particular situation so that it corresponds to reality.

The article which is excerpted below was published in 1955 in Psychotherapy. Robbins was chairman of its editorial board.

Although it antedates the 1960-1968 time period which is this book's proper scope, the editor has included it because nothing of comparable viewpoint could be found that was published during the aforementioned years. The portions of Dr. Ullman's 1958 article on "The Dream Process" (which appear in Chapter 7) were used for the same reason.

The Myth of Latent Emotion: A Critique of the Concept of Repression

Bernard S. Robbins, M.D. *

The cornerstone of Freudian theory is the concept of Repression. The basis of its therapeutic practice is the "return of the repressed."

In this paper we propose to reexamine, on the basis of clinical material obtained through therapeutic sessions, the construct of an enclosed psychic structure—the "unconscious" operating dissociatively in motivating human activity and generating human psychopathology. By this means we hope to lay bare the essentially untenable character of the concept of dormant, latent, intrapsychic emotional forces, motivating human activity and generating psychopathology.

. . . Through a contrast between the traditional approach and our own suggested departures we shall try to establish:

1. That neuroses are not diseases of the emotions, but are disturbances in "consciousness".

2. That the emotion presented by the patient at any one time is not the expression of a "reemergence from dormancy" —a mere repetition—but is a feeling always consistent with his prevailing consciousness.

3. That we are always dealing with *change*—change in personality, in ways of living, in ways of thinking, in contrast to the principle of "immutability," which is involved in the concept of "repression."

In our first illustration we present a clinical case that would

* *Psychotherapy*, Vol. 1, No. 1 (Fall 1955), pp. 3-11, 17, 28-29.

generally be regarded as showing evidences of repressed hostility, and we suggest a differentiated approach, which, to our mind, may lead to more appropriate theoretical conclusions (which are incorporated in the text).

A young man comes into a therapeutic interview session in a mild euphoric state. He has been struggling with the problem of an autocratic, domineering attitude toward his wife, and gleefully reports a situation which he believes he has coped with in a manner that augurs a profound change in himself.

Briefly, he recounts that his wife, during the course of this struggle with him, has come to learn the true meaning of "independence," and has laid down the following ultimatum: She is eager to renew her premarital interests, particularly in other men, and demands his consent to her decision, even to the extent of his acquiescing in her indulgence in indiscriminate sexual promiscuity. The young man insists that a change has occurred within him, for in contrast to his previous violent reactions to even mild suggestions of similar conduct, he now feels no jealousy, but only happiness at the fact that his wife now has the opportunity of fulfilling her needs, and that he is equipped to recognize and accept them. He feels exalted at the change within himself, for in his own eyes he is now treating her not like a "pup," but like "a human being."

The practised eye of the objective therapist, regardless of his theoretical presuppositions, will at once observe clinically that this activity and its accompanying emotion appear inappropriate. There prevail too many transparent and unresolved contradictions. A man does not, if he is rational, on the one hand protest a great love for his wife, and on the other, accept her announcement of proposed infidelity with ostensible joy. Even if we do make allowances for some of the constructive forces at work here (for example, the increasing necessity on the part of the patient to recognize the equality of his wife), his patently inappropriate response to this specific irrational demand of his wife (which does indeed reflect her own irrational conception of freedom), immediately strikes the therapist as spurious. No man can be quite so "noble"; nor can such "nobility" be deemed rational. Therapists, we are sure, would all agree that at this particular moment in the patient's history such activity reflects an irrational approach to the problem of establishing a more mature and humane relationship between his wife and himself.

Our problem then, as psychotherapists, is to understand the conditions that make for this irrationality, and to assist the patient in achieving a more rational approach and acting upon it.

The traditional Freudian view of this problem from the standpoint of the "inappropriateness of the emotion" and an "overdetermined reaction" would assume, and correctly, that a more rational response on the part of the patient to such a demand of his wife's would ordinarily be either bewilderment or anger, or both. Since the patient appears to be exhibiting inappropriate glee, it follows, from that standpoint, that the appropriate emotion, "hostility," must be "repressed" or "unconscious"; and that for reasons peculiar to himself, the patient dare not allow himself to be "conscious of his hostility to his wife," and that this "repressed hostility," operating *in situ,* within the psyche, accounts for the peculiar euphoric quality of his current behavior. The traditional approach then would be directed toward uncovering this "unconscious hostility." Historical material would be explored, centering around the patient's jealousy directed against a brother preferred by his mother; the remembered anger of the patient toward his mother would be stressed; similar situations would be recalled, and the connection would be established between these and the patient's anger toward his wife. The traditional view then would consider the original theory of "repressed hostility" as established, and the task completed so far as understanding of this episode is concerned.

Of course, the Freudian analyst may venture more "deeply" —that is, he may try to show that the patient's "repressed hostility" toward his wife, now returning, and originally surrounding his mother, was itself not directed toward the mother-sibling relationship, but was only a return of the "repressed hostility" surrounding the oedipal situation with castration anxiety about the father; and this, in turn, was itself a return of the "repressed hostility" associated with the pre-oedipal configuration—maternal, oral frustration, weaning, and so on *ad infinitum*. There is in fact no end to the possible constructions, which can carry (as one schizophrenic "recalled" to me) the resentment back to the hostility experienced by the ovum on being penetrated by the sperm.

Yet, even in the above formulations, one element remains clear: The patient discussed above *did* become aware of anger toward his wife where none had existed before. Need one actually employ such an elaborate construct as described above to account for the appearance of a specific emotion in its previous absence?

The answer is affirmative only if the therapist refuses to accept the therapeutic development as a *process* that involves *movement* and *change*.

It is our contention, however, that (1) the therapist, whether he is aware of it or not, is concerned solely with *activity* that reflects the state of interaction between the patient and his external world. This is the patient's *conscious existence;* and (2) that the emotion which is itself a part of this conscious existence is *always appropriate* to the character of the patient's consciousness at that particular time, and is always an accurate reflection of how the patient himself is reflecting the real world.

In the light of the above considerations, let us briefly reevaluate the activity of the traditional therapist with our patient. Our patient reports his wife's demands. He feels "exalted" at his understanding their rationality, and at being advanced enough to recognize her desire for "freedom." But now, what has the traditional analyst in reality been demonstrating, under the impression that he has been searching out the patient's "repressed hostility?" Has he not actually demonstrated one objective fact about the patient's external world: that this demand of his wife's is not in reality a correct pursuit of genuine freedom, but in all probability irrational? So that that entire formulation, with its stress on unconscious forces operating at the present time, its stress upon all that past history still lying dormant, and working out its evil now—*communicates only one* reasonable and probably correct reflection of reality: that his wife's activity, despite her husband's oppressive and exploitative treatment of her in the past, is "crazy" and unreasonable. When the husband becomes aware of the correctness of this view, when he contrasts his picture of his wife now with his image of her before his psychoanalytic interview, anger at her demands replaces his former euphoria. She appears different to him now as a result of the analyst's influence; and *now that he sees her differently, his feelings too are different*. So that the *anger* and *hostility* he now manifests are not evidences of a return of the "repressed," but actually *evidence of an alteration in perceptual consciousness*.

What has actually taken place? *Consciousness has changed; and with it feelings*. The theory of repression must appear then as a theoretical construct of a metaphysical view which holds that *nothing changes*. Hence the necessity for the conception of "dormant emotion" to account for current emotion.

Now, on the other hand, how do we approach this phenomenon of inappropriate euphoria?

We proceed from the following premises:

1. We are deeply concerned only with what *exists*—that is, the current activity of the patient himself.

2. We regard this activity as accurately reflecting the consciousness of this patient in his total life situation, his interaction with the world outside.

3. We place consciousness at the center. We regard the accompanying emotion or its absence as always appropriate to the particular consciousness of reality at that particular time—though not always appropriate to the *total* life situation. Thus, if a false consciousness of the reality exists, it will be accompanied by a feeling appropriate to the particular false prevailing view, but not appropriate to the true reality. For example, a schizophrenic who giggles at a funeral of a beloved person reflects not repressed hostility, but an incorrect awareness of the reality. His hostility is appropriate to his false consciousness

of the nature of the events taking place—but is thoroughly inappropriate to its *actual nature*.

4. We are guided by the necessity of assisting the patient in achieving an accurate reflection of reality; i.e., in changing his consciousness. In the course of this change, his life too undergoes a change.

It seems to us that once these principles are grasped, there appears small need to resort to an "unconscious" or to the "repressed" in order to effect a cure.

Alerted by what appears an inappropriate feeling of exaltation and nobility in the patient, we then carefully scrutinize and require an accurate account of his wife's demands. We wish first of all to determine the nature of the external forces operating upon our patient (in this instance, reflected by the person of his wife), and on the basis of this material, we come to the tentative conclusion that the wife's demands at this time reflect a contradictory understanding of the question of "freedom": it is a mixture of a personally and socially valuable striving for "independence," and destructive means of achieving it. Her *necessity* to achieve "freedom" negates and denies the existence of her husband's and her children's needs, in that it tends to deny the responsibilities associated with true freedom, and in fact tends to equate "independence" with an absence of these external necessities, and is blind to the principle that one's own "freedom" is bound up with the "freedom" of others.

Once we have come to this conclusion, we advance the thesis to the patient; not for *acceptance,* but in order to initiate such *cooperative activity* between us as will determine its accuracy and correctness, or the reverse.

Both therapist and patient now enter upon the task of compiling evidence both of historical (past) and current activity, either to support or refute the contention about his wife. As the evidence accumulates, through a consideration of the wife's social practices and behavior toward others as well as her husband, the latter comes to the "inescapable" conclusion that there is considerable truth in the therapist's view, and that his wife is indeed making, in his own words, "very excessive and irrational demands" upon him.

He suddenly alters his view of his wife. He comes to regard her as an inimical force, intent on denying him his rights as a person. In altering his view of her, he becomes furious with her, hostile toward her, and begins to act accordingly.

Let us pause here for a moment.

The traditional Freudian therapist will regard the appearance of hostility as "return of the suspected latent or repressed hostility." So far as he is concerned, his work with the patient on this problem is completed at this point, although he may continue, in the interviews, to pursue various metapsychological investigations into hetero-sexual origins of this "unconscious hostility."

So far as we are concerned, our work has only begun with this abrupt change in the patient's feelings toward his wife, which reflects *the coming into being of a new consciousness of reality*.

We are challenged by the question of how accurately this "new awareness" of his wife on the part of our patient reflects and corresponds to reality. True, his hostility augurs a change in perspective; it is consonant with and appropriate to the patient's new outlook. But does the new outlook really correspond to objective reality?

Now, the total situation includes not only the wife, but the patient too, as an active force in this process. Heretofore we have concentrated on his wife. But the patient also has his part to play. We are faced by two questions: What were the forces that operated to exclude his wife's irrationality from the patient's awareness? And why did he respond to her unreasonable demand with an anger that was equally unreasonable, since he suddenly came to regard her *in toto* as his enemy?

The first question concerns the particular elements in the patient that determined his false reflection of reality. What was obvious to everyone else, including the therapist, was that the wife was making unreasonable demands. For the patient, his need to distort this aspect of his wife's irrational activities into a rational movement for freedom was bound up in his need to maintain a vested interest in preserving a false image of himself as unblemished, eminently noble, and human. So that his view of himself was as distorted as his view of the outside world. His irrational behavior therefore is governed not only by an incorrect consciousness of the external world, but also of himself. This is the case, since self-consciousness is an aspect of total consciousness; and where one falsely reflects reality, the other necessarily follows.

Actually, he was far from being the kind of husband he imagined himself to be. Whatever may be said of his wife's unreasonableness, her criticism of him was based upon his actual behavior and practices, and was essentially correct. These practices were manipulative, domineering, and exploitative; they were essentially dehumanizing, as was his "acceptance" of her dream of "freedom," which robbed her of any remaining conviction that he still loved her.

We have pursued the case in some detail because it bears directly upon the second problem: his rage at the discovery of his wife's irrational exactions. Assuming that his rage was accompanied by his "new" outlook upon her as an inimical force that was in some way threatening him, we may ask: What was it that was being threatened? And why must he respond to that excessive demand with an excessive rage that the therapist must consider irrational since it contributes nothing to the resolution of a difficult marital problem, but must lead to counter-recriminations, greater bitterness and frustration?

The traditional analyst might try to dispose of this rage on the basis of its being "unconscious hostility," associated with past parental indignities, weaning, etc., and in reality as not directed toward his wife but rather toward a "mother image."

However, the particular approach we are here suggesting does not try to dispose of the patient's rage by denying *its actual existence*—by claiming it to be a fiction, relevant only as a "return of the repressed" and hence not to be taken seriously.

On the contrary, we contend that this rage does have an objective reality; that it is directed against his wife, and that it has serious consequences for the relationship. Furthermore, we contend that it must be eliminated, not by being relegated to some "encapsulated unconscious," but by having the conditions for its *genesis at the present time* determined. These conditions consist not only of the husband's recognition of his wife's excessive demands, but also of his recognition of his internal inability to cope with them except with the weapons of violence. So long as he regarded his wife's demands as rational (fantastic though they really were), they appeared to be in harmony with his own false image of himself as one of Nature's "noblemen," and they constituted no threat to the internal-external equilibrium predicated on that kind of conscious existence. As soon as he perceived their fantastic character, his entire *modus operandi,* the whole nature of his interaction with others—in short, his whole conscious existence was threatened. He had been betrayed by his totally false picture of reality; he was enraged by the betrayal of it (for what right did his wife have to ask him to accept what she demanded, when he had been thinking only of her?); he was helpless to cope with this threat, and in desperation he resorted to an irrational and violent rage (the final response when a collapse is imminent), in order to reestablish his old vested interest patterns, preserve his image of himself, and above all continue to maintain his obtuseness to his wife's legitimate needs. To recognize fantastic demands as such requires discrimination and an understanding of legitimate human demands. The patient's *status quo* depended upon the denial of the existence of any objective necessities, including his own, and hatred of his wife *comes into being* with his recognition not only that she has made irrational demands upon him, but also that she should make any demands upon him at all. It is this recognition of the existence of objective human necessities, including his own, that threatens his entire structure. His wife, by her very assertion of her human existence and needs (strangely as they were expressed), was putting to the test his whole fiction of nobility, that could be maintained only in a world that made no demands upon him. The hatred of his wife disappears as soon as he recognizes the existence of her rational necessities: that she might well be hostile to his current *modus operandi,* but was not hostile to his actual rational needs.

His hatred of her disappears when in the struggle in which he is engaged with her in *real* life, and under the influence of therapeutic necessity for obtaining accurate consciousness, he recognizes the following:

1. That helplessness prevails only so long as he has the need to preserve his vested interest position (in this instance, his "nobility").

2. That rational necessities of two individuals are not necessarily contradictory, but either compatible or capable of becoming reconciled without violation to either of the parties involved.

3. That these individual necessities can only be fulfilled through mutual cooperative activity; that that which is right for the development of his wife as a human being is compatible with that which is right for the husband's growth as a mature human being. So that "freedom" in this sense is indivisible. The freedom of one person activates the freedom of the other.

As a consequence of this growing consciousness of his wife as a partner in the satisfaction of his genuine needs, as a friend and lover, *he ceases to hate her.* His previous hatred is not repressed or suppressed. *It ceases to exist* by reason of his altered consciousness and tenderness—the reflection of their new form of existence—comes into being.

The movement from his initial "euphoria," through subsequent rage and hostility, to an eventual evolution of a degree of tenderness, concern, and seriousness is the reflection of a changing consciousness and a changing way of life. . . .

The scientific thinker always proceeds from that which exists. In these instances, what exists is the contradiction between the actual thinking and behavior of the patient and what is demanded by the objective requirements of the situation.

The patient here acts not in accordance with the real situation, but in accordance with his consciousness of it, which is false. We contend that his *irrational activity is determined by an irrational consciousness.* . . .

Let us now try to summarize some of our theoretical conclusions:

The concept of repression, in our opinion, cannot account for sudden changes in behavior or thinking associated with traumatic childhood experiences, and fails in its attempt to grapple with the problem of how the outside world affects an individual adversely for the following reason:

1. It does not recognize the actual interplay and coexistence of consciousness and social existence;

2. It does not recognize the fact of evolution of consciousness out of existence; and

3. It refuses to recognize the existence of change.

We propose in its stead a theory that would place life itself as the core of the neurotic process. Since human living consists not only of experience, but also of reflection upon experience, i.e., of what we call a "conscious existence," it is our belief that consciousness is at the core of functional disturbances.

We regard irrational activity, therefore, as being motivated by distortions of consciousness rather than "infantile emotions." We have also tried to show that the prevailing emotion always reflects consciousness, and is a relatively sure index and a useful tool in determining how accurately a particular consciousness reflects reality. If the emotion is what we regard as appropriate, then we assume that the reflection is accurate: if the emotion is inappropriate, then we assume that there is a disturbance in the consciousness of reality. Such a disturbance points up the existence of a contradiction between the objective, external world and the particular consciousness of the person reflecting it. Furthermore, we have tried to show, using emotions as clinical indices to the nature of a particular consciousness, that radical abrupt and intense alterations in feelings do not indicate return of the "repressed infantile," but are indicative of changes in consciousness.

It appears to us then that in postulating an "unconscious" and in clinging to "repression" as a therapeutic tool, in failing to recognize the relationship between feeling, consciousness, and external reality, the traditional psychotherapist is depriving the patient of a most useful instrument for achieving an accurate picture of the outside world; that is, he robs the patient of *reason;* for the very unreasonableness that has brought the patient to the therapist is aggrandized as reasonable, so that very frequently the patient leaves the therapist more comfortable in his unreason, but utterly unchanged.

In the final analysis one might venture the notion that the concept of the "unconscious" is itself no more than an inaccurate conceptual *conscious* reflection of something that exists in the objective world, by placing destructive and irrational human activities, destructive relationships, such as today characterize many segments of our human society, within the individual unconscious, by taking our eyes away from examining the structure of our society, and by falsely representing our task to be merely the reorganization of the psyche.

Once we think in terms of *change,* we cease thinking in terms of repression. There can be no *status quo* in the neurotic process any more than in the healthy one. As psychiatrists, psychotherapists and analysts, we ourselves are constantly preoccupied with the problem of what constitutes change.

When, therefore, we grasp the principles (1) that new things *can* come into being; that the present is not always merely a repetition of the past; and (2) that life not only acts upon the individual, but that he also acts upon life, and that in this process of interaction changes take place: then our therapeutic practice will be governed by the real existence of the patient and the external world, the contradiction to his conception of himself and it, and "cure" will consist in changing his *consciousness,* and not in some legendary recovery of his "unconscious."

REFERENCES

1. Sigmund Freud, "The Interpretation of Dreams," *The Basic Writings of Sigmund Freud* (New York: Random House, Modern Library, 1938).
2. Bernard Robbins, "Consciousness: the Central Problem in Psychiatry," *Psychotherapy*, Vol. 1, No. 2 (1956), p. 150.
3. *Ibid.*, p. 153.
4. Heinz Ansbacher and Rowena Ansbacher, *The Individual Psychology of Alfred Adler* (New York: Basic Books, 1956), p. 232.
5. Rollo May, "Existential Bases of Psychotherapy," *American Journal of Orthopsychiatry*, Vol. 30, No. 4 (October 1960), p. 688.

3

Causes of Emotional Difficulties: I

Paranoid States

In Henderson and Gillespie's *Textbook of Psychiatry*, [1] we are told the views of Freud and his co-workers and pupils concerning paranoid states:

> They state that paranoia and paranoid states are dependent upon homosexual fixation which is repressed, but when a failure of repression occurs the paranoid symptoms develop as projection phenomena. Freud's views stemmed from his analysis of the case of Dr. Schreber. He showed that in the genesis of delusions of persecution the persecutor is the one who, before the illness, had a great influence on the emotional life of the patient, or was an easily recognizable substitute for that person. The person who, on account of his supposed persecutory activities, is hated and feared, is the one who was formerly loved and revered. Schreber, for instance, had had at one time a great trust in and affection for his physician, Flechsig, but during his illness he called Flechsig a "soul murderer," and also exhibited a feminine wish fantasy (passive homosexuality) which had taken Flechsig for its object. The person longed for had become the persecutor. Eventually Flechsig became replaced by God, and this seemed to afford a way

of escape from the unbearable homosexual wish fantasy. Flechsig and God both probably symbolized the father. Freud then came to believe that all the recognized forms of paranoia could be represented as contradictions of the proposition "I (a man) love him (a man)."

Dr. Leon Salzman sees the primary origin of the paranoid state not in a repressed homosexual tendency but in an extremely deflated self-esteem. This poor self-image in *some* cases may be caused by sexual pathology, but Salzman does not see sexual pathology as its main cause in the majority of cases. He makes out a thoughtful case for the following propositions: (1) feelings of deflated esteem can arise from many different sources, sexual and nonsexual; (2) an individual may try to overcome these feelings of worthlessness by grandiose behavior which antagonizes the environment; (3) anxiety-producing rebuffs from the environment can provoke the organization of a self-protective delusional structure, i.e., a paranoid state.

Paranoid State—Theory and Therapy
Leon Salzman, M.D. *

For the purpose of this paper, paranoid state will refer to those delusional techniques, mild or extreme, which attempt to secure certain and universal acceptance because of a grandiose feeling of personal uniqueness. This is accompanied by secondary defensive externalizations, projections, and transference of blame made necessary by the environment to support these claims. In their most extreme form, these maneuvers produce delusions of grandeur and delusions of persecution, but are also manifest in everyday living as paranoid transfers of blame, or neurotic externalizations of self-doubt, or failures in living.

Some aspects of the paranoid process are more striking than

* *Archives of General Psychiatry*, Vol. 2, No. 6 (June 1960), pp. 679-681.

others, and the sexual pathology appears to be the least significant issue in the largest number of cases. This fact was also
noted in a study made by Klein and Horwitz of a large number
of case records of hospitalized paranoid patients who had psychotherapy. A search was made not only for evidence of homosexual content, or erotic needs or feelings or conflicts, but also
of fears of being or becoming or being attacked as a homosexual.
Klein and Horwitz found such content in only one-fifth of the
group. It is my impression that the grandiosity and the messianic nature of the patient's behavior, however, is very common.
The Schreber case highlighted this issue most dramatically.
Freud, in quoting Dr. Weber's report about Schreber, said:
"The culminating point of the patient's delusional system is his
belief that he has a mission to redeem the world and to restore
mankind to their lost state of bliss."

A patient from whom much of the material for this paper is
drawn stated it in a less striking fashion. She said: "Most of my
insecurities were handled by considering myself a great leader,
a superman type of character, determining the lives of others
without needing to relate to them." The mission which charac-
terizes these patients is one of great humanitarian concern, fulfilling the greatest benevolence for the world as they see it. They
feel themselves always opposed by forces of evil. . . .

Essentially, then, the paranoid development as I see it, is
characterized by a grandiose development, frequently messianic
in nature, which is an attempt to deal with extreme feelings of
worthlessness through a process of denial and reaction formation. The unreality, lack of humility, and arrogant presumptuous-
ness of the grandiose state alienate and antagonize the environment. The environment then belittles, denies, derogates, scoffs,
or simply disregards the claim. This may be sufficiently humiliat-
ing and infuriating and damaging to the grandiose structure to
encourage the development of a feeling of conspiracy, cabal, or
generalized malevolence which at its worst becomes organized
into a systematic plot. Briefly, it states that the denial of a low
self-esteem through grandiosity produces rebuffs from the environment. A defensive, projective transfer of blame through

delusional structure is organized in order to deal with this threat.

This thesis, then, is the reverse of the traditional thesis, which postulates that the paranoid development is based on a latent or repressed homosexual wish and the gradiosity is a secondary development, which is an attempt to rationalize the delusion and to explain the attention of the world on the patient. My notion is the reverse—that grandiosity is primary, and that the paranoid developments result from the realistic rejections or frustrated failures to achieve the grandiose claims. The paranoid development is thus a secondary response to the failure of a defensive technique.

There is considerable evidence in the extensive literature on paranoia to suggest that the paranoid mechanism can result from the anticipated attacks and retribution which would result from an attempted homosexual assault by the individual. While I do not deny the significance of these findings in the development of paranoia, I maintain that these expectations of attack by others are not simple reversals or displacements, as implied in these formulations, but follow a definite, grandiose development, and are initially attempts to deal with a deflated esteem based on many causes, sexual and nonsexual. Thus we find that in the development of paranoia the patient feels that he is being looked down upon, considered weak or impotent. He may feel that others consider him a sissy, or a homosexual, or a man who is unable to maintain himself in the competitive struggle of existence. Such feelings of deflated esteem first produce grandiose feelings of varying degrees, the patient's consideration of himself varying from a figure of special prominence to one of magnificent, omnipotent stature. In each instance it is an attempt to reinstate the low self-esteem by a display of strength and power, which will overwhelm one's adversaries and clearly establish one's stature. Ovesey, in the summation of [a] paper on homosexuality, says: "I would go so far as to suggest that it is the pure power (aggression) motivation without any pseudo homosexual elaboration that is the constant feature in paranoid phenomenon and that the related anxiety is, therefore, a survival anxiety." I extend this thesis by emphasizing that it is the power element so frequently expressed in messianic terms that stimulates the environment to rebuff and reject, rather than a mere semantic reversal which follows the formula: I want to subjugate, defeat him, etc., which becomes altered into: He wants to defeat or subjugate me. Such a profound alteration needs to be comprehended in more dynamic, adaptational terms than mere semantics.

This thesis may alter the therapeutic pessimism which has always accompanied paranoid developments, since it allows for an organized attack, based on data which can be arrived at without extensive hypotheses about homosexuality or questionable symbolic interpretation about latent homosexuality.

Obsessive-Compulsive Reaction

The obsessive-compulsive reaction consists of irrational behavior and/or thought which is beyond voluntary control: anxiety; persistent doubt and vacillation; and the fact that understanding the unreasonable nature of one's act or thought does not alter it. Freud and subsequent psychoanalysts appear to agree that the symptoms of this disorder represent an individual's attempt to control unacceptable sexual or aggressive impulses. In their view, compulsions or obsessions are symbolic substitutes for unconscious impulses and wishes intolerable to the individual's consciousness. The persistent thought or action (e.g., repeated handwashings) serves to keep something else out of his mind; the "something else" is the material repressed into his unconscious, the existence of which creates anxiety. The persistent thought or action also serves to reduce this anxiety and constitutes "a sort of magic ritual by which he undoes or annuls the possible effect of his unrecognized impulses and achieves a distorted satisfaction, self-punishment, and atonement." [2]

In an article dealing with obsessive-compulsive reactions, Salzman, [3] as in his preceding discussion on the paranoid state, again postulates the origins of an emotional disorder in non-Freudian terms. He points out that in earlier years the obsessive-compulsive disorder was also called *Manie de Doute,* or the doubting mania, since this symptom often occupies the fore-front of the malady. This is illustrated by the compulsion of an individual to try a doorknob a dozen times in an effort to assure himself that the door is really locked. Salzman contends that the primary source of the disturbance is excessive feelings of insecurity which require absolute guarantees before action is pursued. Although such guarantees are not necessary or pos-sible and interfere with normal living, the individual dares not take the ordinary risks and chances implicit in any decision any-one makes in his daily life. This extreme insecurity can develop from all kinds of life experiences, not only from fear of losing control of sexual or aggressive impulses. There is no single cause. Rather, there takes place a long process of conditioning in which the ritual comes to be used as a guarantee against risk. By performing a ritual such as washing his hands a cer-tain way a specific number of times, the individual believes he is following a proven, automatic procedure that takes care of a particular problem. He thereby eliminates the doubt that comes from making a choice of action each time.

Sociopathy

In the next paper, Richard C. LaBarba re-examines the tra-ditional psychoanalytic theory that, because of a developmental defect of the superego, the sociopathic individual shows no anxiety over his pattern of antisocial behavior. He makes a tentative case for the proposition that the sociopath's ruthless and selfish behavior actually is generated by anxiety and con-stitutes a major overcompensatory defense against it. In this view, the sociopath is a person who feels incapable of achiev-ing success in life through cooperative relations with others. He alleviates the anxiety engendered by this sense of inadequacy through attempts to be successful in antisocial ways.

The Psychopath and Anxiety: A Reformulation

*Richard C. LaBarba, Ph.D.**

One of the so-called classic signs of the psychopath or socio-path is his failure or inability to exhibit any behavioral or clini-cal anxiety. Social constraints, and the implicit and explicit threat of punishment for transgressing these constraints ap-parently do not prevent anti-social or otherwise disruptive be-havior. Such individuals are described as immune to the typically anxiety-evoking structures of society, both legal and moral. They are further characterized as ruthless, selfish, impulsive people who show no anxiety or guilt over the effects of their behavior.

Traditional psychoanalytic theory "explains" this personality disturbance generally as a developmental defect of the superego, the anxiety-generating and restraining component of the psy-chic apparatus. This paper is not so much concerned with the etiology of psychopathic behavior as it is with the concept of concurrent anxiety among such individuals.

The consensus that psychopaths bear no anxiety is not en-tirely correct. While often quite true that such persons when interviewed do not show any significant clinical anxiety which is typically interpreted as lack of anxiety, conscience, or super-ego, this interpretation reflects a wrong approach to the assess-ment of anxiety in these cases. The psychopathic syndrome which McCord and McCord have synthesized from the work of other investigators—the psychopath as asocial, driven by prim-itive urges, frustrated, impulsive, aggressive, and yet free of remorse, anxiety, and guilt—is seen by this writer as actually the consequence of an overwhelming anxiety arising from what we should like to call global organismic inferiority feelings.

As we see such individuals in the interview situation, they indeed display the McCord syndrome. Yet the "pure" psycho-path, as an anxiety-free, guilt-free individual probably does not

* *Journal of Individual Psychology,* Vol. 21, No. 2 (November 1965) pp. 167-170.

and cannot exist. The rich fantasy life, intense obsessive rum-
inations, pervading inadequacy feelings, and pathological ego
involvement inevitably augur deterioration characterized by
poor judgment, slips of memory, and underestimation of others
—all disastrous mistakes for the "successful" psychopath. The
dynamic system of the psychopath is in precariously sensitive
balance, and it is extremely prone to disruption in the vicissi-
tudes and stresses of daily living.

What evidence can we draw upon in support of a hypothesis
of concurrent anxiety in the psychopath? Experimental evidence
is, unfortunately, lacking, but there is some behavioral evidence
in the form of case histories, and there are some formulations of
personality theorists.

Adler, in a discussion of criminal behavior, states:

> We know that they (criminals) are cowards, and if
> they were sure we knew it, *it would be a big shock to
> them.* It swells their vanity and pride to think of them-
> selves as overcoming the police, and often they think,
> "I can never be found out." In all this we can see the
> criminal's inferiority complex. He is running away from
> the tasks of life in association. *He feels himself incapable
> of normal success. . . . He hides his feelings of inade-
> quacy by developing a cheap superiority complex* (italics
> mine).

Although Adler is referring specifically to the criminal, his
statement is broadly applicable to most cases of psychopathy.
Note the strong overtones of neurotic anxiety implicit in Adler's
description. The italics should be kept in mind when reading
the case history which follows below.

Sullivan states similarly that "psychopathic manifestations
include characteristically a more or less distinct awareness of
personal defect or abnormality, and this is accompanied by an
exaggerated tendency to rationalize."

A brief case history to which the author was exposed lends
some plausibility to a hypothesis of subjective anxiety in the
psychopath.

A 38-year-old white, single male who had been committed to a mental hospital some 20 years ago was seen in group psychotherapy for seven months. His behavior prior to hospitalization was characterized by repeated petty larceny, attempted robbery, and generally disruptive, antisocial, and unmanageable behavior. The patient was considered to be an incorrigible sociopath. Over the years of his hospitalization, he quite cleverly and adeptly escaped from his ward twice, once posing as a physician, and once as a state food inspector. So successful was his second deception that he enjoyed three days of attentive catering by anxious, threatened hospital personnel in another part of the hospital before he was discovered!

Superficially pleasant and friendly, his behavior on the ward was marked by obsequiousness to the professional staff and an overzealousness to help with the daily ward routine. His every act, however, was designed to provide himself with extra privileges, self-imposed authority, and opportunity, at the expense of other patients on the ward. All attempts to change his behavior by group therapy failed. Threats, punishment, and exhortation from both staff personnel and other patients were futile. Here was truly a case where anxiety was apparently absent and where none could be generated.

As a last resort, the therapist confronted the patient with direct interpretations of his behavior, first in the presence of the group members, and then in the presence of the ward nurse. The pupose of this approach was to "expose" the patient both to his peers and to the staff. His clever plans and ulterior motives were revealed to him as fruitless and not so clever. The group was warned as to future attempts by him to manipulate others for his own gains.

This approach destroyed the patient's image of bravado and grandiosity, and seriously undermined his "cheap superiority complex" by inhibiting future pyschopathic behavior on the ward. This last result is important, for now the future became uncertain for the patient, resulting in a growing apprehension bordering on a catastrophic reaction. Any future behavioral reinforcement by successful psychopathic maneuvers became less probable, leaving the patient with what appeared to be a serious degree of uncompensated anxiety.

In the second week of this approach, the patient began exhibiting physiological and behavioral signs of anxiety: mild hyperactivity, fidgeting, periodic manneristic behavior involving the face and hands, and mild stuttering, all of which had been absent before. Behavior on the ward was now seen to be meek, submissive, and subdued. Amount of verbalization in the group sessions declined sharply.

Unfortunately, the patient was soon transferred and further work with him was discontinued. No follow-up information was obtainable from that point on. It seemed, however, that this patient was now amenable to a more traditional approach of psychotherapy, perhaps with some degree of success.

When the sociopath is questioned about his behavior, he responds without much apparent anxiety. But this must not be construed as an absence of anxiety. He is anxious, but does not manifest this when talking about his behavior, because this is the very thing which alleviates his feelings of inadequacy, inferiority, frustration—his organismic anxiety. His casual admission and description of his behavior is not only necessary but vital for maintaining his sense of superiority, his distorted sense of self-worth. We cannot expect the psychopath to exhibit remorse, guilt, or anxiety over behavior which constitutes a major overcompensatory defense against organismic inferiority feelings. So powerful and all-consuming is the anxiety-produced striving to preserve and rebuild self-esteem that all socially oriented behavior is ruled out.

In sociopathic behavior the absence of overt anxiety is proportional to the degree of utility of the act in enhancing the feelings of self-worth and superiority. At the same time, any felt anxiety is covert and can be detected or elicited only by a different approach. As long as the approach remains behaviorally oriented, dealing with the external acts of the individual, no anxiety will be elicited.

It is contended here that anxiety is a concurrent component of the psychopath or sociopath, and that a sustaining arousal of anxiety is the only therapeutic tool we have to restore empathy towards individuals as well as groups or society in general, and to facilitate a change of the life style. These individuals must be exposed to something akin to stress interviews and procedures designed to bypass the affectively neutral, externalized components of their behavior.

The following four propositions for eliciting anxiety in the psychopath are cautiously offered. They would seem to be experimentally testable, and it is hoped that they will stimulate research in this area.

1. Group therapy is the treatment of choice for the psychopath insofar as the group members will contribute to the interpretation of his behavior.

2. Deliberately "pushing" the psychopath with early dynamic interpretation by the therapist will elicit anxiety.

3. Exposure of possible future psychopathic behavior to both peers and staff is very important in evoking anxiety.

4. Reinforcement of anxiety when it is exhibited for any period of time will aid in sustaining it and thus permit a more traditional therapeutic procedure.

The reader is reminded that these propositions are, for the most part, theoretical, and that good judgment is essential to guard the interests of the patient.

Pressures from Society

We began Chapter 1 ("The Nature of Man") with a brief sketch of Freud's outlook on man and his concept of the origin of emotional disturbance. It is clear that Freud viewed emotional difficulties as having intrapsychic origins and little direct relation to one's life experiences after early childhood or one's current environmental situation. It is suggested that the reader review these pages before going on to the next three readings, which deal with the impact of culture on the individual. These three readings make the point that emotional problems are very much related to one's present living situation and all the forces in his background, including, but not limited to, the interpersonal relationships and the events of infancy and childhood.

In the first paper, Dr. Irving Markowitz shows how the inconsistency, hypocrisy and pressure of adults in our culture pushes young people into unwholesome reaction patterns.

Culture's Impact on Adolescence

Irving Markowitz, M.D.*

Biologically, the latency period of development is thought of as that period starting after the early full development of the personality—roughly age six—and ending when this development is capable of being harnessed to its biological purposes at puberty. Socially, the latency period may be conceived of as the period between full physical maturation—puberty—and the time when the individual is considered capable of full acceptance into social institutions—adulthood.

Thinking of adolescence as a period of social latency simplifies our understanding of the impact cultural phenomena have on adolescent problems. The greater the discrepancy between the society's adulthood requirements and the capabilities of the child at puberty, the longer the adolescent period; the smaller the discrepancy, the shorter the period. In different cultures this gap widens or narrows in accordance with the complexity of the culture, the artificialities introduced, and the degree of recognition and aceptance of different individual rates of growth. Thus, in the culture of yesteryear, the young man who was required to drive a horse and buggy did so early in his development. Today, however, he may not drive a car until he is at least sixteen. Likewise, a young scholar may not perform in a given capacity until he has gone through all the ritual performance required, regardless of his degree of competence. The fulfillment of his social obligations is delayed until he has met all the initiation requirements, no matter their meaningfulness.

Gaps and discrepancies tend to foster distrust and suspicion, and adolescence is an especially fertile period for the develop-

* *Medical Opinion & Review,* Vol. 3, No. 9 (September 1967), pp. 66-69.

ment of paranoid distortions. Is it any wonder that the segment of the population most perceptive of hypocrisy finds untrustworthy a society that professes democratic ideals while practicing male chauvinism; that boasts of the superiority of its manufactured products while their production becomes increasingly slipshod; that advertises its interest in the consumer's convenience while its marketplace increasingly demands Caveat Emptor rather than Caveat Venditor; that encourages everyone to vote while it gerrymanders districts? Adolescents would have a far greater tolerance of the discrepancy between their growing capabilities and the requirements of society's institutions if they felt that these requirements were not exaggerated by such injustices and inequities.

Additionally, there is a marked intolerance for adolescent idiosyncrasy in the American culture. Parents hope to have the previously charming child pass as quickly and painlessly as possible through this awkward and parentally embarrassing period. Early child care is accepted as a valid responsibility, but the necessity for continued active participation in the lives of their teen-age boys and girls is judged to be an interference with the parents' unbothered use of time. The adolescent does not reflect enough credit on his parent to be a companion in all the adult activities in which the parents participate. This begrudging tolerance makes a demand on the adolescent to grow as quickly as he can.

If the period is one to be passed through quickly, then the young person must make use of "get-rich-quick" methods. These methods are generally the sickest ones in the culture, which may explain why adolescents often reflect the most baleful aspects of their society. In many European cultures, adolescents are considered children. Although their potential is recognized as being greater than it was before they attained puberty, they are not required to fulfill the social amenities of adult relationships. In our culture, however, they are expected to play the role of adults without the privileges of full membership. The tendency here has been for socially accepted adult customs to filter down to progressively younger and younger persons. Thus lipstick is now used by very young girls. Although the adolescent girl is encouraged to make her lips kissable, she must not allow them to be kissed.

Recently a father told me that he was planning to go camping with his adolescent son. He liked anchovies and even though they were going to "rough it," he wanted to take some canned anchovies along. His wife was tickled by this and in a rather belittling way told some of their neighbors, "Imagine, my husband is going camping and taking anchovies with him." The husband was furious. He discussed the situation with his son and was surprised that he also snickered at this aberrant behavior. After more talk he realized that taking anchovies did not seem incongruous to him because he was secure in his skills as a camper; they did spoil the "roughing it" aspect of the trip for his son who had not yet acquired this sense of security.

Training practices in both civilian and military life have long fostered the belief that the hard way is the only way a person can develop himself and his skills properly. He must brave the jungle clad only in a loin-cloth or crawl under actual machine gun fire in order to learn his capacity to survive when he meets the "real thing." What is often forgotten is that the endurance of necessary discomfort is very different from the endurance of simulated discomfort. Unnecessary emphasis on artificialities often causes the adolescent to concentrate on passing tests rather than on developing their capacities.

The notion that there is a special virtue in having done it the hard way is very pervasive in our culture. Although it may be true that atomic physics can be learned by a person forced to write with charcoal on the back of a shovel, it is a most uneconomic method of computation, and there is no special distinction conferred on the physicist who learned this way. It is also true that his contribution to society would occur much later that it would if he were able to employ less arduous methods. If we insist that the adolescent learn "the hard way," meaning that he repeat methods of learning common to his father's era, then instead of developing skills, he is only competing with his parents. This generation has to learn atomic physics—not just arithmetic.

Instead of trying to increase his learning the youngster often basks in easily acquired, dubious accomplishments as a way of proving his right to adulthood. He can hold his liquor as well as his father. He has more girls than his father did. He knows his "way around" as well as his father. These "get-rich-quick" methods are more appealing than the slower methods prescribed by his schooling. Unnecessary prolongation of training makes these methods seem even more attractive. The adolescent having learned these methods can say with some degree of right that he is thereby entitled to all the privileges of any adult around him. This leads to cockiness, resentment, and attempts to oust the oldsters rather than to develop himself. When adults say that what really matters is how well the game is played, they are talking not of the profundity of ethical values but of how well the spurious facade of good sportsmanship can be maintained. Parents who concentrate on form rather than substance must accept the responsibility for their children's tendency to confuse piety for conscience, politeness for courtesy, manner for feeling.

A young patient recently said to me, "It's not good to be better when you are in your teens, it's good to just get along." The same thought was expressed by another boy: "The good American boy should not be a student." Both attitudes result from warped cultural values: the belief that only through self-effacement can the individual be tolerated by his society.

The notion that he will get along best by hiding his light under a bushel may have especially unhappy consequences for the adolescent struggling to establish his individuality. Often the only way is to find common expression with other adolescents or to adopt stereotyped viewpoints sanctified by parental edict. Since he tends to believe that his own efforts have little to do with the attainment of manhood he settles for a ready-made identity and thus takes on much too readily the dignity gained for him by his peers, his school, his church. He joins causes not because they always express his views but because they hallow them. He expresses his rebellion en masse and may become a juvenile delinquency statistic.

In the past few years, there has been an increasing number of juveniles involved in major crimes in both suburban and rural areas. Arrests of juveniles have increased ten times as fast as arrests of adults; the number is rising faster in the United States than in England, but France, Austria, and West Germany show a decline in such offenses. What differences in these cultures have caused the changes in patterns of juvenile delinquency?

In the case of Japan, possible answers may be found in its adoption of Western customs and in its transition from a yesterday-oriented culture steeped in the notion of man's ineffectuality in the midst of his uncertainties to a today-oriented one. In the former both adult and child are chained without too many differences to the same observances and the same limitations. As Japan has moved into the present, new opportunities have developed, but their tendency has been to favor older groups in the enjoyment of these new dimensions. This has encouraged the young to grab what they can as the only way to attain something close to their previous stature.

That the adolescent in England is able to find more of a place for himself may be attributed to "unhealthy" factors such as the lack of higher educational facilities and resulting diminution in social mobility. Partly, however, it may be attributed to "healthy" factors: there is not as much pressure in England for the adolescent to "join up" while he is being denied adult privileges. It is not clear why France, Austria, and West Germany have shown a decline in numbers of juvenile offenders. Two possible interpretations might be that the complete disruption of old patterns has given young men more of an opportunity to gain the privileges of adulthood through study and concentration and that the shortage of manpower has permitted acknowledgment of the young men's contributions.

The increase in the seriousness of offenses committed by juveniles we may attribute, *in part,* to the greater variety of opportunities available and the increasing restriction of adolescents in their enjoyment of these opportunities. We say in effect, "Here is a big world available to you but you cannot enjoy it until we adults judge that you are ready. You may pretend you are part of it but you are not." To the young man not likely to be as well equipped as some of his peers to *ever* reap these full benefits, this tantalizing prospect may lead to intense fury and the determination to thrust his unwelcome self upon society. This is even more true when that society has set him few examples of equity and justice, and when he feels that little attempt is being made to find a place for him.

Is the answer then for us to become less complex and to pay for it with some diminution of the intensity of our joys and sorrows? I suggest that a more pleasing solution would be to lend ear and heart to understanding the adolescent's difficulties and to cooperate with him in establishing a place for himself in society.

Parents are useful in guiding the growth of adolescents just as they are important in guiding the growth of younger children. Parents have hesitated—and been discouraged—from offering their concern and help to their teen-age boys and girls. They have relinquished this role to society's organizations. Only as we re-emphasize the value of parental involvement with adolescents, separate from and indispensable to more specialized organizational help, can we make parents proud of their contribution.

By helping parents to fulfill their role comfortably and competently, we may well help the adolescent to a more fulfilling concept of *his* role. A chief difficulty is that until our social practices are much improved, the adolescent will often reject his parents' advice and thereby hinder collaboration. This does not mean that parents should be discouraged from offering their help, nor does it mean they should inflict it heedlessly. They may just have to keep trying without expectation of any great immediate impact.

The major area to which we all should address ourselves is the remedy of those social inequities and injustices that heighten the sense of futility and cynicism in adolescents. As we become more vital in our practices, as we yield less to connivance and manipulation, we may convince the adolescent that the rewards of his society are attainable by diligence and by honesty rather than through opportunistic behavior. In a world where weapons of complete and total destruction are available, we may avoid complete defeatism only through the development of just practices. If we insist instead that the adolescent mimic our ritualistic and anachronistic practices, we can only convince him that society must be tricked or defeated in order for him to survive and flourish. If, however, we make a place for adolescents and show that we are mutually united in similar struggles for growth and development, that we are as eager to remedy our own sins as we are to remedy theirs, and that we would appreciate their help and cooperation in the task, then perhaps the emotional problems of our adolescents would tend to decrease.

Richard and Katherine Gordon have done careful studies of suburban living to try to discover the sources of emotional difficulties in the residents of such communities. In a well-known book, *The Split-Level Trap,*[4] and in other writings, they concluded that the period of rapid suburban community growth during the early 1950's, was particularly hard on young married women at the child-bearing period. These women and their husbands migrated from larger cities to suburban towns and developed emotional problems from the stresses that arose. Their spouses got caught up in the high-pressure rat race toward the top of the socio-economic ladder, which interfered with family closeness. The women themselves had to bear alone the considerable strain of adjusting to a new and unsettled community.

In the later 1950's and early 1960's, these suburbs slowed down in their rate of growth, and more facilities of various types came into existence to help prevent emotional problems and involve the newcomers in community life. Around this time, percentages of young married women with emotional problems subsided, but percentages of adolescents with difficulties increased, and the suicide rate rose among middle-aged men in New York State.

The Gordons [5] suggest that the rise in adolescent difficulties was connected with the increased emphasis on education and the much greater pressure applied to this group to achieve academically, as a result of the launching of Sputnik I by the Russians in 1957. Marginally adjusted young people might have had trouble coping with this pressure. The notable increase in industrial competition and automation in the American economy of the 1960's resulted in greater job stress and unemployment of marginally prepared workers, and might partly account for the rising numbers of suicides among middle-aged men.

These observations of the Gordons underline dramatically the impact of culture on mental health, and present new evidence that the pattern of a community's psychiatric disorders may be related to its socio-economic conditions. This concept is distinctly different from that of classic Freudians, whose interest in environmental influences on the personality is usually confined to relationships with family members during infancy and early childhood.

In another paper, portions of which are presented below, the Gordons and Marcia Singer expand the above concept to the larger premise that emotional disorders are related not only to present-day stresses in the lives of individuals, but also to various kinds of background stresses over and beyond those of the first few years of life. In a study of a large number of cases of both psychiatric patients and "normals" (controls), they investigated several background stress items, beginning with *death of a parent* and *parental separation and divorce*. *Parental separation and divorce* was important in the lives of both married and single young adult patients and child patients significantly more than norms. *Parental separation and divorce* among young married and single men and women was very significantly more related to their emotional disorders than was *death of a parent*. Married patients of both sexes and all ages reported significantly more divorce in their own previous marriages than the comparison group.

Severe personal physical illness was reported by all patients very significantly more than by the comparison group. Patients of all ages reported very significantly more *previous personal emotional disturbance* than did normal young men and women. A *family history of alcoholism or mental illness* also occurred significantly more in the lives of patients. Patients *failed to complete their educations* significantly more than did normals of comparable age.

Social Psychological Stress

Richard E. Gordon, M.D., Ph.D., Marcia B. Singer, and Katherine K. Gordon *

... Many of the authors' previous studies have concentrated upon the important on-going stresses in emotional and physical disorders. In *The Split-Level Trap* they summarized these earlier investigations, showing relationships between present-day stresses, particularly those associated with social mobility, rapid educational and socio-economic advancement, and emotional and psychosomatic disorders in the lives of children and adults. The present report will explore more fully the importance of background, as well as present-day, stresses in the lives of patients.

In several studies, particularly of women who developed post-partum emotional problems, it appeared that the development of an emotional difficulty was related quantitatively to the numbers of background and on-going stresses. It appeared that accumulations of past and present traumata conditioned painful emergency behaviorful mechanisms in many susceptible persons. However, response to therapeutic or preventive measures was very significantly related to environmental as well as personality features. Those who had been educated to use their intelligence in facing and coping with the stresses of their lives did better than the falterers and quitters. For those individuals

* *Archives of General Psychiatry,* Vol. 4, No. 5 (May 1961), pp. 459-460, 464-470.

who made efforts to help themselves and/or received some practical assistance and encouragement from others, extinction of the maladaptive emotional responses took place readily, if the individual's life situation permitted removal of on-going stress.

The stress of "getting ahead" or just plain survival in a changing, increasingly crowded suburb or larger world, may serve acutely and chronically to activate emergency neuroendocrine reserves. This activity of humans (and/or lemmings) caught up in the "Rat Race" is often associated with disturbing emotional and psychosomatic processes. But if an individual has won by his struggle, or by good fortune has had thrust upon him, the power to control and influence his environment and life, he may readily quiet the psychophysiologic disturbance. Even patients who suffered a coronary artery thrombosis were more likely to survive if they had achieved higher socio-economic positions, as compared to those whose status was lower, or was declining.

This paper will examine the evidence regarding patients in other groups—children of both sexes, single young adults, married young men and women, the divorced and widowed, the middle-aged and older. Several hypotheses will be investigated. They are as follows:

1. General stresses, individually and in the aggregate, are associated with the occurrence of emotional disorder.
2. Certain other stresses may be related specifically to the life-role of an individual.
3. Whether an individual responds to therapy or not is related to the modifiability of his social environment. If environmental stresses can be reduced, either by his own efforts, or by those who have power and control over his life, he will tend to benefit from therapy.

These hypotheses have previously been tested in controlled experiments with new mothers who developed postpartum emotional difficulties. The affirmative findings will now be re-examined with other patient groups. However, this present report will deal with less controlled observational data which can only support these theses, or fail to do so. Thus this study is larger in scope, though less rigorous in design. More refined experimental tests must come later.

Eight hundred and ten case histories of adult private psychiatric outpatients and 114 records of child patients were analyzed for objective background social history data. Similar information was obtained for comparison from 232 normal parents of young children and from 325 normal school children in the first, fifth, and eighth grades of a public school in the same community.

The patients' subsequent course of therapy was determined from their case records. There were four types of treatment: (1) outpatient psychotherapy (sometimes combined with meprobamate); (2) referral for inpatient care in a psychiatric hospital; (3) tranquilizers—predominantly chlorpromazine; (4) psychic energizers—iproniazid and later phenelzine (Nardil). . . .

Modern social psychotherapy combined with pharmacotherapy has helped many patients remain outside hospitals and in their homes. However, marked differences occurred between patient groups.

Certain social history features associated with emotional stress regularly discriminated between patients and normals. Scores made from these items were much higher than those of the norms, but differed between the groups.

Some items, particularly those specific to patients of various socio-economic groups, were associated with better or worse response to therapy. Generally, it appeared that patients whose life situations were less subject to improvement, despite a combined outpatient therapeutic attack, were more likely to become hospitalized. Hospitalized patients included (1) older people more than younger; (2) unmarried (single, widowed, or divorced) more than married women (but not true for men); (3) older and single young men who were having job and financial difficulties; (4) older women who had no children or whose grown children had left the area, more than those whose grown children still lived in the same county; (5) older women who had no job skills and experience more than those who did.

Study of the general and specific items associated with emotional disorder in various patient groups suggests that preparation for one's position in life and anxiety about the role one must play are important in the development of emotional problems. For example:

1. Young married men seemed to be bothered by stresses associated with their bread-winning and marital role responsibilities. Business, financial, and family physical and mental health difficulties concerned them more than they did single men. They, as other men, had more difficulties when they lacked a completed education and/or an American-born father in their childhood home to prepare and guide them. They were overloaded with quantitative stresses more than any other group. However, they usually were upwardly mobile socially, more rugged and competitive. They responded readily to therapy.

2. Young married women reported stresses related to preparation for the feminine homemaking role. Disruption of their parents' home by divorce or mother's death and a previous marriage ending in divorce were more frequently reported in their social histories. Foreign birth, with its implications of separation from mother, family, and childhood friends and customs, was important in the disorders of some women, mostly war-brides. They were almost as much overloaded by background stresses as the young married men. Earlier studies indicated young married women were also particularly affected by the stresses related to geographic, socio-economic, and cultural mobility. If these items were counted and the numbers added to the scores from background items, the mean score for this group would be 5.5. For comparison, the new total score, including both background and mobility items, for young married men would be 5.7. Scores for other age, marital, and sex adult groups were relatively unchanged by the mobility item. Social mobility was not too important as a source of stress in the lives of other groups, except for children, particularly boys. Young married

women, just as young married men, were usually overloaded with stress. They responded well to therapy, particularly if an understanding husband was available temporarily to help reduce the burden of stress, and to increase their number of rewards.

3. Single young men had problems related to poor preparation for the competitive world of school and business affairs. They succumbed to less total stress, indicating they as a group were less inured to, unable to cope with, stress than the tougher, more successful married men of the same age. They often had European-born, working-class fathers, who were themselves oriented to the stable but often authoritarian values of the Old World. Such fathers were usually poorly equipped to guide their sons for the competitive educational and social rising expected of the American middle class to which their sons tended to aspire. Incomplete educations and personal illness were common features in these patients' social histories. Pushed aside by the tough competition of more aggressive young married men, they more frequently became hospital patients.

4. Single young women, although almost all were working, were relatively less concerned with problems in this sphere of activity. They reported stresses related to their feminine and family problems. Romantic difficulties, family mental and physical illness, and parental separation were more important to them. The mean scores related to stress which they underwent were the lowest of all the groups. This suggests a relative lack of toughness of character, which is not surprising. However, they generally responded to therapy. The environment is not so harsh on them; they can often obtain employment, and thus build self-esteem in this area. A less rugged, competitive attitude is expected of them. They can feel a sense of personal advancement and success after smaller accomplishments than can single men.

5. Middle-aged and older men had problems with work, personal and family illness, and previous personal and family marital troubles. Foreign birth was a handicap to them. Their stress scores were lower than the middle-aged women's. They, like the single young men, were often being pushed by the competi-

tion of aggressive young married men. Less inured, with few outside interests to distract them, they often became depressed, sometimes attempted suicide. They required more hospital care. They, as a group, frequently had tried to prevent themselves from becoming overloaded with stress, not by learning to cope and manage, but by compelling others, including their wives and children, to bear and help relieve them of burdens.

6. Middle-aged and older women were especially incapacitated by loss in any or all of their three main sources of security. With no husband, no work abilities, or no children it was difficult for a woman to gain a respected position in society and maintain self-confidence. With few outside interests to distract them, their worries made them tense and sleepless. The tension resulted in muscular pain; this increased worry and a vicious cyle set in. Their mean stress scores were among the highest. They as a group tended to be unassertive, though more inured than the men patients of comparable age. They frequently had become involved in situations beyond their control. Without special resources to fall back upon they became depressed, and often required hospitalization.

It is apparent that personal and family illness, both physical and emotional, particularly necessitating hospitalization, was important in the development of all patients' emotional disorders. Separation and divorce, personal or parental, also were important to most groups of patients. Among younger patients, failure to complete one's education was regularly associated with emotional disorder.

This study has provided evidence in support of the three hypotheses.

1. General stresses—related to personal illness, family illness, early death of a parent (particularly of the same sex), parental separation or divorce (even more than death of a parent in the younger groups), previous personal or familial emotional disorder—were common to most patient groups. The

sum total of items which indicated potential stress was related to the occurrence of emotional disorder in an individual.

2. Certain stresses, usually related to their role in life, were specific to each of the various groups.

3. Finally, response to therapy, as measured objectively by ability to remain in outpatient psycho- and pharmacotherapy, was related to the personality somewhat, but particularly to the life-situation of the patient, and the role and position he held. Patient groups that responded best were those with best modifiable social environments. Improvability of the environment with consequent decrease in total numbers of stresses seeemed to be the important factor.

These observations are in accord with simple *principles of learning,* conditioning, and extinction in general psychology. They support the findings of previous more precise experiments which, however, were limited in scope. They indicate that, when large numbers of cases are used, objective social history data can be used in psychiatric investigation. These data may be treated statistically and electronic data processing equipment are useful. Relationships and interrelationships may be determined and new inferences suggested by the findings. These not only may be useful to the clinician, but also suggest new correlational and experimental researches.

The term "stress," as used in these studies, has been used analogously to its use in physiology. It is highly possible, and subject to experimental test, that the quantitative overloading described in these studies has parallels in neuroendocrine processes.

This report also demonstrates the usefulness of *combined pharmacologic, psychologic, and social therapy,* particularly in decreasing need for hospitalization of psychiatric patients. This was not the principal purpose of the study and no effort was made to investigate the relative importance of each of these aspects of therapy. This task must await further research.

The findings of this report do not justify many cause and effect conclusions. They do provide indications of relationships which suggest practical clinical measures. Important recommendations that may be derived from the findings of this study would include:

Physical Health.   Since physical disorder, familial and personal, is strongly related to emotional problems, patients who have had severe physical illnesses in their own family members' lives might be advised to undergo regular repeated physical checkups for preventive purposes. New ailments can be found and treated early, before they tend to become severe. Thus sound medical practice may have psychiatric prophylactic effects of greater importance than was previously realized.

Education.   Educational quitters frequently have emotional problems. Physicians might strive to encourage not quitting. Experience has shown that the person who does continue, even with only one or two courses, in night school perhaps, is less likely to suffer subsequently in job opportunities, as well as socially and emotionally. In time many such educational falterers may even resume a full program of studies. The enormous importance of continuing education in this modern era of increasingly automated industry cannot be overemphasized. The employee must continually not only do his job but prepare himself for a better one. Only then can he free himself from fear of being displaced by either man or machine. It is far easier to prepare in advance than to wait until he is out of a job. Once he has suffered the loss of self-esteem, which the findings of this and other studies have shown to be so frequently associated with work difficulties, he is much harder to help. Anxiety then interferes with the concentration needed for pursuing studies.

Marriage and Divorce.   Divorce is highly associated with emotional difficulties of children and of the divorced, even if the latter remarry. The difference in importance between death of the parent and parental separation and divorce, in the emotional disorders of children and young married adults, was striking. Nowadays a first marriage often is between infatuated teen-agers poorly prepared for the responsibilities of marriage. Perhaps physicians can help control this problem by counseling long engagements of minors. Those who continue their educations tend to divorce less. Sometimes a pregnant teen-ager compounds rather than remedies her errors and misfortunes by marrying her careless lover.

Emotional Health.   Previous familial and personal emotional illness, particularly when complicated by hospitalization and ECT, is frequently associated with a tendency to recurrence. These patients, too, may benefit from periodic prophylactic psychiatric conferences. They may learn to respect their physiologic limitations, not allow themselves again to be overloaded. Biennial psychiatric checkups might help them guard against new stress and prevent further psychiatric illness, which is not only a response to stress but is in itself stressful in our society.

Continuation at Duty.   It is usually easier to help the emotionally sensitized who stays at his job, or at her household tasks. Except for the overprivileged, who do not need to earn their own livings nor care for their own homes, a patient with emotional problems may find his difficulties compounded by financial strains, or anxieties about her children's care in the case of the housewife. As with those with educational difficulties, some of the burden of responsibilities might be curtailed temporarily until the other stresses which helped acutely overload the patient are reduced. Then the full load of necessary duties can be resumed, with care and caution.

Much tolerance of temporary deficiencies, willingness to help, patience, tact, and perseverance on the part of family and friends are necessary. Meanwhile the patient's emergency emotional reactions subside as more easily removable strains are reduced, and he accustoms himself to bearing the necessary stresses of his responsibilities. Unfortunately, in this mobile world many people are often too preoccupied with their own affairs to provide the understanding and help such patients require. They resent what they consider having to assume another's burdens permanently. But there is a great deal of difference between an *endless handout* and a temporary *helping hand*. Very few persons need or deserve the former; most everyone has required and benefited from the latter in the process of gradually learning habitually, automatically, and relatively effortlessly to bear responsibilities.

Preparation for Work and Other Interests in the Future. People—men, women, children of all ages—do well to prepare for diversified roles in their futures. Women in particular were prone to emotional difficulties with loss of their homemaking, childrearing, and marital roles, especially if they lacked work skills. In a changing, increasingly automated, industrial and mobile world, this problem will probably continue, and even get worse, before it gets better.

Physicians are probably well-advised to counsel their patients in declining industries, and children as well—boys and *girls*—to prepare for job skills in industries and professions *with a future.* As mentioned earlier, it is better to prepare in advance for a new position than to wait until the situation has become an emergency.

Moreover, men, as well as women, should prepare for community, home and off-the-job interests. Men whose self-respect is sustained by accomplishments in other spheres than business readjust more readily in periods of business decline. Men might continually ask themselves whether they are getting too much involved in the competitive economic struggle. Oftentimes they pursue from habit activities that no longer are necessary for security or enriched living, yet are potentially injurious to both physical and emotional health.

Mobility. Even as we counsel patients to "prepare for anything" in their lives, we might caution a little less frenzy about assuming new responsibilities, having more children, moving about. The young housewife leaves her home community to follow her husband's job opportunities, and has her babies, and suffers emotionally and physically from the lack of family help and guidance with her children and other new responsibilities. Her mother remains behind and gets depressed for the lack of uselful services to perform. Perhaps Greeley's famous advice might be rephrased: "Stay home, young woman!" In the modern era many leave needlessly just for the sake of being on the go— to everyone's disadvantage. Others, of course, leave purposely, to be free of domination of a mother who is of little help and causes much confusion by her lack of understanding and no-longer appropriate values.

Speculative Boom and Bust.   Let us learn from our unfortunate patients in declining industries who became physically or emotionally incapacitated and did not recover. The economists caution us that the epidemic of speculative mania, the consume-now, pay-later morality which we observe in the present era, has always led eventually in the past to economic depression, with its counterpart—epidemic psychological depression. Physicians can caution their patients against speculative recklessness in their lives. They can help prevent the development of too many and too much power to the overprivileged, decrease the efforts of patients to emulate their envy-inspiring excesses. With the cooperative efforts of others—scientists, educators, lawyers, who are both educated and ethical—perhaps a new economic and medical calamity may be averted.

The Sensitized.   Whether the early traumatized become emotional casualties or sensitive, intelligent, and creative individuals depends upon how their experiences were handled. Life's stresses, if not overwhelming, can bring out the best in us. The well-guided can learn from his own griefs, and the mistakes of others, how better to prepare for and avoid similar troubles in the future. Punishment, combined properly with reward, results in better learning than either alone.

Physicians may counsel a one-at-a-time facing of, and not running from, problems, with loving support and assistance of family in reserve. Anxieties about possible recurrences of past griefs stir plans and preparations and intelligent constructive efforts in those who are encouraged and helped to continue moving forward carefully. Emotions, properly guided and controlled, can inspire intelligent thought, as well as produce painful symptoms. The example and training the sensitized has received has much to do with his subsequent personality, intelligence, and behavior.

Training Children.   Children in our present materialistic society often have high expectations for pleasures and rewards and low tolerance to frustration, punishment, or stress. Younger ones, particularly overprotected girls, often become phobic after physical illness; older ones are demanding, undisciplined, poor students, and temperamental. Just as we often immunize against many severe physical illnesses by repeated doses of antigens, we might recommend "inurization" against emotional illness, gradual facing responsibility, toughening up in order to face a not so gentle, competitive world. As the child recognizes he must assert himself tactfully, face some hardship, strive, persevere, develop patience, consideration of others and self-control, he is better prepared to cope with life's stresses without developing emotional illness. The learning principles by which he can be trained have been demonstrated clearly in the laboratory. They are quite applicable in life.

The differences in social stress scores indicate, among other things, that some age, sex, marital groups are more susceptible to emotional difficulty than others. Probably the more susceptible have had less preparation for the rigors of modern life. Children need less protection and smothering "love" and more toughening and preparation for life.

Reassessment of Values. Some tasks are more important than others. The overloaded individual who strives to do everything personally and equally well may keep his emergency neuroendocrine mechanisms straining. Conference with others and a good deal of thought will help him discriminate between what is less important (such as keeping up appearances, conspicuous consumption, less profitable responsibilities, chairmanships rather than lesser responsibilities on committees, etc.) and what is essential. The less important need not be forgotten, but postponed until a less stressful period of life, or delegated to a subordinate employee in the office or child in the home. Much of the effort compulsive and perfectionistic people were taught to make as children has relatively less survival value in the world of today. Continual discrimination between the important and the trivial, and laying aside of the less valuable, permanently or temporarily, helps keep down the burden of stresses.

Therapeutic Responsiveness.   An individual's therapeutic responsiveness depends upon (1) the economic skills he has learned; (2) the improvability of his life situation and the role he plays in it (age, sex, marital, economic, social factors); (3) the availability of helpful resources to assist, enrich, and reward him (both agencies or institutions and family or friends); (4) the total number of stresses to which he has been subjected, his constitution, and the type of reaction he developed to the stresses. Certain reaction patterns are less amenable than others, especially when associated with lifelong, repeated stresses; (5) his personality and social skills. A more skillful, usually better educated individual copes with his environment by study of what has succeeded and what failed in his life and others' lives. He learns from his past history and improves his present and future; (6) how much he is inured to hardship. Medical science has a challenge to discover how to harden persons, and how inured an individual can become to life's stresses, without interfering with longevity. Some, usually less-educated, patients think their symptoms will just go away somehow, especially if they take their medicines. But they must both remove some of the stresses that aggravate them and inure themselves to the rest. Unfortunately, they cannot buy courage in a bottle.

Diagnosis.   Psychiatric diagnosis has been recognized to be unsatisfactory for some time. Many patients appear similar to each other symptomatically, yet they respond with varying success to psychotherapy. It seems reasonable to develop a more functional and systematic statistical approach to psychiatric classification. The approach used in these investigations may be helpful.

The six categories used in describing therapeutic responsiveness above may serve also a diagnostic purpose. Each of these categories contributes in large measure to the amount of stress or pleasure with which an individual's life is associated. Statistical probabilities of his achieving a happy, healthy life, or responding to therapy might be obtainable for each of these categories. With large numbers of subjects formulas could be set up and combined probabilities determined.

Many single young men, sons of foreign-born parents, are labeled schizophrenic. So are acutely disturbed young married people, temporarily overloaded by the burden of new stresses or old. Both groups of patients may be similar symptomatically, but they differ enormously in therapeutic responsiveness.

Housewives married to men of different ethnic background often respond differently, depending upon the combinations, despite similar clinical symptoms. Protestant girls married to Catholic, particularly Italian-American, husbands do not do as well in therapy as do Catholic girls, including those of Italian descent, married to Protestants.

The tendency of middle-aged men and women to hypochondriasis and paranoid symptoms is also more readily understood in the light of these studies. The functional usefulness of a social psychological type of diagnosis, as compared to a symptomatic, becomes more apparent in the light of these few examples.

This study investigated features in social histories that discriminated between psychiatric patients and norms. Environmental factors related to therapeutic response were explored.

Certain background items occurred significantly more in the lives of each age, sex, marital groups of patients. Other features were related to the life histories of specific groups. Similarly certain features were related to poorer therapeutic response of patients in general, others to response of specific groups.

It appeared that preparation for one's life role and anxiety about performance were related to occurrence of emotional disorders. Not only personality and social skills but environmental opportunities were associated with favorable response. Implications of the findings were suggested for both medical practice and research.

The third of our three readings on the impact of culture deals with occupational stresses, and makes the point that work pressures can trigger emotional upsets. What follows is an excerpt from an unsigned statement prepared by a pharmaceutical company as part of an advertisement appearing in medical journals. The selection speaks for itself and indicates that human behavior cannot be understood without a knowledge of each individual's total current life situation, including the conditions under which he works.

Occupational Stresses Leading to Depression and Anxiety*

How prevalent is emotional and mental illness in the country's working population? McLean cites studies suggesting that over 30 per cent of the work force may present mild to severe symptoms of emotional difficulties at any given time and that 2 per cent annually must change jobs or lose significant time from work because of major emotional disturbances. It has been called industry's top medical problem, costing billions annually in absenteeism, employee turnover, accidents, and lowered productivity.

Among the work pressures and stress situations that may precipitate depression, anxiety, paranoia, and other signs of neurotic and psychotic disorders are: (1) difficult adjustment to job transfers including those involving geographical moves; (2) assignments calling for new skills or displacement of old skills by machines; (3) inability to meet deadlines, quotas, altered production schedules; (4) changes in bosses and company policies; (5) overt or covert competition for promotion and failure to obtain promotion; (6) discharge or demotion with its threat to self-esteem.

In the belief that rest and change are health promoting, an employee who appears overly anxious and depressed is often told to take a few days off to help him "snap out of it." Is this practice advisable? Not always, although a change of pace and scene may be beneficial for some. Many, however, depend on their job for a feeling of belonging, of accomplishment, of social acceptance. Telling an employee he can't work for a while may make him feel that he must be sick, may increase his feelings of

* Used with the kind permission of Schering Corporation, Union, N.J.

unworthiness, dependence, and helplessness, may aggravate the depression and anxiety which they triggered.

Executive crack-up may not be as prevalent as modern business myths and catch phrases suggest. Psychiatrists report that executives often display above-average mental as well as physical stamina and that their emotional health is as good as and perhaps better than that of others. However, when emotional breakdowns do occur in executives, the effects may be far reaching on the morale of subordinates and the economic health of the business. The special pressures on executives—frustrations in goals, feelings of insecurity or inadequacy, fear of failure, summit loneliness—should not be overlooked or underestimated. Under these stresses, severe disabilities may occur with chronic anxiety or other psychoneurotic disorders in which depressive reactions (sometimes well concealed) play a prominent part. . . .

REFERENCES

1. David Henderson and R.D. Gillespie, *Textbook of Psychiatry,* 9th ed. (London: Oxford University Press, 1962), p. 211.
2. Charles Brenner, *An Elementary Textbook of Psychoanalysis* (Garden City, N.Y.: Doubleday Anchor Books, 1957), p. 48.
3. Leon Salzman, "Therapy of Obsessional States," *American Journal of Psychiatry,* Vol. 122, No. 10 (April 1966), pp. 1139-1146.
4. R.E. Gordon, K.K. Gordon, and M. Gunther, *The Split-Level Trap* (New York: Bernard Geis Associates, 1961).
5. R.E. Gordon and K.K. Gordon, "Psychiatric Challenges of the 1960's," *International Journal of Social Psychiatry,* Vol. 10, No. 3 (Summer 1964), pp. 228-231.

4

Causes of Emotional Difficulties: II

Phobias

Friedman, in his chapter on "The Phobias" written for the *American Handbook of Psychiatry*, gives the Freudian concept as follows:

> The processes involved in the formation of phobic symptoms are especially well illustrated in Freud's "Analysis of a Phobia in a Five-Year-Old Boy," commonly known as the case of "Little Hans". . . .
>
> Freud's classic case study deals with a child who refused to go out into the street for fear that a horse might bite him. At the root of the phobia, as the analysis revealed, was a conflict between the boy's instinctual strivings and his ego demands. His oedipal conflict and strong hostility toward his father gave rise to intense fears of punishment, that is, to castration fears, which became transformed into the phobic fear of being bitten by a horse. In other words, the horse was substituted for the father; an internal danger was changed into an external one, and the fear was displaced onto the substitute. It is easier to avoid an external danger than to cope with an inner danger that cannot be avoided.

These processes are characteristic of the phobic structure in general.

In phobia the original object of the fear is typically replaced by some other subject, and the original source of the fear reaction becomes repressed. In the case of "Little Hans," death wishes against the father and fear of punishment for such wishes were repressed, because consciously they were unacceptable to the boy who also had strong positive feelings toward his father. However, his death wishes and fear of punishment (as well as still other psychic components) re-emerged in the form of a phobia consisting of fears that a horse would fall down and that a horse would bite him. The choice of a horse as object of the phobia appeared to have been overdetermined by various factors, including the fact that prior to the onset of that phobia Hans once had actually seen a horse fall.

The child was unaware of the symbolic meaning of his fear, thus the displacement provided a double advantage: he could go on loving his father, while the fear could be concentrated on an object more easily avoided.[1]

Kolb [2] summarizes the psychoanalytic view of phobias in this fashion:

In general, one may say that the patient's anxiety becomes detached from a specific idea, object, or situation in his daily life and is displaced to some situation in the form of a specific neurotic fear. The fear that he feels in the presence of a certain object or experience is really the displaced fear of some anxiety-producing component within his own personality. The situation about which he is phobic symbolizes or represents the incidents arousing affects of rage or shame, affects which must be prevented from coming to the surface, usually out of anxiety of rupturing an important relationship. The patient is not, of course, aware of the psychological source or significance of his fear, and while he may acknowledge that his fear is irrational, he is quite unable to regulate his life except as dictated by the phobia. He is constantly attempting to control his anxiety by avoiding the object or situation to which the anxiety has been displaced.

One non-Freudian concept of phobias stresses that they are learned reactions. In such a non-Freudian framework, a phobia is seen as a fixed, unrealistic fear response, which originally began as a fear of a specific object or situation which the individual could justify in his perception of it at the time. Because of the highly charged emotional atmosphere in which the original S-R (stimulus-response) bond was formed, or because there were early repetitions of the encounter to reinforce the connection, the reaction became entrenched and the S-R bond did not dissolve when the individual later came to see that the object or situation was no longer dangerous to him.

In this view, the anxiety has not been displaced to an object or situation other than its true source. The phobic object or situation is what he truly fears, albeit without factual cause. The individual cannot reason himself out of his phobia because it has become a function of his nervous system and is now a physiological rather than a mental phenomenon.

Another non-Freudian view of phobias, by Leifer, is interactional and is presented in the next reading. Leifer states that phobias need not be viewed as defenses against innate sexual and aggressive drives, but rather are desperate attempts of an individual to maintain a sense of mastery over various presumed dangers in the external world. This is done by investing something which is possible to avoid with the dangerous qualities of something which is more difficult or impossible to avoid. The danger can thus be symbolically controlled. Note Leifer's comment on the case of "Little Hans."

Avoidance and Mastery: An Interactional View of Phobias

*Ronald Leifer, M.D.**

. . . Phobias are generally defined as fearful and avoiding responses to apparently harmless objects, situations, or actions, or as exaggerated fears of relatively harmless objects, situations, or actions. Prior to the writings of Sigmund Freud, they were thought to be caused by subtle cerebral degeneration. Freud's explanation of phobias (as of the neurotic process in general) was rooted in a conception of human nature as fundamentally conative and driven. According to his view, which has been widely accepted in psychiatry, human nature is primarily sexual and aggressive and is repressed, controlled, and sublimated by social training and social structure. Avoidances, therefore, are considered to be secondary and defensive and can be analyzed and reduced to sexual and aggressive strivings; in fact, the more vigorous the avoidances, the stronger the drives which generate them are presumed to be.

According to psychoanalytic theory, phobias are the result of the repression, transformation, and displacement of aggressive and sexual drives. The motive force for the symptom is the anxiety which is associated with the belief that punishment (castration and loss of love) would result if the forbidden impulses were expressed. The phobic symptom represents a symbolic and defensive avoidance of the unacceptable wish and the unpleasant consequences of its enactment.

The importance of drives in psychoanalytic theory would seem, on the face of it, properly to place human psychology in a biological perspective. However, the view that animal behavior is primarily governed by aggressive or seeking instincts is contradicted by the facts of evolutionary biology in general, and of human behavior in particular. The concept of the instinctual basis of behavior places undue emphasis on the organ-

* *Journal of Individual Psychology*, Vol. 22, No. 1 (May 1966), pp. 80-81, 83, 84-91.

ism, by attributing to it a primary nature which is relatively independent of its relationship to environment. It thus ignores a major theme of Darwinian biology, namely, that animal behavior is ecological; that is, it is to be understood in terms of its interaction with environment. Further, it assumes that this primary nature is fundamentally positive or aggressive, while in fact, there are three possible reactions of all matter, both living and non-living, towards its surroundings: approaching (or aggressive); repulsion (or avoiding); and neutral (or indifferent). Each reaction depends both on the properties of the organism and the properties of the external world *in interaction with each other*.

It is the purpose of this paper to present such an interactional view of phobias. In their general character, phobias constitute one of the above three universal types of reactivity: avoidance . . .

Symbolic reactivity . . . is specifically human and is the basis for all of those qualities by which man has been characterized. The simplest example of this stage of minding is symbol formation in which the organism actively relates two or more stimuli to each other independently of their intrinsic properties: that is to say, arbitrarily. Upon this basic design culture and society, myth (shared fictions), and character (personal style) are elaborated.

The employment of one stimulus to represent another is called symbolizing or symbolization; and the stimulus employed for this purpose is called a symbol. Anything whatever that can be perceived is eligible for this use. The relationship between the symbol user (the person), the symbol, and its use is a relationship of meaning. The capacity to symbolize enables the human animal to react to his own movements (and those of other persons) not in terms of their intrinsic properties, but in terms of their meanings which depend on their connection with other symbols past (remembered), present (perceived), and future (anticipated). It is this capacity which transforms bodily motion into conduct, antecedents into history, and ends into purposes. It is this capacity which frees the human being from driving causes and immediately impinging stimuli, and sparks him with the situational flexibility that is choice and the fictional variety that is culture. As we climb the evolutionary scale we may observe that with the increase in flexible reactivity there is a corresponding decrease in the automatic reactivity of instinct. . . .

The multi-dimensionality of human nature is associated with three general threats to its existence which are based as much on that nature as on the external sources of danger. First, there is the inevitability of the death of the organism as a biological being. While this fate is shared by all living things, only humans can anticipate it, give it meaning, and contrive instrumental and symbolic means for its avoidance.

Second, there is the possibility of conflict with the group to which one is socially bonded and from which one derives his identity as a person. The result of this conflict may be derision, punishment, or banishment from the group, acts which are often tantamount to social and even biological death. Psychoanalysts customarily link the subjective fear of the first two threats under the single heading of castration anxiety: the fear of punishment, concretized with respect to the genitals, for the violation of social rules of conduct.

The third threat to the creature of fictions is the possibility of the loss of meaning. As has been indicated, the narrow sense of meaning refers to the relationship between the symbol user, the symbol, and its use. In a broader socio-historical context, it refers to the relationship between personal identity, the systems of socio-cultural fictions, and the patterns of individual behavior by means of which they intertwine. The loss of meaning thus refers to the loss of a coherent symbolic framework—dramaturgically, the loss of the central elements of the plot which binds past, present, and future into the unified design within which life's action can be sustained.

The fear of this loss has been called separation anxiety because for the relatively helpless child, life's meaning is monopolized by his parents, the loss of whom would deprive him of the central reference points for his experience. However, this paradigm of separation is only one component of the larger anxiety about meaning-loss. Anything which has meaning can be lost: objects, persons, modes of relating, parts of the body, goals, or causes. The more central that meaning is to the individual's life style, the more devastating the loss of it will be. The more limited the individual's range of meanings (or plots), the greater his anxiety will be about the possibility of their loss; the more transcendent and enduring his meanings, the less he will be threatened by the possibility of their loss. It is from this desire for eternal meanings (or everlasting plots) and not from the submissive child in man in search of a dominating father that the belief in God springs.

In order to maintain a satisfactory life the individual must be capable of mastering these threats. First, he must be able to maintain biological life, either by means of automatic bodily mechanisms or with the aid of medical intervention. Second, he must master the rules of deportment which are required by his society; this does not imply strict obedience and conformity with them, but rather a consciousness of them and the capacity to resolve conflicts decisively whether they be social or intrapersonal. Third, he must live in (and contribute to the creation of) a society which provides adequate meaning for its members; and as an individual, he must develop the skills necessary to mould and maintain meaning for himself.

Avoidance is as necessary a component to these three forms of mastery as is execution. From the physiological perspective, it is important to the maintenance of life that reflex and conditioned avoidance mechanisms function properly; it is also vital that certain known dangers to life and health be avoided, for instance, poisonous foods, precipitous cliffs, and penetrating missiles.

From the perspective of social conduct, an individual must not only master the skills of social communication, etiquette, and work; he must also learn self-restraint, control, and discipline. Acts of commission and acts of avoidance are both included in the catalogue of obligations and prerogatives which a child learns during his socialization. Failures in either may create conflict between the child and his parents or the individual and his society which may result in anxiety, guilt and punishment. Success in either is likely to bring a warm sense of self-esteem, mastery, and social reward.

Finally, avoidance is as necessary to the preservation and nurturance of meaning as is positive action. For the animal whose unique nature is forged out of significance, the threat of meaninglessness can be more devastating than even death or social exile. The avoidance of meaninglessness is therefore the supreme task of human life.

Psychoanalytic orthodoxy postulates that avoidances are defenses against the dual instinctual thrusts of aggression and sexuality, and that it is their infiltration into all areas of life, which must be followed by their repression, transformation, and sublimation, that accounts for the ubiquity of inhibition. However, avoidances are not reactions against pre-existing evil. Avoidance and evil are the dialectical co-creators of one another: That which is to be avoided is given the significance of evil, and the existence of evil signals the desirability of avoidance. The distinction between good and evil, manifested in conduct by prescriptive and prohibitive rules, is a prerequisite of social life.

Avoidance is therefore an essential ingredient of all social conduct and has equal status with the perpetrated deed. Its social value derives not in the recoil from evil instincts, but in the definition of evil which, when it is shared, contributes to the creation of the social bond. Avoidances thus have a social value which is independent of the reality of the evil they oppose. They may also serve as social strategies which, for instance, in the form of nonviolent passive resistance may promote social reform, sympathy, or self-aggrandizement. Or, they may serve to enhance the sense of mastery and self-esteem by demonstrating conformity with rules of conduct that marks one as deserving the praise of important others (current or "internalized" authority figures) for a job well and obediently done. In fact, avoidances are often more conducive to a sense of mastery than positive action: First, because in a collective society, the majority of rules tend to be prohibitive, rather than prescriptive; second, because errors of omission are usually considered to be lesser sins than errors of commission; and finally, because, since the activity to be avoided is assumed to be harmful, the sense of safety from evil can be accomplished without the risks of direct confrontation.

Avoidances can become prominent and distracting characteristics of behavior in three ways: They can dominate the life style; they can dominate a particular sector of behavior; or they can become specific and caricatured avoidances of the type we designate as phobias.

The human organism, as a creature of meanings, can be taught or become convinced that he ought to be an avoider; that effort, assertion and encounter are evil and that repose, caution and detachment are desirable. Avoidance can become the mark of an individual's life style not as a defense against the seeking "instincts," but by his learning to believe that the social world belongs to others who do not look approvingly at his stamping his mark on it. Such a person may become so radically encrusted with self-inhibiting and negating armor that by refusing to risk danger, he may lose himself as a growing self-altering, participating human being. Such a person is the paradigm of inferiority, and suffers such a profound sense of guilt about self-affirmation that he may feel himself to be an alien form in a strange and hostile world.

Avoidances or inhibitions may dominate certain areas of behavior rather than the entire life style. For instance, in a society with vestiges of puritanism, young girls may be taught that sex is evil and dirty and at best a marital duty which is to be discharged with haste and a minimum of pleasure. Later in life, such girls may de-emphasize their sexuality and avoid physical relationships with men, including their husbands. This inhibition may generalize to other areas of their lives which are tinged with sexual meanings such as in the display of tenderness, warmth and affection. Yet, such persons may be aggressive and assertive in other ways, for instance in the pursuit of a career.

Exaggerated avoidance devices may be employed to increase the individual's sense of mastery over danger when his life, social relations, or meaning are in jeopardy. Dollard and Miller

write about the combat pilot who developed a phobia of airplanes after a near-fatal mission. By an exaggerated avoidance
of the machine which he so closely associated with his demise
he could both symbolically and actually (by being grounded)
master his fear of death which had reached such disasterous
proportions. It is misleading to explain this phobia as the result
of conditioning, for while it required learning (i.e., antecedent
experiences) for its accomplishment, it was also perpetrated and
purposive. The conditioned avoidance of a stimulus which is
associated with pain is the combined result of antecedent experiences and automatic, physiological mechanisms. However,
this flier tried to avoid death, an event which he had not experienced and which requires a discriminating symbolic capacity
to anticipate. He associated death with airplanes rather than
with noise, turbulence, height or the myriad of other stimuli
which impinged on him at the zenith of his fear; airplanes were
the single stimulus of all of these, the avoidance of which could
be expected to preserve his life. His phobia thus must be construed as an active attempt to enhance his feeling of mastery
over the threat of death, by avoiding a selected stimulus to
which the meaning of death was ascribed.

Exaggerated avoidances may also occur in situations in which
it is difficult for an individual to avoid conflict, and hence, the
anxiety and guilt associated with it. In a socially strained
society, many activities may be both prohibited and recommended; or they may be prohibited at one stage of life and
recommended at another, without a clear and meaningful rite
of passage to mark the transition. An individual may thus want
to do what he ought to avoid, or he may want to avoid what
he is obliged to do; he is then faced with the task of wanting to
practice and avoid the same activity. Under these circumstances,
the unskilled social performer will either experience anxiety and
guilt for violating a taboo, or he will feel a lack of fulfillment
and a longing for a desirable and pleasurable activity.

For instance, a patient who had been taught to avoid sex
and also to be a compliant and dutiful wife was confronted
with a dramatic emergency. Her solution to submit blandly to

her husband's sexual advances on the condition that immaculate cleanliness be maintained was a virtual stroke of creative genius. She avoided the sexual act symbolically by avoiding the pollution which she took for its major quality; this avoidance, in turn, placed preconditions on the sexual act which were so inconvenient and irritating to her husband that his spontaneity, passion and patience were quickly exhausted and his demands on her gradually ceased; and as a result, the requirement to participate in sex was radically diminished without her violating the obligations of her wifely duty. The price of this strategy came high with her husband's infidelity, but she repressed the connection of this to her eccentricity and thus could shift the blame for her broken marriage fully to her husband.

Or, it may happen that conflict is impossible to avoid. For instance, a mother may teach her child the importance of honoring his parents and avoiding any action which might hurt them. However, she might also unpredictably accuse him of wounding her deeply when he engages in assertive and independent actions. He is thus placed in the position of not being able to avoid hostile behavior towards his mother because *anything* he does may be defined by her as an instance of it. He stands perpetually guilty of crimes for which the convicting evidence is his accuser's suffering. Such a person might fashion an exaggerated fear and avoidance of doing harm to living things such as insects and animals, as well as persons. At least then he could convince himself and perhaps others, that he is not a mean and destructive person who deserves to be reviled and punished; and he can maintain a semblance of self-esteem which is derived from his caricatured goodness.

Another example of this predicament is the case of Little Hans who was given contradictory instructions for the use of his penis: he was warned not to touch it under the threat of castration and he was simultaneously encouraged to urinate by himself. Unable to comply with his parents' expectations, Hans attributed the qualities of the penis symbolically to horses: they had the largest organs he had ever seen and were also, at the turn of the century, equally as difficult to avoid, at least on the streets. The avoidance of horses, sustained by the fear that his encounter with them (touching) would lead to injury (castration) enabled Hans at least to be symbolically obedient to his parents' prohibitions. It thus served to bolster his threatened self-esteem and gave him a sense of mastering the rules of conduct.

Finally, phobias may be employed by a person who finds it difficult or impossible to avoid changes in his life which would radically alter familiar meanings. Perhaps the best example of this is the small child who develops a school phobia when he is suddenly thrust from his habitual home surroundings into a strange school environment. The phobia serves as an exaggerated attempt to avoid new and unfamiliar meanings and to preserve meanings to which he had become accustomed.

When an individual's life, social acceptance, or meanings are threatened, the forward momentum of his action is obstructed and his sense of self-esteem and mastery are jeopardized. Yet, life must continue. When the symbolic animal is balked by his own fictions, he may transform or distort them in order to permit the continued flow of action, no matter how grotesque or eccentric the new fiction may become. Of the great variety of fictional transformations of which man is capable, two lie on the reactivity continuum: There is the counter-phobic maneuver in which the individual charges ahead in the zealous, indiscriminating confrontation with the dangerous activity; and there is the phobic maneuver in which the individual retreats in an exaggerated avoidance of a threat, or of a symbolized representative of it, or of an activity which is a prerequisite of it.

Phobias need not be viewed as defenses against drives which obstinately press for expression. They are desperate attempts to maintain a sense of mastery when the individual would otherwise be confronted with anxiety or meaninglessness. By investing something which is possible to avoid with the dangerous qualities of something which is more difficult (or impossible) to avoid, the danger can be symbolically controlled. For finite man, the dangers to life, social function, and meaning are ubiquitous. Indeed, we may postulate that the greater the inability to master these dangers, the more frequent and exaggerated the resort to phobic avoidance will be; conversely, the greater the sense of mastery, the less the need for phobias will be. Thus, childhood phobias are so common as to be considered a natural stage in growth and development; and while superstitions and private, idiosyncratic fears are common among adults, they tend to diminish where science and education replace the mastery of magic with the mastery of practical knowledge.

For the most part, phobias are neither conspicuous nor inconvenient; often they are thought of as no more than personal idiosyncracies. However, the woman who fears to walk on public avenues, the child who is terrified of his school, the businessman who dreads his automobile—these people live under conditions in which it is difficult to discharge life's daily routines and obligations; they create burdens for themselves and others which lead to conflict and the disruption of affectionate, cooperative living. Once phobias have been instituted as devices to sustain a meaningful existence, they become social actions themselves which are then subject to a social evaluation upon which the worth and esteem of their creators depends. It is out of the desire to remedy the intolerable conditions caused by the phobia that medical or psychiatric aid is sought. It is not the phobia itself, but its undesirable social consequences that marks it as an "illness"; judgments about these consequences are moral and not medical in nature and depend as much on the evaluations of others as on the phobic individual's own verdict that his life is unsatisfactory. . . .

Depression

Grinker [3] states: "Since Freud's original paper in 1917, melancholia has been considered a form of self-reproach intended as anger against a lost loved object whose image has shifted onto the patient's own ego." Brenner gives the psychoanalytic view of depression as "a clinical condition in whose psychopathology unconscious identification with a lost object regularly plays an important role."

Other psychoanalytic writings hold that depression can be triggered in adult life by various kinds of losses, such as the death of a loved one, the loss of a positive relationship with one's spouse, or the loss of self-esteem because of failure on one's job. These and other deprivations in adult life can precipitate depression when they are associated unconsciously with object loss, i.e., the loss in childhood of parental love.

Aldrich [4] has commented that "depression can result when grief is not directly expressed and remains buried in the patient's unconscious."

According to Henderson and Gillespie, "In many depressions a precipitating cause is not recognizable. In others, the depression results from disappointment or deprivation. In a third group, the precipitant is the reanimation, often by some external event, of an unconscious trend ('wish') which, if allowed to reach consciousness, would ultimately destroy the personality. Hence a gigantic effort is made at repression (inhibition), and the inhibition becomes generalized, so that all thinking is interfered with." They go on to say that, if a wish has a strong guilt feeling attached to it, it is repressed and "depression appears as the conscious correlate of the now unconscious guilt-feeling. The depressive ideas which appear in consciousness are largely rationalizations, but may have also some disguised relation to the repressed wish." [5]

Henderson and Gillespie [6] also tell us that the psychoanalytic view of the psychopathology of depression is that the following factors are involved: a constitutional one in the form of inherited accentuation of oral erotism; a special fixation of the libido at the oral level; early disappointments in love, especially love of the mother; the occurrence of the first disappointment in love before the Oedipus wishes have been overcome; the repetition of the primary disappointment in later life as the exciting cause of the depression.

In the next reading, Beck does not deal with the precipitating causes of depression. He concentrates on the nature of the thinking processes carried on by patients *after* they have become depressed. His thesis is that certain conceptual orientations (schemas) based on a conviction of inferiority, feelings of ill health, self-blame and pessimistic expectations become activated with the onset of depression, distort the person's perceptions, and maintain affective responses such as sadness, anxiety, guilt, loneliness, pessimism, and anger. In a section of his article not reprinted, Beck discusses how the patients view their distorted thought processes (depressive cognitions): they generally consider their thoughts to be automatic and not the result of reasoning; while their cognitions seem plausible to them, they have an involuntary quality and intrude even when the patient is trying to think objectively. The application of this cognitive-affective model of depression to treatment calls for the correction of the patient's distorted thinking, which in turn will reduce sadness, anxiety and other typical depressive feelings.

Thinking and Depression: II. Theory and Therapy

*Aaron T. Beck, M.D.**

The cognitive distortions and the idiosyncratic thought content of depressed patients have been described by me in a previous article. It was suggested on the basis of clinical observation that many of the phenomena in depression may be characterized in terms of a thought disorder. This conclusion was drawn from the consistent finding of systematic errors, such as arbitrary inferences, selective abstraction, and overgeneralization in the idiosyncratic conceptualizations of the depressed patients.

The present paper will present a theoretical analysis of the thinking disorder observed in depressed patients. The formulations will be limited to a few broad areas in which the relevant clinical material was considered adequate to warrant a formal theoretical exposition. The discussion will be directed toward two salient problems: first, how the typical idiosyncratic content and cognitive distortions become dominant during the

* *Archives of General Psychiatry*, Vol. 10, No. 6 (June 1964), pp. 561-562, 565-568, 570-571.

depressed phase; secondly, the relationship between the cognitive organization and affects in depression. Finally, suggestions regarding the application of the theoretical formulations to psychotherapy will be presented.

The main thesis to be developed is that *certain idiosyncratic cognitive structures (schemas) become prepotent during depression, dominate the thought processes, and lead to cognitive distortions.* . . .

In conceptualizing a particular life situation, composed of a kaleidoscopic array of stimuli, an individual has a number of alternatives as to which aspects of the situation he extracts and how he combines these into a coherent pattern. Individuals react in varying ways to a specific complex situation and may reach quite dissimilar conclusions. A particular individual, moreover, tends to show consistencies in the way he responds to similar types of events. In many instances these habitual responses may be a general characteristic of individuals in his culture; in other instances, they may represent a relatively idiosyncratic type of response derived from particular experiences peculiar to him. In any event, stereotyped or repetitive patterns of conceptualizing are regarded as manifestations of cognitive organizations or structures.

A cognitive *structure* is a relatively enduring component of the cognitive organization, in contrast to a cognitive *process* which is transient. Cognitive structures have been postulated by a number of writers to account for the observed regularities in cognitive behavior. Piaget's "schemas," Rapaport's "conceptual tools," Postman's "categories," Bruner's "coding systems," Kelly's "personal constructs," Sarbin's "modules," and Harvey's "concepts" are examples of such postulated structures.

In the present formulation, I have preferred to employ the term schema to designate a cognitive structure because of its relatively greater usage and familiarity than the other terms. A cognitive schema has been defined by English and English as "the complex pattern, inferred as having been imprinted in the organismic structure by experience, that combines with the properties of the presented stimulus object or of the presented idea to determine how the object or idea is to be perceived and conceptualized." The term is broad and has been applied to the small patterns involved in relatively discrete and concrete conceptualizations, such as identifying a shoe; or to large, global patterns, such as ethnocentric prejudice, which causes one to regard the behavior of persons from another social group in an unfavorable way. In this discussion, the focus is on the broader, more complex schemas.

In current usage, a schema is conceived of as a structure used for screening, coding, and evaluating impinging stimuli. In terms of the individual's adaptation to external reality, it is regarded as the mode by which the environment is broken down and organized into its many psychologically relevant facets; on the basis of the matrix of schemas the individual is able to orient himself in relation to time and space and to categorize and interpret his experiences in a meaningful way. . . .

. . . A highly successful research scientist had a chronic attitude (schema) "I am a complete failure." His free associations were largely concerned with thoughts of how inferior, inadequate, and unsuccessful he was. When asked by the psychiatrist to recall a single experience that did not constitute a failure to him, he was unable to do so.

In this case, it is postulated that a schema with the content "I am a failure" worked over the raw material of his recent and past experiences and distorted the data to make it compatible with this premise. Whether the particular cognitive process was recollection, evaluation of his current status or attributes, or prediction of the future, the thoughts bore the imprint of this schema.

A cursory examination of the typical thoughts of depressed patients might lead to the observation that they are not very different from notions that normal people occasionally entertain and then dismiss. This fact raises certain questions: Why does the depressed patient appear to cling so tenaciously to his painful ideas in the face of contradictory evidence? Why does he appear refractory to alternative explanations of his experiences? While the various factors involved in the breakdown of certain intellective functions (judgment, self-objectivity, reality testing, reasoning) are obscure, an attempt can be made to answer these questions within the framework of the theory advanced in this paper.

As has been already indicated, one of the primary assumptions of this theory is that certain idiosyncratic schemas acquire an increased potency or intensity in the state of depression. It is further suggested that this intensity is substantially greater than that normally possessed by schemas. Because of this increased intensity, the cognitions resulting from the interaction of these schemas with the raw material of experience tend to be unusually intense; i.e., they are exceptionally compelling, vivid, and plausible. The other nondepressive cognitions tend to be relatively faint in comparison with the depressive cognitions. Hence, in scanning the various possible interpretations of the situation, the depressed individual will be affected by the idea with the greatest intensity rather than by that with the greatest "truth value"; i.e., the ideas with the greatest relevance to reality will be subordinate to the idiosyncratic ideas which have a far greater intensity.

In the more severe states of depression, the patient appears to have lost voluntary control over his thinking processes; i.e., even when he makes a determined effort to direct his focus to neutral subjects and to ward off his depressive ideas, the depressive cognitions continue to intrude and occupy a central position in his phenomenal field. At this stage the idiosyncratic schemas are so active that they are continuously producing the idiosyncratic cognitions. In such severe cases, the cognitive processes may be analogous to the processes during dreaming. When an individual is dreaming, the imagery of the dream totally occupies the phenonmeal field and is accepted by the individual as reality. The individual has no voluntary control (or at most only limited control) over the content of the dream or ability to gauge its viridicality.

Similarly, in severe depressions the individual's ability to direct or modify his thought content is drastically restricted. His ideas rather than being regarded by him as thoughts or interpretations of reality are viewed as reality. It may be speculated that in such a state, the intensity of the hyperactive schema is so strong that it obscures or excludes the operation of schemas involved in the process of reality testing. Even when he makes a determined effort to examine his depressive thoughts objectively, to check back on the details of the external stimuli, and to consider alternative explanations, the ideas associated with these processes are relatively weak and constantly crowded out by the much stronger depressive thoughts.

My previous paper presented a summary of the characteristic thoughts and affects of depressed patients, and indicated that there was a definite temporal contiguity of thought and affect. It was noted, furthermore, that there was a logical consistency between them; i.e., the specific affect was congruent with the specific thought content.

My thesis, derived from these clinical observations, is: *The affective response is determined by the way an individual structures his experience.* Thus, if an individual's conceptualization of a situation has an unpleasant content, then he will experience a corresponding unpleasant affective response.

. . . the cognitive structuring or conceptualization of a situation is dependent on the schema that is elicited. The specific schema, consequently, has a direct bearing on the affective response to a situation. It is postulated, therefore, that the schema determines the specific type of affective response. If the schema, for example, is concerned with self-depreciation, then a feeling of sadness will be associated with it; if the schema is concerned with the anticipation of harm to the individual, then anxiety will be produced. An analogous relationship between the content of the schema and the corresponding feeling will hold for the other affects, such as anger and elation.

In clinical syndromes, such as depression, this relationship between cognitive process and affective response is easily identified. When the affective response appears inappropriate to a particular stimulus situation, the incongruity may be attributed to the particular schema that is evoked. Thus, the paradoxical gloom in depression results from the idiosyncratic schemas that are operative. This may be ilustrated by the example of a depressed patient who wept bitterly when he received praise. His predominant attitude (schema) was that he was a fraud. Any praise or other favorable comment tended to activate this idea about himself. Receiving praise was interpreted by him as confirmatory evidence of how he consistently "deceived" people.

As was pointed out in my previous paper, the specific types of depressive affects are related to the specific types of thought patterns. Thus, schemas which have a content relevant to being deserted, thwarted, undesirable or derelict in one's duties will produce, respectively, feelings of loneliness, frustration, humiliation, or guilt. The relative absence of anger among the more severely depressed patients, particularly in situations that uniformly arouse anger in other people, may be attributed to their tendency to conceptualize situations in terms of their own supposed inadequacies. The currently popular explanation for the relative absence of overt anger in depression is that this affect is present, in fact intensified, in depression but is repressed or inverted. The present explanation seems to be more parsimonious and closer to the obtained data. It is postulated that the dominant schemas are concerned with the idea that the depressed patient is deficient or blameworthy. Proceeding from the assumption that he is unworthy or culpable, the patient is forced to the conclusion that insults, abuse, and deprivation are justifiable. Remorse rather than anger stems from these conceptualizations. The schemas that are dominant during depression tend to force the patient to regard insults, abuse, or deprivation as justifiable because of his own shortcomings or mistakes.

For purposes of comparison, it may be expected that in other clinical syndromes characterized by an abnormal intensity of a particular affect there is a dominance of the cognitive patterns corresponding to the specific affect. The anxious neurotic demonstrates the dominance and inappropriate use of schemas relevant to personal danger. The hostile paranoid is dominated by schemas concerned with blaming or accusing other individuals (or external agencies) for their perceived abuse of him. The manic patient is influenced by schemas of positive self-evaluations.

It could be speculated that once the idiosyncratic schemas have been mobilized and produce an affective reaction, these schemas are in turn affected by the affects. Hence, a circular mechanism could be set up with the schemas stimulating the affects and the affects reenforcing the activity of the schemas.

The preceding formulation of a cognitive-affective model of depression has a practical application in the psychotherapy of neurotic depressive reactions (as well as other psychoneuroses). Through the procedure of focusing on his distortions of reality and his unrealistic attitudes, the patient can loosen the grip of his erroneous ideas and sharpen his perception of reality. In this way he can become less vulnerable to the instrusions of his repetitive depressive thoughts and can formulate his experiences in a more realistic way. Consequently, the unpleasant affective consequences, such as depression, anxiety or agitation are reduced. . . .

I have presented a cognitive-affective model of depression based on systematic clinical observations of 50 depressed and 31 nondepressed patients during psychotherapy. It was postulated that the characteristic thoughts and affects of depression are determined by persistent cognitive patterns, designated as schemas. The schemas are attitudes, beliefs, and assumptions which influence the way an individual orients himself to a situation, recognizes and labels the salient features, and conceptualizes the experience.

The idiosyncratic schemas in depression consist of negative conceptions of the individual's worth, personal characteristics, performance or health, and of nihilistic expectations. When these schemas are evoked they mold the thought content and lead to the typical depressive feelings of sadness, guilt, loneliness, and pessimism. The schemas may be largely inactive during the asymptomatic periods but become activated with the onset of depression. As the depression deepens, these schemas increasingly dominate the cognitive processes and not only displace the more appropriate schemas but also disrupt the cognitive processes involved in attaining self-objectivity and reality testing. It is suggested that the affective reactions may facilitate the activity of these idiosyncratic schemas and, consequently, enhance the downward spiral in depression. The relative absence of anger in depression is attributed to the displacement of schemas relevant to blaming others by schemas of self-blame.

The application of this conceptual model to psychotherapy consists, first, in an attempt to shift the patient's mode of judging himself and his world from an exclusively deductive to a more inductive process; i.e., to form his judgments more in terms of objective evidence and less on the basis of biased assumptions and misconceptions. This approach consists initially of a precise pinpointing and discussion of the patient's distortions and illogical conclusions. Then, an attempt may be made to correct his erroneous judgments by focusing on the nature of his observations and logical operations and by the consideration of alternative hypotheses. Secondly, the patient's systems of premises and assumptions are examined to determine their validity. By correcting the underlying misconceptions and biased assumptions, the patient is enabled to proceed from a more realistic basis in forming his specific judgments.

Kurt Adler, son of Alfred Adler, uses his father's theory of personality to formulate a different concept of depression. Kurt Adler maintains that depression is a device utilized by an individual for a purpose: to safeguard himself, because of deep inferiority feelings, from having to face the outside world. The depressed adult tends to be someone who, in childhood, got his way by crying and acting helpless and weak. Such a person can develop a life style which in adulthood brings him into conflict with society, because he has not learned to live cooperatively. As a grownup he tries to exploit others just as he did in childhood, but the others reject him, frustrate his desires, and threaten his hopes to achieve his goals. He loses confidence in his ability to be successful in the world and acquires a strong sense of inferiority. To preserve his self-esteem, he adopts a series of alibis and evasions which engender a state of depression: he feels physically weak and without energy; compels his family to cater to him out of worry and compassion; expresses guilt about being a burden; but makes it clear he is too sick to carry any responsibility such as a job in the outside world.

In the following article, Kurt Adler elaborates his view that the depressed person uses his depression to exploit and control others, avoid failure in the outside world, alleviate feelings of worthlessness, and excuse his retreat from life.

Depression in the Light of Individual Psychology

Kurt A. Adler, M.D.*

Psychiatry, today, is confronted with the same urgency in the treatment of depression, as it was when Adolf Meyer substituted the term "depression" for "melancholia" in 1904. Despite the introduction of anti-depressive drugs and electro-convulsive therapy, the therapist is faced with the same pressures and emergencies, and patients and their families with nearly the same amount of suffering as before. Most schools of psychiatry have not attempted to develop a theory of depression, and most of the theories which have been set forth contain questionable formulations. It therefore seems important to consider the nature of depression, its development and its therapy in the light of a comprehensive theory. It is the purpose of this paper to show how Alfred Adler's theory of personality accounts for the facts of depression, and supplies ways for treating it.

According to Adler's theory most problems confronting the individual are problems of relations with others. All problems in life are answered by the individual with his tested methods, attitudes, and symptoms, and all his responses are in the service of his goals for self-enhancement. Depending on the degree of his developed social interest and courage, he will tend to face the problems of his social reality, and attempt to solve them

* *Journal of Individual Psychology*, Vol. 17, No. 1 (May 1961), pp. 56-60, 61, 62-64.

as best he can, or tend to evade them, seeking detours and distance from the expectations of the community, in order to escape a real evaluation of himself, which looms as a threat to his self-ideal.

Whenever the feelings of inferiority are great, the goals of superiority are correspondingly high, in compensation. Then their achievement becomes increasingly difficult, and the individual becomes increasingly discouraged. If at the same time he has not learned to cooperate as a method of gaining satisfaction in life, and, instead, exploits others, he will soon experience increasing opposition once he steps beyond his more tolerant family circle. The outside world will, therefore, seem to consist of enemies who frustrate his desires, and thus threaten his hopes to achieve his goals. The individual then adopts alibis and evasions to safeguard his self-esteem. Adler called these "safeguarding devices"; others later called them "defense mechanisms." Adler says, neuroses and psychoses have "the ultimate purpose of safeguarding a person from a clash with his life tasks, that is with reality, and of sparing him the danger of having the dark secret of his inferiority revealed. . . . What appear as discrete disease entities, are only different symptoms which indicate how one or the other individual considers that he would dream himself into life without losing the feeling of his personal value."

The special safeguarding device or symptom called depression has, of course, specific characteristics. To be sure, most cases encountered in practice will not show the clear-cut picture which will be described here. Together with depression, the patients employ other defenses, such as hysterical, phobic, compulsive, or schizoid reactions which modify, each in their own way, the picture of the pure depression.

Exploitation. One prominent characteristic is that the patient's goal of superiority is not readily detected. To all appearances he depreciates himself, accuses himself of being the greatest failure, and expresses guilt for all sorts of evil doings and happenings, local or family calamities, or even world catastrophes. Where, then, is the goal of superiority?

Actually, the patient exploits the greater social feeling and empathy of others; he forces them into his service, extorts the greatest sacrifices from them, compels them to express their devotion and love for him and to worry about him constantly. All this serves his hidden goal of superiority for it places him in the center of attention, underlines his importance, gives him license to do whatever he wants, and relieves him of all obligations. Only in fairy tales can a prince or princess command such a privileged position.

Since he is, of course, unable to acknowledge that this is his secret purpose, he expresses guilt feelings about exploiting others and being such a burden to them. Such guilt feelings were already recognized as "mere wickedness" by Nietzsche. Adler explained their purpose and function as a device for appearing to oneself and others as noble and socially minded, while persisting in exploitative actions. Nevertheless, these guilt feelings are still often considered as basic and honest by the general public and many psychiatrists.

Depression, with its unique superiority ideal, has, like all adult behavior, its prototype in childhood. It is not devised on the spur of the moment, just when some exogenous factor seems to threaten the individual's prestige and self-ideal. Adler says: "The discouraged child who finds that he can tyrannize best by tears will be a cry-baby; and a direct line of development leads from the cry-baby to the adult depressed patient." The patient tries "to approximate the well-tested picture of a helpless, weak, needy child, for he discovered from personal experience that it possesses a great and most compelling force."

Many psychiatrists see in this employment of methods that were used in childhood, something that they call "regression." But this betrays a rather mechanical view of the functioning of the human mind. In the first place, as Adler says, "We can never speak of regression in the Freudian sense; otherwise every psychic act would be a regression, since it is always based on experiences from the past." A second point which contradicts "regression" is that all symptoms and methods of action are directed towards some goal; they are therefore relentlessly *forward*-pressing, and never directed backward.

The history of the depressed patient shows that he has depended since childhood on the efforts and aid of others, to an excessive degree, and that he does not recoil from stressing and exaggerating his weaknesses, illnesses and inadequacies. He does this in order to force others to compliance with his wishes, and to extort sympathy and active help from them, as well as to spur them on, often to unheard of sacrifices. He will use his power ruthlessly where and when he can, often adorning his actions with ethical postulates, only to turn around and point to his needs and his weakness, when he can not prevail with his will alone.

Depreciation. In his depression-free days, the patient's thwarted but exaggerated ambition urges him to chase after glory and after successes which can be attained without much effort and risk of failure. As soon as failure seems to threaten, however, he shrinks from the task, and stresses that he has failed again as he always has. Indirectly he blames this on the wrong-doing of relatives or friends, on his upbringing, on an unlucky star under which he was born, or, as a last resort, on his sickness, his depression. He ascribes his depression to heredity or other unknown causes, while laboriously—though largely unconsciously—generating this depression within himself. He anticipates a dire fate, from which he cannot save himself or be saved by others, despite all their strenuous efforts.

Thus he frustrates all efforts to help him and thereby depreciates others. This is one of his methods for feeling superior. The therapist, I may add, is of course, frequently one of the patient's chief targets. Characteristically, the depressed patient will say, "Now it's too late," or find some other spurious reason for rejecting the very thing he had complained had been denied him. We are reminded of the child who, after much fussing and crying, is finally offered what he wants and responds, "Now I don't want it."

Certifying the sickness. To demonstrate to himself and all others that he is really sick, the depressed patient is ready to go to any length and to pay all costs. He can sit for hours painting in his mind the evils that will befall him, and then act as if they had already happened. He thereby produces a shock effect with the utilization of all his emotional potentialities— primarily fear and anxiety, and always rage against someone near him. He neglects himself and his outward appearance; he disturbs his bodily functions, his sleep and his nourishment; he presents a pitiable condition, always stressing his grief-stricken state. Adler remarks: "We want to stress especially that toxins are released by the endocrine glands thorugh the affect of rage and grief by way of the vegetative nervous system." In such a condition, then, social relations, and with it, all obligations, are safely excluded, and the patient's proof of sickness, irreponsibility, and need for those who will serve him are firmly established.

This, then, is the relentless effort of the depressed: to prevail with his will over others, to extort from them sacrifices, to frustrate all of their efforts to help him, to blame them—overtly or secretly—for his plight, and to be free of all social obligations and cooperations, by certifying to his sickness.

Suicide threat. If the patient is still dissatisfied with the effect his illness has on some significant person in his entourage, a threat of suicide will usually terrorize his environment into compliance with his wishes. If this, too, fails, he may in his rage and in revenge go so far as to attempt or commit suicide. He expects the particular person involved to be shattered by this act, and suffer guilt for not having acceded to his wishes. In addition he indulges in a romantic delusion, a beau geste, designed to point up the worthlessness of others, and to absolve himself of all criticism: *De mortuis nil, nisi bene.* He will no longer have to carry on the Sisyphus work of covering up his own responsibility for his failures, which he feels is in danger of being exposed, and of upholding his illusory superiority ideal, in the service of his vanity.

The symptom of suicide also has its prototype in childhood where it has been tested out as a method. There are all sorts of ways for children to hurt themselves, in order to hurt others.

Essentially we find this in the child who says: "It serves my mother right, if I break my leg." The implication is always: "Then she will be sorry and suffer." Similarly the adult suicide says: "See what you have driven me to do; now you will suffer the rest of your life for it and, missing me, realize what a rare and sensitive person I was". . . .

. . . As for the depressed, does he enjoy his symptoms? Since he is firmly dedicated to the proposition that life is designed to bring him suffering, and since his suffering is the most formidable weapon in his battle against his opponents, he cannot possibly enjoy his depression; that would annul all his efforts. The patient does endure the most severe agonies. But we should never forget that he is largely not aware of the fact that he creates them, and for what purpose he does so. Sly and secret smiles of triumph are, however, frequently encountered among patients when they report the sacrifices others are obliged to make as a result of their depression, or when they report how they frustrated others. Evidently the patient's secret enjoyment of depression was recognized a long time ago. The very insightful Viennese playwright Nestroy has, according to Fenichel, a character say: "If I could not annoy other people with my melancholia, I wouldn't enjoy it at all."

The proponents of the libido theory have had a particularly difficult problem in the interpretation of depression. According to Jones, Freud failed in his first attempt to explain the genesis of depression.

Abraham recognized the superiority feeling and contempt for people in the depressed, but failed to see in them, and even denied, any basic inferiority. In fact, he believed that they have genuine self-appreciation. Together with Freud, he constructed a system, wherein the libido, loosened from its attachment to a love object (after its loss), was repressed, and reappeared in the form of depression.

Rado, according to Fenichel, gave the final touch to this theory by having the libido break in two, in its agony over the loss of its love object. One half becomes repressed as latent aggression, while the other half is turned like a boomerang against the self, in the form of depression. He also added fear of re-tribution as cause of self-punishment, and finally that all de-pression contains a fear of starvation, originated in infancy.

Eventually Freud had to introduce the death instinct in order to explain the tendencies toward self-destruction in depression and other conditions. . . .

There are also many researchers in the fields of biochemistry, physiology, and endocrinology who, on finding changes in one or another organic constituent in depression, believe to have found its cause. We, like others who stress unity of the person-ality, with psyche and soma totally integrated, expect physio-logical changes in any neurosis or psychosis. But we believe that the question of the primacy of these changes has been answered long ago to the effect that neither organic nor psy-chological symptoms come first; they generate each other. The principle of multiplicity of causes, all of which are interrelated and influence each other, must be considered basic here, as in any other area. And this holds true equally for organic, envi-ronmental, interpersonal, or conditioning schools of thought. . . .

The schools of interpersonal relations, as might be expected, come closest to our views. Sullivan states that there is only a superficial similarity between grief and depression, and that in the latter all constructive situations are cut off, while stereotyped destructive ones are maintained. He also sees goal-directedness in the depressed suicide: "Our impulse to live . . . in these peo-ple is vanquished entirely by a hateful combination of im-pulses, which leads to destroying oneself in order to strike at some other person." Clara Thompson, too, in criticizing Freud's theory of the death instinct, recognizes that "suicide is usually stimulated by motives other than self-destruction. Spite and punishing the loved one are almost invariably factors."

I recall one patient, a highly intelligent college girl, who told me that she was always depressed and unhappy, even in child-hood. But, she added: "I was actually not as unhappy as I pretended to be; I felt more interesting being unhappy." She also told me how she always used to lie about having pains of all sorts, and never would allow her mother to leave her. She had enuresis until the age of eleven, when, much against her will, she was sent to a boarding school. She admitted not liking anybody, and that any friendship would be a positive danger to her. Her earliest recollection was that, when she was four, a car ran over her toe. She wasn't hurt, but a big fuss was made over it. The patient added: "It was a pride of mine."

You can see in this short description the early childhood preparation for a pattern of life of hurting herself, or at least appearing to hurt herself, in order to gain recognition, have her way, achieve an illusory superiority, dominate others, and never attach herself, really, to anybody except for exploitation. At the same time, there is, of course, a deep-seated feeling of inferiority with its compensatory superhuman ambition as her guiding line. She totally lacks belief in her ability to achieve anything by her own honest efforts; therefore, she feels constantly on the brink of exposure as a sham and a failure. This, in her vanity, her exaggerated self-image can not permit. And so, the tenacious clinging to the safeguarding device of depression, despite the high cost to herself.

Another patient, after prolonged treatment, admitted that she could stop her depression any time she wanted to. But, she added, she could not afford to do so, because her husband would immediately resume treating her like a door mat, as he had done before her depression started; now, she had the upper hand. When she was cautiously asked, if she could not just play-act to her husband, as if she were depressed, but otherwise enjoy her life, she acted offended at the proposition that she be so dishonest. She also constantly bemoaned the fact that she was such a burden on her environment, including her husband. Here, again, one can see the goal-directedness of the depression, the battle for superiority, and the safeguarding of the idealized self-image.

Masochism

The final reading in this chapter deals with masochism and is excerpted from an article by Salzman, who was represented in Chapter 3 by a portion of his paper on the paranoid state. The text which follows is the first half of an article in which Salzman discusses both masochism and psychopathy. Our text omits the section on psychopathy because LaBarba's article on that subject, also reproduced in Chapter 3, presents a concept of psychopathy very similar to that of Salzman.

Salzman offers an alternative to the Freudian concept of masochistic behavior as "unconscious guilt seeking for punishment." He believes that the masochist is not seeking punishment but reward. The masochist repeats behavior or remains in a situation that causes him suffering because, feeling inadequate and powerless to reach his goals by assertive action, he hopes to stimulate another person to benevolent response by the appeal of his helplessness. In this sense, masochistic behavior is an attempt to solve a problem.

Masochism and Psychopathy as Adaptive Behavior

*Leon Salzman, M.D.**

The concept of the unconscious was Freud's major contribution to the theory of personality development. He postulated that there must be an area in the mental apparatus which stored, or maintained under rigid control, feelings and attitudes which had great influence on mental operations without ever appearing in consciousness except under special circumstances. This area he called the unconscious, and in spite of all his warnings and safeguards, it has been treated as if it had topological reality and has become a "thing-in-itself," instead of being considered a process or a conceptualization. The unconscious was thought to be an area which was occupied by primitive forces as well as repressed ideas or feelings, and exerted its influence through dream states, certain pathological states, parapraxes, behavior which appeared to be contrary to the individual's conscious desires, and various unrecognized ways.

Almost from the start many theorists, notably Adler and Jung, disagreed with Freud's conceptions, especially with regard

* *Ibid.*, Vol. 16, No. 2 (November 1960), pp. 182-185.

to the nature of instinctual forces and thus the contents of the unconscious. Among recent theorists Sandor Rado and Bernard Robbins, particularly, have visualized the unconscious in a less mechanical fashion, considering it to be a process which deals with mental activity that is currently, but not permanently, out of awareness.

To Rado, who has developed his views in an adaptational framework (adaptational psychodynamics), the unconscious of Freud appears like a department of the mind which is "below" or "outside" awareness, like another, mysterious, mind. Freud based the metaphysical conception of unconscious mind admittedly upon Kant's "philosophy of *Ding an Sich* (thing-in-itself, which lies outside the conditions of possible experience)." Rado, in contrast, views the unconscious as a "non-reporting (in contrast to the conscious mind which is reporting) organization of causative links between processes of which we are aware." The concept of non-reporting level of activity avoids the error of making a thing-in-itself of an extrapolated concept and gives it real operational usefulness.

Robbins, the recently deceased prominent member of the Karen Horney group, at the extreme of ego-psychoanalytic theorists, has raised even stronger doubts about the validity of concepts which permit ideas, attitudes and feelings to be encapsulated, outside the influence of time or change. He considers this impossible, since all human processes participate in the change which time and experience produce. A patient's reactions and emotions are always part of his conscious existence and always appropriate to his way of looking at the world at that time. An apparently inappropriate attitude or feeling becomes understandable in terms of the individual's current distortions of the real world, rather than as a residue of an early inappropriate response to a parental figure. While recognizing that we are influenced by "out of awareness" feelings and attitudes, Robbins feels that these are neither time exempt nor incapable of being altered.

In this paper I should like to examine the unfortunate consequences for theory and practice of some of the implications of

Freud's concept of the unconscious as these apply to masochism and psychopathy, and offer alternative interpretations.

It was the practice of Freud and many of his followers to assign the label of unconscious to certain forces which could not be identified in consciousness. For example, if an individual manifested behavior which appeared to be guilt-appeasing, self-punishing, or otherwise self-defeating, it was assumed that he had unconscious feelings of guilt if the basis of such behavior could not be identified in consciousness. Like other occupants of the unconscious, their presence could only be identified by interpretations of manifest behavior. The assumption of their presence ran into two frequent difficulties: (a) self-contradictory concepts, like unconscious anxiety or guilt, and (b) the necessity of a prior acceptance of other unvalidated conceptions like the death instinct.

(a) Freud himself had serious concerns about the matter of unconscious feelings. He said, "We then come to speak, in a condensed and not entirely correct manner, of 'unconscious feelings,' to keep up an analogy with unconscious ideas, which is not altogether justifiable." But in the same work he speaks of a "newer discovery, which compels us, in spite of our critical faculties, to speak of an 'unconscious sense of guilt'."

Such mixed concepts like latent or unconscious anxiety are by definition impossible, since anxiety is defined as a *felt* state of mind, and this cannot be unconscious. This criticism applies to the notions of unconscious hostility as well as unconscious guilt.

(b) It is apparent that much human behavior is self-defeating and self-destructive and often results in repeated failures or successive punitive responses from the community. While in the framework of the concept of the pleasure principle such behavior was incomprehensible, it became understandable with the formulation of a death instinct, as direct evidence of the activity of this instinct. The effect of the death-instinct hypothesis and the concepts of unconscious guilt and the need to fail was to restrict and close off further efforts to understand such behavior rather than to open it to clarification and correction. Eventually the death-instinct hypothesis became largely discredited through philosophical and theoretical elucidation of its premises; but many still cling to such concepts as unconscious guilt.

The notion of an area of mental functioning entirely out of control of the individual and populated by forces and attitudes which are destructive (aggressive instincts), self-defeating (need to fail, unconscious guilt), and antisocial has lent support to the tendency to feel relieved from responsibility for one's behavior. Such a concept encourages the foolish notion that hostility outwardly manifested is healthy since it avoids the internalization of this hostility, which may lead to depression or suicide. It encourages pessimistic attitudes towards the potentialities of the therapeutic process and justifies the notion of the untreatability of some patients, because they produce a "negative therapeutic reaction." Philosophically, it encourages a view of man which is essentially destructive, and considers the humanistic and optimistic view of man as sentimental romanticism. The concepts of need to fail, etc., encourage in the mind of the therapist, as well as the patient, an irresponsible attitude towards the unproductiveness which maintains and reinforces the neurotic pattern.

We can no longer be satisfied with a psychological concept which tends to throw blame or responsibility on our parents, our heredity, or our instinctual drives and unconscious motivations over which we have no control.

Let us examine some alternative explanations for the self-defeating behavior of the masochist and the psychopath.

We approach the problem from the point of view that human behavior is adaptive and adjustive. Thus we recognize that masochistic behavior, although it always tends to berate, belittle, or actively destroy the self or part of the self, may yet be an attempt at mastery and an adjustive maneuver designed to deal with certain personal and social conditions. In this event masochistic behavior would seem an intrinsic part of all neuroses where self-derogatory behavior fulfills some psychic goal, i.e., where it is the lesser of two evils, or the consequence of the neurotic's inability to fulfill his goals. It may also be the inevitable consequence of the neurotic's failure to fulfill or achieve his idealization. Consequently, there is no need to postulate a need to fail or a destructive instinct.

I believe that the masochistic defense is a particularly effective way of dealing with certain problems of existence, namely, guilt, aloneness, helplessness, and powerlessness. The masochist appears to be someone who, like the psychopath, feels cheated and abused and is attempting to get justice and compensation for his claims.

The usefulness of the masochistic defense in dealing with feelings of powerlessness depends upon man's continued belief in primitive magic and its powers of expiation, as well as on the human propensity to stimulate another person to benevolent action by the appeal of helplessness and suffering. The masochist hopes to gain higher rewards through his suffering. Like neurotic behavior in general, his behavior is distorted and does not achieve its expected results. Thus masochism can demonstrate a kind of behavior which appears to be punishment-seeking, yet actually is reward-seeking. Although it often appears to be "unconscious guilt seeking for punishment," the guilt may well be secondary rather than primary, since the brazen, exploitative, and righteously indignant behavior patterns may frequently produce sadistic rejoinders from the community, and thus stimulate guilt feelings. . . .

REFERENCES

1. Paul Friedman, "The Phobias," *American Handbook of Psychiatry*, Vol. 1, edited by Silvano Arieti. (New York: Basic Books, 1959), p. 296.
2. Lawrence Kolb, *Noyes' Modern Clinical Psychiatry*, 7th ed. (Philadelphia: W.B. Saunders, 1968), p. 101.
3. Roy Grinker, Sr., "Reception of Communications by Patients in Depressive States," *Archives of General Psychiatry*, Vol. 10, No. 6, (June 1964), p. 577.
4. C. Knight Aldrich, *An Introduction to Dynamic Psychiatry* (New York: McGraw-Hill, 1966), p. 242.
5. David Henderson and R.D. Gillespie, *Textbook of Psychiatry*, 9th ed. (London: Oxford University Press, 1962), p. 211.
6. *Ibid.*, pp. 211-212.

5

Anxiety

Calvin S. Hall,[1] in discussing Freud's ideas concerning anxiety, makes the point that Freud saw anxiety as a conscious emotional and physiological phenomenon. The emotional component is the frightening expectation of imminent disaster either from the external world or from within oneself. The physiological manifestations might include rapid heart beat, heavy breathing, dryness of the mouth, or sweating of the palms. Anxiety is always consciously experienced, although it often serves as a danger signal to the ego that it is being threatened by unconscious forces of which the individual is unaware. Anxiety of this type may be triggered by a primitive wish of the id to commit some act or think some thought which will prove harmful or which will evoke punishment from one's conscience.

In practice, Freudians have given almost all of their attention to the kind of anxiety which they claim is a signal of threat from unconscious forces. Henderson and Gillespie [2] have commented on this kind of anxiety as follows: "The anxiety tends to attach itself to an idea, since affects can hardly remain unrelated in consciousness. This idea to which the anxiety attaches is apt to be one consciously very far removed from ideas associated with originally repressed material—this is the so-called 'displacement of affect'."

In the next reading, the existential theory of anxiety is presented by Frederick C. Thorne, editor of the *Journal of Clinical Psychology*. Dr. Thorne declares that the master motive of man is to live as fully as possible. His success in life will be determined by how much he accomplishes in relation to his potentialities, by what he does with his constitutional and environmental resources. The life of each individual has several departments and he cannot possibly excel in all; most people show a mixed profile of success and failure in different areas, and "get along" through generally acceptable performance or superior performance in single fields.

The existentialist hypothesizes that anxiety is generated by a fancied or actual failure in any important department in the business of running one's life. The threat which triggers anxiety is the fear of not achieving "full-existence." It is postulated that the only real antidote to anxiety is success.

Freudian theories about sexual conflicts as a primary cause of anxiety are regarded as only a special case of the existential theory of anxiety. The existential theory views sex as only one department of living: failure to attain sexual satisfaction is not always the main or the only source of anxiety.

An Existential Theory of Anxiety

Frederick C. Thorne, Ph.D.*

From the existential viewpoint, the master motive of Man is to live as fully as possible, to have the best possible life, to actualize potentialities and opportunities to the utmost. Existentially, the good life does not occur by chance. It is not inevitably the result of a maturational growth process in which positive resources inevitably triumph over negative forces. It is not necessarily the result of mechanistic patterns of environmental stimulation, since environmental stimulation is typically chaotic until organized through selective perception and learning. It is not basically determined by chance even though some seem to

* *Journal of Clinical Psychology*, Vol. 19, No. 1 (January 1963), pp. 35-38, 41-42.

have more luck than others. It is not easily produced by conditioning and training since the best educational institutions do not produce it invariably. The good life seems to require special effort and commitment on the part of each person, not only to mean well but also to act out good intentions consistently in practice. Only solid accomplishment pays off in achieving the good life.

Phenomenologically, strivings to secure the best possible life for one's Self may be likened to the processes of running a business (which is only a special example of running one department of life). In running a business, one starts out with a collection of assets and liabilities and sets out to make the most of them. In general, a business is successful if it results in an appreciation of capital or, at the least, breaks even. If there are consistent capital losses, the business cannot continue and is bankrupt with insufficient assets to meet liabilities. Some people are willing to subsidize a business which is creative or artistic even though not financially successful, but usually not for long.

Phenomenologically, each child starts out in life with definite constitutional assets and liabilities which tend to limit what he can become. Thus, a female has certain limitations, a congenital cripple has others, and a person with a black skin color has others. Undoubtedly, differences in physical attractiveness, energy expenditure levels, physical strength and innate ability contribute important factors of individual variance.

Phenomenologically, the environment provides large opportunities in the form of general and specialized education, training and tutoring. Some children can command larger resources of wealth, cultural background and sheer coincidental opportunities than others, but almost everyone is offered much environmental stimulation and growth. Phenomenologically, each person has his own distinctive quota of time, energy, ability and effort with which to make the best of his environmental and constitutional resources. What the person does with these resources is a matter of fundamental personal and social importance.

Existentially, what a person accomplishes (or fails to accomplish) in relation to his potentialities determines his relative success or failure in life. In upward striving societies everywhere, but particularly in America, there is great pressure put on almost every child to "make the most of himself." Self-improvement has been elevated to the status of a major motive in life with the bait of the possibility of becoming President of the United States being held out at least to every young male. From a very early age, almost every child is tested, rated, examined and judged as to his relative accomplishments. He is made consciously aware at every possible moment of the importance of "succeeding" and of "getting ahead" as rapidly as possible.

Ultimately, existential success appears in large degree to be a function of how well a person runs all the important departments of his life, rationally and deliberately making the most of every resource and opportunity, with the eventual goal of the fullest possible self-actualization. What man can become, he must become, personally and socially. And this is only possible with maximal commitment and investment of all resources. Existentially, to become completely self-actualized through self-improvement is the major motive.

Because of constant pressure to succeed, and because of constant confrontation with marks and other evaluations of the quality of behaviors, every child continually is made aware of the discrepancy between his ideal self (what he could be) and his actual self (what he is).

Every act of a person may be considered as contributing to some kind of success or failure. In school, each child is marked daily for his effort and production. In the business world, each employee is rewarded financially in terms of the quality and quantity of his work. In society, each person wins acceptance or rejection in relation to the significance of his contributions.

Under such circumstances, it is inevitable that every child early develops a progressive awareness of the cumulative record of what he has done in life. In early childhood, a child has very little productive resources but experiences some success if he is praised by others because of attractiveness, growth and size, intelligence, or other socially desirable qualities. The developing Ego is like a small fire which starts out as a spark and is either (a) fed by praise and encouragement, or (b) put out by rejection and criticism. Later, as the young person becomes productive, he receives more recognition for his actual accomplishments and level of adjustment, and develops more self-esteem.

The important thing is that no one who is aware of the importance of becoming a real person can ignore the significance of the cumulative record of success and failure, achievements and defeats, which constitute his own particular success-failure ratio. Early in life, the relative balance of successes and defeats may not loom too importantly, since the child is still learning, and hope for the long period of adult productive life is still ahead, but even in early childhood most children are aware of "how they are doing." The status of the success-failure ratio becomes critically important in the prime years from 20 to 50 when the foundations for any real success in life are laid, and ultimate levels of achievement become pretty clearly established. After 50, relatively little opportunity for improvement in the success-failure ratio exists since constitutional resources begin to be impaired, vocational opportunities become fewer, and chances for "hitting the jackpot" become less. By age 65, the record is largely in, and the person must try to live with what he has done. Throughout life, every person carries with him the cumulative record of his success-failure ratio.

Only an Olympian personality could be universally successful in running all the departments of his life, self-actualizing potentials in all the roles of student, worker, leader, executive, sex and marriage partner, parent, social and civic person, creative artist, etc. Most people show a mixed profile of success and failure in different areas, and "get along" in life either by virtue of generally acceptable performance or because of peak performance in single fields.

It is hypothesized that a primal stimulus to anxiety is a fancied or actual failure in some important thing(s) which are perceived as threatening to the prime existential motive of living as fully as possible. Anything which blocks self-actualization tends to stimulate anxiety. Failure in any important department in the business of running one's life generates anxiety. Anything which inhibits or frustrates "full-existence" generates or releases anxiety. The great fear is of failure, i.e., not to become self-actualized, thereby missing out on a full life.

It is postulated that the level of anxiety stimulated by any fancied or actual failure is a function, relatively, of the status of a person's success-failure ratio in life. Persons with a predominantly successful balance of achievement can tolerate small failures with production of minimal anxiety. Persons with a predominant balance of defeats in their ratio, cannot tolerate even the smallest further failures because they exaggerate an already hopeless position.

It is postulated that the only real antidote to anxiety is success. In general, one unit of success counterbalances one unit of failure, but this holds true only if the unit of success is in the same department as previous units of failure. Thus, success in business may not compensate for failure in love or as a marriage partner.

It is postulated that existential anxiety tends to be tolerable as long as the ratio of success to failure is at least 51-49% so that the person can realistically perceive himself as at least to some degree "getting ahead" and making at least average progress in actualizing himself. A person really becomes self-confident when he has accomplished a well-rounded success in all departments of his life. No exact ranges can be delimited, but 60% success in life is unusual, 80% success is phenomenal, 90% success is Olympian, and even God is not 100% successful. Actually, superior levels of achievement usually fall far short of perfection. Thus, a baseball player who bats at a .400 rate (4 hits out of 10 at bats) is sensational. In a competitive culture, anybody who scores above average can be well pleased with himself.

Existential anxiety becomes progressively intolerable under conditions where a person (a) achieves progressively less than 50% successes, (b) cumulatively loses ground in relation to the convoy of his age peers, (c) loses his resources such as time, energy, health or wealth, and (d) has diminishing future prospects as in old age. Anything perceived as a major catastrophe such as expulsion from school, losing an important job, breakup of a marriage, loss of reproductive fertility, prison sentence, loss of reputation, loss of money, or crippling of health, may stimulate incapacitating psychoneurotic anxiety reactions. This is particularly true where the loss is irretrievable. In World War I, neurotic breakdowns were regarded as reflecting cowardice and a "yellow streak." Many soldiers were shipped back from the front and never given a chance to redeem themselves so that the psychoneurotic reaction became irreversible with resulting lifelong incapacitation. In the Korean War, fear was regarded as being normal and anxious soldiers were held in the front line where they could learn to control their neurotic reactions.

Each person shows differential thresholds and reactivities to various kinds of stimuli causing existential anxiety since levels of anxiety are always relative to the assets and liabilities and situational stresses existing at any time. In general, threats to security can occur in relation to all the levels of factors organizing personality integration, ranging from threats to raw biologic survival to threats to the highest level creative activities.

Existential anxiety tends to develop when one tries to be something which one is not. In order to be genuinely solid and health producing, success must reflect solid achievement rather than being a shallow facade of trying to act-out the roles of worldly success.

Existential theory stresses *authenticity* and *genuineness* as the criteria of existential success. One can surround one's self with the trappings of success such as stylish clothing, fine cars, luxurious homes, displays of wealth and family background, etc., but unless these are genuinely earned, they contribute only to phoniness. A *phony* is a person who acts out or imitates something which he is not.

The person who is not genuine and authentic tends to generate existential anxiety over anything which threatens to topple his house of cards. No one knows better than the person himself how phony and flimsy his pretenses may be. Having offered one's self publicly to be something which one is not, there is the constant fear of detection and defrocking. Nothing can replace solid accomplishment. Success in life cannot be borrowed or transferred. To pretend anything else is self-defeating and actually inhibits positive self-actualization by starting the person off "on the wrong track."

In this case, existential anxiety arises because the person consciously or unconsciously recognizes that he is actually a failure no matter how hard he may pretend otherwise. Complicated defenses and rationalizations against the recognition of failure tend to become top-heavy and generate anxiety as their collapse becomes increasingly imminent.

Mental disorder is always characterized by various degrees of breakdown of self-control and personality integration. Loss of control is a constant symptom of all kinds of breakdown, and it is always associated with levels of anxiety proportionate to the degree of loss of integration.

Dissolution of personality integration is always threatening and anxiety-producing because it implies a breakdown of the functional integrity of the conscious Self. It is significant that hypochondriacal fears of mental breakdown, death, heart attack or some other somatic disorder are symptomatic of most anxiety states. Most people fear mental breakdown more than any physical disease because they would prefer death to "loss of my mind."

Awareness of loss of control, or tentative control, stimulates anxiety because it implies that the person is no longer in control of his life. . . .

In our opinion, psychological theorists have not given sufficient attention to the role of money in personality states. Money is the life blood of modern business and commerce. In more primitive rural societies, a person could get by with direct barter and exchange of goods and services, with little or no money necessary to complete all necessary transactions. In complicated urban society, direct exchanges of services no longer are possible, and all commercial transactions depend upon money as a medium of exchange. Unless a person learns to handle money properly, he is in constant difficulty with society.

In the same manner as a person has only so much blood in his body and if this is allowed to drip away, he inevitably dies of circulatory collapse, so a person has only limited material resources and if these are frittered away he ends up bankrupt. We constantly remind clients that "Little leaks sink big ships." Careless handling of capital resources results in poverty and bankruptcy. Usually, the only material things which a person has after a life-time of hard work are some small physical properties and life savings in money.

In spite of all the calamitous tales which are told of the disastrous effects of the unwise use of money by unhealthy or immature personalities, the fact remains that it requires money to participate in most of the better things of life. Money, wisely used, can buy most of the more gracious things of life such as comfortable shelter, better foods, enjoyable luxuries, higher education, nice cars, trips to Europe, personal privacy, fine art and jewelry, and admission to all the performing arts. The mass advertising media are always holding up to the entire population the joys of gracious living which can be bought with money.

Every child early learns that he is powerless to command the better things in life without money. To be certain, he is told that he can have anything if he is willing to work hard enough for it, but that is not always so easy. Some children learn the sociopathic style of life of "taking" forcibly what is not given them. Most people just "give up" in their attempts to get the bright baubles which are dangled in front of them. A fortunate few can create wealth and taste the fruit of the earth.

In our experience, the failure to be able to accumulate wealth, or to preserve it, is an important stimulus to anxiety and guilt. Even though it is currently philosophically unpopular to equate success with money, the fact is that without money many attributes of the richest life are impossible to attain. To the extent that the fullest and most gracious living depends upon money, failure to acquire money represents a failure to be able to possess the fullest and most enjoyable conditions of living. While the title of a popular song tells us that "The Best Things in Life are Free" and there are many poor people who are very happy, this may not be very consoling to the young person who can't go to college, or have a good car, or live in a nice house, or have the nice things, or keep up with the "Jones's" who have been more successful in acquiring and stewarding wealth.

In our clinical experience, a large amount of reactive anxiety and guilt can be traced directly to poor handling of money.

A 67-year-old retired small businessman had acquired about $125,000 by the time he retired, in life savings. Against advice, and because he became restless doing nothing, he bought into an automobile agency. Within one year he lost $50,000 and had to close down. Shortly thereafter he developed a severe neurotic depression expressing great anxiety over what this loss would do to his standard of living, what would his associates think of his mistake, and much guilt over being so stupid. He gradually recovered when he discovered that with his remaining $75,-000 he still could spend at least $5,000 annually for 15 years before his capital ran out. . . .

Freudian theories of the role of conflict and repression in the production of neurotic anxiety and breakdown are regarded as only a special case of the existential theory of anxiety. It is significant that the psychoanalytic emphasis on disorders of psychosexual development arose out of Freud's religious and cultural background. Judaic taboos on sexuality are among the most repressive in the world and lead to special problems not encountered in cultures not holding such views. Freudian preoccupation with sexual disorders as a main cause of neurosis may be regarded as being due to a too-one-sided concern with breakdown of self-actualization in only one department of life. The existential theory of anxiety recognizes that normal sexual life is one component of full self-actualization, and that failure to actualize sexual potentialities and opportunities to the utmost may stimulate feelings of deprivation and frustration which may be very anxiety producing. But they are not always the main or the only source of major failure in life. . . .

Our second reading about anxiety is a paper by Krauss in which he affirms that anxiety is the psycho-physiological feeling tone associated with the "fear of something about to happen." This is—like the existential theory presented by Thorne in the previous reading—a phenomenological approach. The ideas of Thorne and Krauss are quite compatible, with each writer concentrating on different aspects of the subject.

Krauss points out that, while anxiety has essentially a future orientation, Freud turned to the individual's past to uncover the source of his present anxiety. Therapy on the basis of a future-oriented concept of anxiety consists of changing future events, changing the individual's expectations of the future, or changing his goals. Krauss disagrees that the future is largely unstructured. He believes that much of it can be predicted and altered.

Anxiety: The Dread of a Future Event

Herbert H. Krauss, Ph.D. *

Phenomenologically, anxiety must be seen as the psycho-physiological feeling tone associated with fear of the occurrence of an event, fear of something about to happen, rather than fear that something has happened. This can easily be verified through introspection or interviews with patients. You are likely to hear from them, "I'm afraid something will happen," or "I'm scared I'm going crazy," or "They're going to catch me," and so on. You will notice that when the past tense is used by a person with regard to a situation, the accompanying affect is not anxiety, unless there has been a premeditated effort to help the person to "relive" the situation, or there is

* *Journal of Individual Psychology*, Vol. 23, No. 1 (May 1967), pp. 88-93.

worry that the unwanted event might reoccur. For example, a paranoid schizophrenic I have treated could describe the "past events" of his being poisoned by doctors (at this time he no longer believed this was happening) with remarkable calm, matter-of-factness, but, when he would attempt to talk about the effect this poisoning would have when he would look for a job, he would become markedly upset. He was anxious lest his present limitations caused by the "poisoning" would prevent him from ever again functioning as a normal human being.

The essential future orientation of anxiety has, of course, been recognized by most personality theorists, but most have chosen not to emphasize this observation. Although they acknowledge that anxiety serves a signal or warning function, they do not fully attempt to assess the truly far-reaching consequences of such a notion. Freud initially described anxiety as a consequence of the inadequate discharge of sexual energy, often associated with *coitus interruptus*. He came to modify his views to suggest the importance of anxiety as a signal.

According to Thompson:

> Freud's theory assumes that the forces within the Id are of dangerous proportions, the danger being greater or less according to the relative strength of the Ego. The earliest experiences of anxiety occur when the Ego is still weak because it is in the process of developing. This early experience sets the pattern for all later life. Having been dangerously threatened once, the Ego tends to assume that the same situation will always be a danger to it. So in life when similar situations arise, anxiety appears as a warning. This is a signal for the defenses of the Ego to go into action.

But instead of examining the significance of a process directed toward anticipating the future, for indeed anxiety served as a signal for what might come to pass, Freud turned to the developmental history of the individual, the individual's past, to discover what genetic core situation was causing the threatening difficulties. Such a return to the past history of the organism has generally been the technique of psychiatry and psychology, as, e.g., Glasser has pointed out. As Allport has phrased it, "People, it seems, are busy leading their lives into the future, whereas psychology, for the most part, is busy tracing them into the past."

There are, however, notable exceptions to this "past" orientation. These include, in addition to Allport, Kelly, Jung, and Adler. Jung has commented:

> Life is teleology par excellence; it is the intrinsic striving towards a goal, and the living organism is a system of directed aims which seek to fulfill themselves. The end of every process is its goal. All energy flow is like a runner who strives with the greatest effort and the utmost expenditure of strength to reach his goal. Youthful longing for the world and for life, for the attainment of high hopes and distant goals, is life's obvious teleological urge which at once changes into a fear of life, neurotic resistances, depressions and phobias if at some point it remains caught in the past, or shrinks from risks without which the unseen goal cannot be achieved.

The reason that mental science has generally turned to the genetic history of an individual in an attempt to understand him is undoubtedly complex. Ansbacher, in dealing with just that topic, concluded that objective psychology with its dogma that only that which is open to an outsider and is objective is scientific, must, of necessity, deal with the *causa efficiens* or the moving cause of behavior because only the past and present existed or are existing in objective, physical reality. He contrasts objective with subjective psychology, the psychology of phenomenology, of Adler, which concerns itself also with the *causa finalis,* the final cause of teleology and purposivism. Clearly, if one starts out with the position that all behavior is a function of past experience, as positivistic reductionists do, by definition, the future is nothing but the past operating on the present, nothing but what has been learned by reacting to present stimuli. Whether this notion be expressed in terms of past conditionings or reinforcement history, or instinctual development makes no difference.

However, if we accept the notion that anxiety is a signal of future doom, we have let the camel's nose into the tent, and it becomes obvious that the objectivist position needs modification. How far in the future can the events be of which the signal warns? By what solely past and present oriented mechanism does this come about? These questions have to be answered, and they can not be answered sticking to empirical data, without taking into account some notion of expectancy which extends the life space of the individual well into the future.

The only argument that makes the objectivist position with respect to anxiety temporarily tenable is that anxiety is a sort of mechanism like a thermostat, a cybernetic device which allows for change when the present physical tension reaches a certain state. That may well be, but unlike a thermostat, the anxiety device monitors not only the present but the future, or at least monitors expectations of the future and demands upon the future.

For example, announce an examination to a group of students to take place in four weeks. Tell them it is going to determine their grades which will be reported two weeks after the examination and that it may affect their later careers. Watch the anxiety mount. Even the student who has never done poorly before will become anxious if he feels that a goal which he greatly desires is involved. There is no adequate way in which this behavior can be explained by the past oriented objectivist.

Once we recognize that people do expect—and anxiety is the result of an expectation—any analysis of behavior in terms of the past and present becomes inadequate and misleading. This has wide relevance, especially so, since, as many have pointed out, anxiety is the neurotic core symptom, other pathological responses such as compulsions being attempts to deal with anxiety and, therefore, the expected future. Psychopathology can be seen as an attempt to control time, and agreement is reached with Freud when he states, "We have long observed that every neurosis has the result, and therefore probably the purpose, of forcing the patient out of real life, of alienating him from actuality. . . . The neurotic turns away from reality because he finds it unbearable—either the whole or parts of it." Then neurotic takes himself out of reality because he attempts to deny the future of which he is afraid and to substitute for it the unrealness of psychic comfort.

To stipulate that a person fears an event and takes steps to avoid the realization of that doom, is not enough. We must also determine the nature of the feared event. In Adler's sense this would always be "the fear of being proven worthless or the fear of defeat."

Practically, the concept of anxiety as fear of a future event has great usefulness. It allows for the searching of the past to determine what goal the person is afraid of failing to reach, the modification of the present in altering the goal or planning to meet it, and action to modify the future. Often the latter course brings spectacular results.

For example, if an individual is experiencing anxiety with respect to some future event such as an examination, further structuring or restructuring of the event may bring immediate relief. This was so in the case of a student in a panic about the possibility of failing a language examination, until he learned that such an examination had been eliminated as a requirement for an advanced degree. Other cases are, of course, not as simple as this and yield less clear-cut results.

John was a 9-year-old boy referred to the clinic for evaluation. He was diagnosed at one time as having hysterical blindness, though at the time of first treatment contact he apparently was seeing well. In the course of interviews with the parents it became obvious that the boy received a strict, fundamentalist, Protestant upbringing; his father was a minister. Important to the parents and demanded of their children was obedience to what they saw as God's will. And it was God's will for people never to become angry at anyone nor to fight with anyone no matter what the provocation.

When later John attended a public school in which his religious zeal became well known, an attempt to test the virtue of the virtuous soon began, as often happens in such situations. Every day after school, when walking home, the same two children would approach John, subject him to a torrent of verbal abuse, rough him up, and throw him in a ditch. Apparently they view their job as a sort of crusade. John was caught in a bind of not being able to defend himself, nor tell his parents about what was happening, for fear of being judged ungodly. His parents, for their own convenience, chose not to notice the dirt, the cuts, and bruises, or contented themselves with the notion that he had fallen down, fallen out of a tree, or had been splashed by a passing car.

John's teacher began to notice that he became anxious as the end of the day neared. She also noticed increasing withdrawal and uncommunicativeness. John, being quite young, eventually hit upon, as it turns out, the magical solution to his troubles. If he could not see the time, he would not be going home to be jumped, and if he did not see his assailants, they could not hurt him. So, at recesses, he began to stare at the sun, until spots came and until he convinced himself he couldn't see. Then he began to behave as if blind. Thus the hysterical blindness. By considering his future expectations, his strange behavior made sense, and, although it was not easy, changes in his future were made. The events which he had feared were removed: his parents eventually called the parents of the children who were jumping John and asked them to discipline their children. Eventually his parents began to try to understand themselves and their child.

Another case that illustrates the importance of recognizing anxiety as the response to a future threat to an important goal is that of David, a 29-year-old, diagnosed as a manic-depressive. David was totally subservient to his mother. He ran a small business with her, a safe job except that she was intent never to let him grow up and leave her as her husband had done. Much as he hated the situation and his mother, David was afraid that he would fail if he were to try something on his own. His cyclothymic style of life protected him from really acting as an autonomous adult. Whenever he made a move to progress, to take a new job, to try a new future, he would become extraordinarily anxious. Retreating from his future took the form of transmuting his anxiety into mania: He could do all, he could conquer all. But, half-cocked, he soon destroyed his opportunities for advancement, as could be expected. He failed. With failure would come hate, depression, martyrdom, sympathy from his mother, and above all distance from the future. In the course of therapy, working toward realistic goals, making realistic plans, pointing out that failure was not so horrible, and so forth, he started to become less cyclothymic, at first more anxious, and finally less anxious.

In closing, something should be said to the argument that a future-oriented psychology is less scientific for it deals with events that have not yet occurred.

One must acknowledge that all definitions of human "time" are artificial. Man's perception of time is molded rather than imposed. The past-present-future trichotomy is a man-imposed manner of dealing with the changes we see around us. There are many other, just as plausible, views of reality. For example, one might argue that man can directly and totally experience only the now. It is impossible in the present to feel the pain of four years ago or ten years from now. Therefore, all that "exists" is the present. One way to choose from among the many views of time that are available is to determine to what use you want to put the system and see how well it compares with its alternatives.

This paper has aimed at demonstrating that in predicting and understanding behavior the notion of the future must be included. While we think of the future as largely unstructured, it is far from that. Much of it can be predicted. Whether the prediction be that half of the uranium in a rock will be lead at time now $+ x$, or that students will get report cards, the accuracy of that prediction is close to perfect. Humans continually make such predictions and order their lives about them. In many circumstances, it is possible to make predictions for others with considerable accuracy also, for the future is structured to a large extent both by society and the individual. Without taking into consideration this structuring and the fact that man moves through time, no comprehensive scientific psychology of human behavior is possible.

The usefulness of emphasizing the future in anxiety has been found to lie in aiding the understanding of what the individual fears, directing therapy toward changing future events, and more especially, changing the individual's expectations of the future or his goals.

In the third and final paper dealing with anxiety, Sarbin proposes to replace the mentalistic anxiety metaphor with the metaphor of cognitive strain. In Sarbin's view, the concept of anxiety as a mental state or feeling has outlived its usefulness, having been interpreted in so many different ways as to interfere with scientific communication. Regarding anxiety as a condition of cognitive strain will make possible a more objective approach.

Cognitive strain is defined by Sarbin as large increases in cognitive activity produced by a person's inability to classify a new situation or object, find his place in society, or evaluate his performance of life tasks. Therapy, instead of focusing on internal psychic struggles, should focus on the difficulties presented by a patient in coming to terms with his world.

Anxiety: Reification of a Metaphor

*Theodore R. Sarbin, Ph.D.**

. . . As a replacement for the mentalistic anxiety metaphor, I propose the metaphor of cognitive strain. It is drawn, on the one hand, from a derivative of evolutionary theory, and on the other, from a working hypothesis that the world about us is knowable if we work at it. Cognitive strain may be defined

* *Archives of General Psychiatry,* Vol. 10, No. 6 (June 1964), pp. 635-638.

without reference to excessive visceral activity, although it is doubtful whether cognitive activities such as thinking, problem-solving, and imagining can be performed without some subdued or overt motoric activities with their associated autonomic feedbacks.

The first assumption in the model is almost pure Darwinism. In order to survive, living creatures must locate themselves correctly in the world of occurrences—in the distal ecology. If a creature is inaccurate in locating himself, he is likely to become a prey to predators or to wander away from the sources of food and drink and from protective cover. Human beings also must place themselves in the ecology. But, as a result of living in social groups with norms and expectations, and with beliefs about transcendental objects, they must locate themselves in multiple ecologies. If the world of occurrences provides unclear or insufficient cues to solve the problem of ecological placement, then we have the condition of cognitive strain. The referent for the strain metaphor is a large increase in cognitive behavior. This increase occurs in two ways: (a) in attempts to fit what-is-now-happening (inputs) into the summaries of what-has-happened-before (the cognitive organization, the major premises); and (b) in attempts validly to use the multiplicity of major premises that are activated by the sensory inputs. We assume that there are optimal degrees of cognitive strain for efficient cognitive behavior just as there are optimal degrees of muscle tonus for different kinds of motoric activities.

In the present model, we can structure the world of occurrences for any person . . . into proximal and distal ecologies. The proximal ecology is the constantly varying set of stimulus inputs mediated by the somesthetic receptors, the pressures, engorgements, sensations of hot and cold, itches, pains, aches, hurts, and so on, that help to define the form and volume of the body. Under certain conditions of cognitive strain, when the autonomic nervous system is engaged, the proximal ecology may include additional inputs from visceral organs as well as from the skeletal musculature.

The distal ecology may be differentiated into five systems. They may be identified as:

> The self-maintenance ecology
> The spatial ecology
> The social ecology
> The normative ecology
> The transcendental ecology

The self-maintenance ecology includes those objects and events which a person must take into account in order to maintain the self. In a state of nature, self-maintenance would be equivalent to survival. In human cultures, self-maintenance includes such aspects of honor, face-saving, role-constancy, integrity, dignity, etc. To be alert to multifarious stimulus events, an organism maintains an attitude of vigilance, a readiness to classify an object or event as threatening, dangerous, friendly, neutral, etc. It has been suggested that the human or other animals in the vigilant posture, upon noticing a stimulus event, might be described as asking the question *What?* or *What next?* or *What is it in relation to me?* The answer that the person gives to the *what* question in the simplest case is *threat* or *nonthreat,* but the refinements of extended experience, perceptual learning, and linguistic development allow all kinds of modulated answers to be given. When the question is answered verbally, it is in the form of a *qualitative* assessment of the ecological object, signified by adjectives such as hostile, accepting, friendly, unfriendly, helpful, deterring, and so on. The complexities of dimensional attributes in the distal world must be paralleled by complexities in cognitive dimensions to make possible modulated, rather than polar, responses to the *what* question.

The inability to classify the inputs from the distal world of occurrences on dimensions of the self-maintenance ecology produces cognitive strain. Conditions leading to such a resultant include uncertainty, unpredictability, the interuption of expected ecological events, and nonoptimal stimulus inputs (overloading of the perceptual apparatus or insufficiently differentiated inputs). The instantiation of an event as threatening does not lead to cognitive strain *unless* the person has no immediately accessible adaptive techniques for dealing with the object of threat, such as withdrawal, flight, or protective covering. In such cases, *increased vigilance follows* and other *What* and *What next* questions are asked. More acquired major premises are activated with the resultant necessity to decide which conclusions are the correct ones. Under such conditions, organismic involvement may increase. Such involvement is mediated through skeletal and visceral activity and may provide additional inputs which must also be instantiated. The necessity to instantiate multiple inputs, the increase in activated premises, and the interference from proximal inputs may increase the complexity of the cognitive organization. Thus, we may define cognitive strain as large increases in cognitive activity. In another idiom, we might say it is the search for answers to impelling questions.

The same analysis may be applied to the other ecologies, *mutatis mutandis*. In keeping with the metaphor of asking questions, we can pretend that people have readily accessible the question *Where am I?* in order to locate themselves on spatial dimensions. That such questions have a high access ordering is undeniable when a person is in a strange place, or is presented with contradictory spatial cues. The experiments of Witkin, et al. (1954) in which contradictory postural and visual cues to a perception of the vertical were employed show clearly what happens when the *Where am I* question cannot be satisfactorily answered. Some subjects in these experiments reported discomfort, disorientation, feelings of uncertainty, and loss of bearings in the laboratory.

To locate oneself in the social ecology, one has available the question *Who is he* and the reciprocal *Who am I?* or, in alternate terms, *What role must I enact?* In rigid caste and class systems, such questions are asked only infrequently, if at all. In open social systems, for example, where mobility in one social dimension is not necessarily associated with mobility on correlated dimensions, such as socioeconomic level and educational achievement, the question *Who am I* may produce cognitive strain because multiple answers may be contradictory. A recent report suggests a strong relationship between contradictory answers to questions of placement in the social ecology and the incidence of psychosomatic complaints. Jackson (1962) reports a survey study in which the respondents were classified along three social dimensions: education, occupation, and racial-ethnic background. When compared with respondents whose answers indicated consistency among the dimensions, persons whose answers indicated lack of congruence (e.g., high on one dimension, low on the others) were more likely to report the presence of psychophysiological symptoms, such as dizziness, excessive perspiration, loss of appetite, trembling, dyspnea, etc. I would offer the following interpretation: Placement in the social structure is a continuing affair. The continuing need properly to locate oneself in the social ecology in the presence of multiple and contradictory cues produces cognitive strain. High degrees of cognitive strain can involve the entire organism, thus engaging the skeletal and visceral systems and providing proximal inputs to serve as referents for psychophysiological complaints.

To locate oneself in the normative ecology, one must ask the question *How well am I doing?* This question always is asked in respect to some norm, value, standard, expectation, prescription, etc. In all cultures, propriety norms serve as the basis for the evaluation of many sorts of conduct. Guilt and shame are names given to the recognition of performances that do not measure up to certain kinds of norms. In achievement-oriented cultures, the *how well* question may refer to performances gauged against real or imagined standards of competence. When the answer to the *how well* question is difficult to achieve through ambiguities or contradictions in the major premises that comprise norms, then a condition of cognitive strain exists.

The transcendental ecology is an extension of the self-maintenance ecology. For human beings, there exist not only objects of a material sort but also objects that inhabit a shadowy, ephemeral, super-empirical world. Hallowell (1956) has found it useful in accounting for the conduct of various primitive groups to distinguish between the "behavioral" environment and the geographical. The behavioral world includes such entities as ghosts, spirits, windigos, numina, leprechauns, angels, demons, and fairies. Persons who participate in cultures where beliefs are held about such entities engage in behavior that may be described as attempts to answer the question: *What am I in relation to these objects?* Placement of oneself in the transcendental ecology, then, calls for cognitive behavior in which occurrences serve as inputs to instantiate the behavior of these transcendental objects. Religious crises, and autistic conduct in which communication with the deity is involved (sometimes denoted by the term schizophrenic) are events that illustrate this phenomenon. Thus, failure properly to place oneself in the transcendental ecology is another origin of cognitive strain.

Because of time limitations, I have been brief and have tried only to sketch in broad bold strokes the antecedents to cognitive strain. A few comments are appropriate regarding the implications of this model for theory-building and for clinical practice. For the former, a great deal may be said, but it can be summarized under the general heading of economy and efficiency of thought. Occam's razor—the admonition not to multiply entities needlessly—might be cited here when we argue against continuing to use mentalistic metaphors.

The wise employment of the cognitive strain metaphor will point the way to a search for facts that has been absent in the use of the anxiety metaphor. At least in the present formulation, a scientist will direct his attention to antecedents of human problems, to knowable ecological events and to conduct designed to place these events in a cognitive framework. He will not be sidetracked by searching for the dynamics of a mentalistic entity. In the experimental field, related approaches have already been successfully tested. Among these, the metaphor of cognitive dissonance has been fruitfully employed by Festinger (1957).

The implications for psychotherapeutic practice are especially clear. Instead of focusing on anxiety as a mentalistic or as a physiological signaler of internal psychic struggles, the therapist will focus on the difficulties presented by a patient in coming to terms with his world. He will be particularly cognizant that the use of "anxiety-reducing" drugs, for example, is directed at the organismic *effects* of cognitive strain. He will be constrained to ask and answer such questions as the following: under what conditions is it wise—through medication or somatic treatment—to reduce inputs from the proximal ecology? Is the reduction of the patient's attention to proximal inputs a valid criterion of success in therapy?

In proposing the metaphor of cognitive strain, I am painfully aware that it does not produce the dynamic overtones now associated with the anxiety metaphor. Perhaps this is as it should be. For nearly a half century, a romantic mystique has evolved around the professional enterprise stimulated by Freud's colorful metaphors. Experienced clinicians recognize that the mystique is not justified,—and that when therapy is successful, it is not due to the purging of anxiety. Rather, it is because the patient has learned how to minimize, with his finite cognitive capacities, the strains produced in his efforts to find himself in a complex, changing, and often contradictory world.

REFERENCES

1. Calvin Hall, *A Primer of Freudian Psychology* (New York: New American Library, Mentor Books, 1954), pp. 61-69.
2. David Henderson and R. D. Gillespie, *Textbook of Psychiatry,* 9th ed. (London: Oxford University Press, 1962), p. 126.

6

Aggression

Kolb [1] states that one of the theories of aggression, "stemming largely from the later writings of Freud, holds that aggression is a primary, instinctual drive (more accurately a component manifestation of Freud's death instinct). According to this view, each individual requires a certain amount of gratification of this destructive impulse which, if not attained in one way, will be achieved in some other."

Alfred Adler, whose views have been outlined in Chapter 1, originated the concept of an aggression drive and later discarded it. Freud continued with the concept and elaborated on it. In the following excerpt, Dr. Heinz Ansbacher describes Adler's final conclusions about aggression in man, which represent a position antithetical to that of Freud. Dr. Ansbacher, an authority on Adler, is editor of the *Journal of Individual Psychology,* the publication of the Adlerian movement in the United States.

Ego Psychology and Alfred Adler
Heinz L. Ansbacher, Ph.D. *

The uniquely constructive aspect of Adler's theories is today being increasingly appreciated within the fields of clinical psy-

* *Social Casework,* Vol. 45, No. 5 (May 1964), pp. 269-270.

chology and personality theory. Hall and Lindzey expressed this appreciation in the following way: "Adler fashioned a humanistic theory of personality which was the antithesis of Freud's conception of man. By endowing man with altruism, humanitarianism, cooperation, creativity, uniqueness, and awareness, he restored to man a sense of dignity and worth that psychoanalysis had pretty largely destroyed. . . . Adler offered a portrait of man which was more satisfying, more hopeful, and far more complimentary to man. Adler's conception of the nature of personality coincided with the popular idea that man can be the master, and not the victim, of his fate."

Of what, exactly, does Adler's more constructive conception of man consist? Adler views man's most important motivating forces not as his animal instincts, but as his ideas, goals, and values—all of a purely human and psychological nature rather than of a physiological and animal nature. Instincts and their satisfaction are subordinated to goals and values and their attainment. The individual is not blindly pushed by instinctual forces but is pulled by his idea of success, which, in the last analysis, is actually his own creation.

Even sexual behavior itself is not the direct expression of the sex drive; it is behavior that also serves the goals for which the individual is striving. For example, a promiscuous girl is not a girl whose sexuality is of a particular kind. Rather, she is a girl who uses the sexual component of her make-up to achieve a certain goal—to be popular, to have a good time, to hurt her parents, or to demonstrate that she is as independent and free as a boy. She may believe she is compelled by her strong urges and may be completely unaware of the actual mainsprings of her actions.

The content of the unconscious does not consist of inevitable biological facts that have been repressed but of mistaken notions and ideas of success of which the individual has not become aware. These ideas may be corrected once they are seen in their proper context and understood.

Adler was fully aware of the frequently observed aggressive and hostile behavior of men toward one another. However, he did not see this behavior as one of the signs of an instinct of destruction that must find an outlet. Rather, he saw aggression as a way in which the individual mistakenly pursues the goals of personal superiority and power. Far from assuming an innate aggression and hostility, Adler assumed that a positive capacity for social living is an innate component of human nature. Once this capacity has been properly developed, beginning in early childhood, it becomes social interest that assures a constructive life in which all the inevitable conflicting and frustrating situations of daily existence can be successfully handled. In an individual whose social interest is developed, the goal of superiority or perfection will be one that is socially useful; it will make "common" sense.

All maladjustment is characterized by an underdeveloped social interest. In instances of maladjustment the goal is one of personal superiority and power over others; it will be socially useless or harmful, will appear nonsensical to others, and will make only "private" sense. Self-centeredness is not the normal condition of man but a sign of maladjustment. The mentally healthy person, through his developed social interest, will be essentially task-centered or self-transcending. Harmony within the individual and between the individual and society is the normal condition, and conflict with society and other individuals is a sign of maladjustment.

Adler did not see, as Freud did, a necessity for repression. This difference entails an important difference in the philosophy of education and of guidance in general. According to Adler, it is not a matter of the curtailment of wishes but of the encouragement and development of the existing positive forces. Thus Adler could write: "Individual Psychology [the name of his system] demands the suppression of neither justified nor unjustified wishes. But it does teach that unjustified wishes must be recognized as violating social feeling, and that by a surplus of social interest they can be made, not to become suppressed, but to disappear."

Whereas Freud's theory of human nature lends strong support to the cynicism and disillusionment of our time, Adler's theory is in accord with all the liberalizing and progressive tendencies mankind has developed. Toward the end of their lives, Freud, consistent with his theories, became increasingly pessimistic, while Adler described his Individual Psychology as "a gay and optimistic science." Adler's optimism remained unshaken despite the fact that he suffered as much as Freud from Hitler's conquest of Austria. Adler died in 1937; Freud, in 1939.

Non-Freudian views of aggression do not regard it as an instinctual drive requiring ongoing gratification. Instead, aggression is seen as a reactive response that does not take form until triggered off by an object or situation. Aggression is a reaction to frustration, when one feels blocked in the pursuit of just rights, opportunities, or dignity. Aggression is also the response of an individual to what he perceives as an attack upon himself.

In the following paper, Sicher and Mosak support this concept of aggression as a secondary phenomenon. It is not innate and universal. Actual fighting and other forms of hostility, in their view, are secondary to an individual's fear and greed.

Aggression as a Secondary Phenomenon

Lydia Sicher, M.D., Ph.D. and Harold H. Mosak, Ph.D. *

The widespread delight in reading murder mysteries and watching fights, be they boxing or bullfights, is frequently cited as evidence for an innate aggression instinct as postulated by Freud in 1929. Such stories or events would afford, it is held, a vicarious expression of aggression without the responsibility of either killing or fighting oneself. But actual fighting itself, which is found frequently enough in the world, is pointed to as perhaps the main line of evidence for an innate primary aggression instinct.

* *Journal of Individual Psychology,* Vol. 23, No. 2 (November 1967), pp. 232-235.

The purpose of the present paper is to offer alternate explanations for these phenomena, derived from Adlerian theory. While Adler had spoken of an aggression drive as early as 1908, he soon abandoned this concept, replacing it with the concept of a general upward striving which he called variously striving to be a real man, striving for power, superiority, success, and ultimately for perfection and completion—in the mentally healthy person in a socially useful, contributive direction.

People, of course, differ and ultimately each individual is unique. Thus, although there are undoubtedly some who derive gratification from identification with the powerful, the cruel, or the killer, it is unlikely that too many people would really like to be in his place.

What apparently fascinates many, especially the highly intellectual people who read mystery stories, is the skill with which conclusions are formed with minimal clues. The mental processes involved in detective work bear striking resemblance to those engaged in by the therapist when unraveling the "mysteries" of his patients. Unfortunately, few writers of mystery stories possess sufficient imagination to create literary productions involving subjects other than murders to arouse the reader's interest. Poe's *The Gold Bug* is a notable exception.

The hunting dog, in flushing out his quarry, has more appeal than the sheepherding dog who is merely a technician. Likewise, gory movies and television plots are attractive to children and rather primitive grown-ups because they denote action. Yet those more sophisticated pictures in which the gore is merely an accessory to a legal procedure or is an avenue for expressing some ethical ideas, ultimately have a greater audience of mature people, viewers who want something to think about, some values that are at stake.

The excitation of the esthetic sensibilities may also be involved, in addition to the stimulation of the logical processes. In such instances a fight is not interesting because someone is rendered punch-drunk or a bull is killed. Rather the "dancing" skill of the boxer and certainly the "passes" of the matador are appreciated as beautiful, while the gore is an unpleasant, negligible accessory to the beauty of the pageant which the picadors and toreadors are presenting. In Portugal, for example, the bulls are not even killed but are led out of the arena after the fight. Shall we assume that the Portuguese are not hostile or aggressive, overtly or covertly?

There is also the mere desire that the side with whom one has identified may triumph. The yelling that goes on at all of these events—boxing, bullfights, automobile races—is generally not due to the fact (or the wish) that someone might be hurt. In many instances it represents the desire to see one on whom one has placed one's hope and confidence, and in many cases, one's money, emerge victorious. The triumph of the underdog unleashes the yelling for some. The thrill seeker finds his thrill, and he whose life style requires to be in control derives vicarious satisfaction in seeing how close one can get to danger and death (the ultimate controller) without losing control and falling victim to the enemy.

Where does all the fighting in our world start, and why is it so difficult to call a halt to it? What is this hostility and aggression that now threatens to assume primacy even over the sexual drives? Two factors, fear and greed, seem to lie behind it, both directed toward the same two goals—physical survival and psychological survival.

Out of fear for survival and out of the conviction that attack is the safest defense, methods of defense eventually are used in an aggressive manner. There are people who speak of preventive wars, not because they are hostile and aggressive but because their fear for survival calls for the aggressive defense of preventive war. A youngster, asked by his mother why he had hit another boy at the playgroup, explained, "Oh, Mommy, he had such a mean look in his eye. I knew he wanted to hit me, so I hit him back first!"

Although the child is normally protected against the forces of nature, at an early stage he learns to fear and fight the giants in his surroundings, dinosaurs in the form of grown-ups, whom the child for quite some time cannot understand. Yet they have the right to do with him as they see fit without his having a say in it, except for perhaps a cry or scream. Democracy does not intrude in the baby's world. He may legitimately soon come to feel afraid, since he is small, lacks competence, and is incapable of taking care of himself. Consequently, many children who are considered aggressive are probably so in the meaning of self-assertion.

If fear for physical survival is responsible for many acts of hostility among adults, the fear for one's value system, one's psychological survival, generates as many, is not more, anti-social attitudes in human interaction. Psychological survival concerns the status of the person, and its preservation is at least as important as the survival in life itself. At times it is even superordinate to physical survival as when a person chooses to die for his principles.

Both fears, for physical and psychological survival, are re-inforced by greed. If possessions give one status and importance, then the child must be taught to believe in and practice the "have" position as the one which increases one's stature. The self-training in a child along these lines elicits the praise that he is smart and clever, boding well for his future. The misinterpretation takes hold that it might be smarter to get more while doing less. And nothing seems more despicable than to be made a sucker, to be taken advantage of. If one does not get, life is unfair; the individual feels entitled to express his hostility, and feels his greed legitimized.

Is one to believe that these acts of hostility can be attributed to a gene-bound trait? Or are they referrable to an acquired conviction that nothing is enough? Children are trained to worship the false ideas of security, importance, status with which society abounds because of the generally prevalent poorly developed social interest. The associated hostility is the consequence of the acquired greed.

Summarizing, we would say that vicarious aggression is often the fascination for action and its excitement and beauty, or identification with the victor or underdog. Actual fighting and other forms of hostility are secondary to fear and greed, both directed toward physical and psychological survival and self-assertion. These points are further arguments against the Freudian notion of innate, universal aggression.

From this follows among other possible conclusions that the selling of guns and war toys for children can no longer be rationalized as affording them an opportunity to discharge their aggression. Rather, we must ask ourselves, toward what goals are we training our children?

In the next reading, two psychiatrists report on eight boys they studied at the Mayo Clinic: seven had made murderous assaults and one had committed murder. Doctors Easson and Steinhilber conclude that, in all cases, one or both parents had fostered and had condoned murderous assault. This is another confirmation of the non-Freudian view that aggression is not an innate drive but a provoked reaction.

Murderous Aggression by Children and Adolescents

William M. Easson, M.B., Ch.B., and Richard M. Steinhilber, M.D.*

... In response to firm, nonambivalent parental example and direction, the growing child learns to control his impulses and to tolerate frustration. If the parental demand for compliance is supported by warm affection and is clearly delineated by adequate limit setting, the child develops a firm, well-founded conscience structure. Ethics that have no personification in a parental figure have no well-founded part in the life of a child. The child senses when his parent is expressing ambivalent or guilty disapproval. If a parent has no moral scruples regarding some antisocial behavior, the child himself, without guilt, can act in this fashion. Such a delinquent child may show fear, not through guilt, but rather from the prospect of punishment. If the parent is ambivalent, the child may act out the parent's anti-

* *Archives of General Psychiatry*, Vol. 4, No. 1 (January 1961), pp. 2-9.

social tendencies; this type of delinquent has at least vague feelings of guilt. The parent punishing such a misdeed is ambivalent, guilty, and open to covert blackmail by the child. If limit setting is absent or ambivalent and the parental-child relationship is basically rejecting, the child represses those impulses which would expose him to humiliation and punishment from the parent. The child negates his inner impulses to maintain his relationship with the needed parent.

In many studies on homicide there are murderers designated as "normal" psychologically and there are murders classified as being "without motive," often by these same "normal" people. With these designations we would disagree. In our culture, "normal" people do not commit murder. No murder is "without motive." These classifications are most often seen in descriptions of murders by children and young adults. More intensive investigation, in most instances impossible owing to the circumstances of the investigation, would, we believe, have given indication of underlying psychopathology in these cases. . . .

Over a 12-month period we saw in psychiatric consultation 7 boys who had made murderous assaults and 1 boy who had committed murder. These patients were all from socially acceptable "normal" family homes. These patients and their families were the subjects of this study.

Case 1. An attractive 8-year-old boy, during his interview sessions, talked freely about his obsessive thoughts of violence directed mainly against his brother and his mother. He had to pray continually to get rid of these thoughts which he described as "devils." During his play sesssions he showed persistently feminine play with dolls and kitchen utensils. He said that when he married he too intended to have a baby just as mother did.

His father, aged 40, was a busy general practitioner who admitted that he used his work as an escape from a cold, formal marriage. This man was the eldest son of a brutal, sadistic mortician and of an overprotective mother. He married his wife "because she was an efficient nurse." His wife, the patient's mother, also 40 years of age, was a cold, dissociating woman.

Her own father, to whom she was very close, died 1 month prior to the birth of the patient.

This young boy was the middle child of 3; he had a 13-year-old sister and a 7-year-old brother. The mother stated that the boy had been "hard to handle since he was 1 week old." "He refused flatly to take the bottle at 3 weeks of age." He always was an aggressive, antisocial, rather withdrawn boy. He was enuretic and had many nightmares. He did poorly in school, and testing here at the Mayo Clinic showed a specific reading disability. The mother said about his first-grade teacher, "I really think she wanted to pass him to get rid of him." Discipline in the home was vacillating and there was no bathroom or bedroom privacy. The parents brought the child for evaluation of his behavior. A local psychiatrist had recommended residential treatment but the parents had decided that, if residential treatment were advised here, they would take him to yet another psychiatrist.

Six months prior to the clinic visit, over a period of 1 month, the patient made 3 murderous assaults on his younger brother. The first occurred at school where his older sister caught him trying to choke his brother. The young brother was blue in the face and the sister had forcibly to pull the 2 boys apart. The mother found out about this attack 5 days later but felt then "It was too late to do or say anything." She did not tell the father. One week later, again at school, the sister found the patient trying to strangle his younger brother with a belt. The school authorities immediately notified the parents who, however, did nothing and the father felt, at that time, "It was part of growing up." One week later, at home, the mother discovered the boy trying to drown his brother by holding his head under the bath water. Only then did the parents take the child to a psychiatrist.

Comment on Case 1. Cold, formal relationships within this family barely concealed the marked rage and hostility. Vacillating discipline reflected the parental ambivalence. In no way can attempted strangulation or drowning be considered "a part of normal growing up," and the parental ambivalence was clearly shown in the reaction of these parents to this young boy's lethal attacks on his brother.

Case 2. The father of a 13-year-old boy said blandly in his first interview, "I am sure he is going to kill someone and end up in the penitentiary."

During the year prior to his evaluation, the patient had been increasingly violent and aggressive toward his parents and siblings, so much so that on 2 occasions he was removed to the local state mental hospital under police guard. Twice during arguments he had attempted to slash his father with a knife. On one occasion, when his mother rebuked him for teasing his 14-year-old sister, he swore at her and when his father reprimanded him for swearing at his mother, he slapped his father and tried to stab him. The mother became extremely upset when asked by the interviewer to repeat the swear word the boy had used and eventually she flatly refused to reveal this word. The patient freely discussed this episode and the language he had used. He said, "My mother will not stay in the house with me," and "My father is sure I am going to kill someone." This boy had a collection of guns and knives, which he was allowed to retain, and on his 12th birthday he was given a gun as a present by his father.

The patient was the elder son in a family of 4 with 2 older sisters. Within the family there was marked sibling rivalry between this boy and his sisters. During this boy's third year of life he began to have typical petit mal seizures and was started on treatment with phenobarbital and diphenylhydantoin sodium (Dilantin). He had his first grand mal seizure when he was 5 years old. During the ensuing 8 years he had 4 or 5 grand mal convulsions, the last one 15 months prior to his evaluation at the Mayo Clinic. Minor spells had continued once every 2 to 3 months. The results of physical examination at the clinic were normal; the electroencephalogram showed no abnormality. His intelligence was low normal (I.Q. 95).

In this family home there was no door on any room in the house. The patient complained bitterly about his lack of privacy. For 5 or 6 years the mother had been in the habit of getting into bed with the boy and, face to face with him, massaging his back. With his increasing aggressivity over the past year, he had demanded this treatment more and more. The mother had related that the boy's father received exactly similar massaging from his mother, the patient's grandmother. When it was put to the mother that this was rather seductive behavior, she was unable to agree, saying, "I cannot see why it upset this child, as it in no way upset the 2 older children"—both girls. The patient's mother, a very hostile woman, minimized her role in the development of the boy's symptoms. Her own mother was a strict, rigidly religious woman and her father, to whom she was much closer, died when she was 12 years old. She married her husband because "A man who was good to his mother would be good to his wife." This man, the patient's father, was excessively passive and had been impotent for several years.

The patient himself was very glum and initially negativistic. As the interview sessions progressed he was more able to talk of his hostility and anger at the family pattern of seductiveness, permissiveness and rejection.

Comment on Case 2.   Both parents expected that this child would be violent and aggressive. They indicated to the boy the violence expected of him when they called in the police to take him to the state hospital. Yet he was allowed to retain and to add to his collection of weapons. At no time was the local physician consulted.

This pubescent boy was subjected to gross seduction and infantilization in a family setting of marked psychopathology.

Case 3.   The complaint of persistent enuresis brought a 16-year-old boy for evaluation. All physical examinations gave normal results.

During a routine psychiatric collaborative evaluation of this enuresis the patient's mother related how 1 year prior to this clinic visit he had shot at his younger brother during an argument. During the time of this actual evaluation he "shot up" the family farmhouse and killed several chickens. After the first episode of shooting, the mother took the gun from the boy but did not punish him. She did not tell his father, as she felt that the boy would be brutally beaten and injured.

When the patient was 11 years old he stole a knife from the local store. His mother, though aware of the stealing, did not make him return the knife. At the time of this clinic visit she knew that he was still stealing money from the house. He had run away from home several times. Whenever he would threaten to run away, his mother would tell him to go ahead and do so. He always had a violent temper and had been liable to aggressive outbursts. Many times his father had beaten him brutally. Both parents, during their interview, stated that the patient would eventually hurt someone and "end up in a penitentiary."

This young man was the fourth child in a family of 6, the product of an unwanted pregnancy. Because of his enuresis he was the family scapegoat. Physically he was small for his age and rather slow in physical development. His intelligence was average. The patient appeared depressed and agreed with the information given by his parents as to the shooting, stealing, and running away. He described frequent brutal beatings by the father. On the Thematic Apperception Test the patient described scenes of murder in response to 2 cards.

The patient's mother, although sullen and reticent otherwise, talked freely about her hatred for her domineering mother. She described her father as a very passive, self-effacing man. When this woman was 3 years old she was given to an aunt and uncle who were childless. She still wondered why her own parents "gave me away." Inadvertently she let it slip that her own mother insisted that she marry a man 20 years her senior who was falsely considered to be wealthy, when she was 18 years old. This marriage lasted 2 months; she refused to give any further information about this marriage. When she was 24 years old she married the patient's father. The mother denied any pre-nuptial intercourse, but the father revealed that she was 6 months pregnant at the time of the marriage. The father himself was defensive and inarticulate and unable to give a detailed family history. All 4 boys in the family were enuretic into middle adolescence and 2 maternal uncles were also enuretic.

Comment on Case 3.   The relationships within this family showed a marked degree of barely concealed hatred. To the patient, the mother was hostile and rejecting, the father brutal and sadistic. His mother had fostered multiple delinquencies: stealing, truancy, and aggressive violence. Both parents took it as a matter of course that the patient would end up in a penitentiary because he would eventually do physical harm to someone.

Case 4.   A 16-year-old boy was tricked into coming to the Mayo Clinic by his grandmother. She wished an evaluation of his behavior problem but told him that he was coming for an eye examination.

The grandmother was the adoptive mother of this boy. The boy's mother had been a chronic, depressed, phobic alcoholic and had committed suicide on the patient's bed when he was 7 years old. The boy's father had died in a mental institution when the patient was 3 years of age. The father had been repeatedly in and out of jail for reasons unknown to the grandmother. The grandmother did not know the father's final psychiatric diagnosis.

The patient had always been overactive, aggressive, and a behavior problem. He had been expelled from many schools because of his aggressiveness and destructiveness; he destroyed school property and repeatedly assaulted the teachers and his fellow pupils. The grandmother related how he would kill birds with a whip or with firecrackers. Over the previous 2 years he had hit the grandmother with a golf club, he had set her hair on fire, he had thrown knives at her "in fun," and twice he had slashed her arms with a knife after mild reprimands. As the grandmother described his violent outbursts she smiled with obvious pleasure. These actions she passed off as "adventurous." He had been allowed to retain his collection of knives. The grandmother described how she still slept with this boy and how, until he was 11 years old, she bathed him. When his car license was suspended, the grandmother drove the boy around town although her own license had been revoked because she had bilateral cataracts. The grandmother's first husband, after whom this boy was named, had been a brutal sadist. Recently, because of the patient's violent, aggressive behavior, the local authorities had taken the matter out of the grandmother's hands and the patient had been instructed that either he agree to placement in a residential school with psychotherapy, or else he remove himself from the state.

This young man, a depressed, tense adolescent, agreed that he badly needed psychiatric help, and that "things are all screwed up."

Comment on Case 4. The grandmother, the adoptive mother of this patient, was seductive, dishonest, and permissive with this adolescent youth. She gained obvious pleasure from the boy's wanton destructiveness and sadism. The suicide of this boy's mother over his bed was an indication of the mother's barely controlled murderous wishes toward her own son. This adolescent boy showed in his own sadistic, murderous behavior his hostile identification with his mother and his grandmother.

Case 5. A 15-year-old boy was referred by the legal authorities for psychiatric evaluation because of his repeated truancy, stealing, and shoplifting. He was an illegitimate child but his mother had successfully pretended to her family, her church, and her friends that she had once been married. The patient had been enuretic and had sucked his thumb until he was 6 years old. He had slept with his mother until the time of this psychiatric evaluation. Until 14 years of age the patient was bathed by his mother and his grandmother. He related how his mother and grandmother ridiculed his tentative attempts at shaving and how they mocked at his developing axillary and chest hair.

When the patient was 6 years old he began stealing from his mother's purse. She soon discovered this and was aware that the stealing had continued in spite of all punishments. Nevertheless, she persisted on leaving her purse available and open. Repeatedly she told the boy, "You are going to be a thief." She was aware, also, that from about the age of 8 he had been stealing from the local stores. She did not question him nor did she oblige him to return the stolen merchandise. For 2 years prior to this evaluation he had been repeatedly truant from school. His mother had ignored his increasing intake of alcohol over the previous year. One month prior to his psychiatric examination he had choked his mother to the point of near unconsciousness. Only with difficulty had his grandmother managed to separate the two. Two days before this episode the mother had brutally beaten the boy for a minor offense, and as she beat him she had repeated, "I hate you, I wish you were dead."

The boy's mother described a passive, seductive father, a chronic business failure, who repeatedly stole from her childhood savings bank. Her mother was a hysterical woman who greatly favored the younger sister. The patient's mother admitted that she would have aborted the pregnancy that resulted in the patient's birth but for her religious convictions. Spontaneously she admitted her fostering of stealing, truancy, and murderous retaliation in her son.

The patient, normal physically, was obviously depressed. Psychologic testing confirmed this depression.

Comment on Case 5. This boy had been raised in an atmosphere of successful pretense. His mother repeatedly stated in her interviews that this son was unwanted, yet she had kept him. Obviously, in some way, his mother thus gained emotional gratification. Both mother and grandmother were physically overclose to this adolescent boy, although they scorned his developing masculinity. The mother was aware of her hostile, destructive impulses toward the boy and of her role in fostering his delinquency, truancy, and murderous rages. She admitted freely her own murderous impulses toward her son.

Case 6. A small-statured 13-year-old boy talked readily of his terror concerning his uncontrollable rages. He discussed freely his extreme anger at his parental overpermissiveness. Intelligence testing gave him an I.Q. of 120. The Rorschach test showed impulsive swings of mood with some confusion of male sex roles.

Three years prior to his evaluation this patient had his first grand mal seizure. Within the next 2 months he had two further convulsions. He was then started on treatment with phenobarbital and diphenylhydantoin sodium and had no further convulsions. At the time of his birth he had had neonatal asphyxia and a cephalohematoma. He was enuretic until the age of 6 years, and at the time of these psychiatric interviews he still bit his nails. His mother still bathed him and the family all shared the same bedroom. His 7-year-old brother was very much the parental favorite.

Two days after his last grand mal seizure, during an aggressive outburst of temper, the patient first threatened his mother with a gun. Over the next 3 years he exhibited repeated outbursts of extreme aggressivity toward the parents, and several times he threatened them with a gun. He said, "I could always get what I wanted if I made enough fuss. Why didn't they stop me? They were scared of me. They didn't need to be. I am still small." For 6 months prior to his evaluation, the mother had refused to remain alone in the house with the boy. She told him she was afraid he would hurt her. Both parents prophesied many times to the patient that he would end up in a reformatory.

The boy was permitted and encouraged to drive the family truck on the highway although, as both parents agreed, he had on many occasions suggested that he was too young to drive. He had a collection of guns and knives which he had been allowed to retain, although he himself had suggested that his father assume control of this collection. Finally, just prior to his visit to the Mayo Clinic, after an argument at home, he pointed his gun at his father and kept the father as a target for 5 or 6 minutes. The patient repeatedly said that he did not know why he had not shot his father.

The patient's mother appeared emotionally drab and she described a cheerless existence. Her husband, the patient's father, was a passive, tearful man. His brother, a paranoid schizophrenic, had been hospitalized after he had threatened the grandmother with a gun. The patient's parents had delayed having children because they felt that the brother's mental condition might be hereditary.

Comment on Case 6.   Repeatedly this patient had pleaded

for firm discipline and definite limit setting. Despite his murderous outbursts and his requests for control, he was allowed to retain his collection of knives and guns. Repeatedly the parents indicated to this boy that they expected from him aggressive and dangerous behavior.

Case 7. "As he stood behind me stroking my neck he asked, 'Mother, can I have intercourse with you?' I was scared he was going to choke me, so I answered, 'Yes, but it would be horrible.' "

Thus the mother of a 13-year-old boy described her experiences in the hotel room which she shared with this patient during his evaluation at the Mayo Clinic. Since the age of 5 years, this boy had had classic temporal-lobe epileptiform seizures about once every 3 months. He was grossly obese, weighing 205 lb., with a height of 5 ft. 9 in. The results of neurologic examination were unremarkable. X-ray examination and laboratory tests all gave normal results. The electroencephalogram showed frequent sharp-wave bitemporal discharges maximally in the left temporal region; these were increased by hyperventilation and in a recording during sleep.

The patient was the youngest of four children with a sister aged 33 and brothers aged 31 and 20. He was conceived within 3 months of the marriage of his sister. His parents said they had wanted, in this pregnancy, "a roly-poly girl." The boy had had repeated temper tantrums from early childhood. He was enuretic until age 7 and he still bit his fingernails and toenails at the time of this psychiatric evaluation. By the time he started school at age 6 he was obese and was mocked by the other children because of his obesity and femininity. His mother refused to let him fight back against his tormentors. All his life she had controlled his bowels with laxatives and she still bathed him. From the time of starting in school, the patient had become increasingly aggressive and demanding. His father would beat him brutally, at times until he bled, because of his use of swear words with a sexual connotation.

From age 12 he had asked his mother repeated questions about her sexual activities. On many occasions he asked if he could have intercourse with her. Her standard answer was, "Yes, but it would be horrible." This statement was agreed on by the patient and by both parents in their histories. The boy obtained from his mother details of her first intercourse and details as to how she felt during intercourse when his sister was conceived.

During the year prior to his visit to the clinic, his aggression had been much more marked and there had been at least 10 episodes during which he stabbed or attempted to stab members of his family. He had knifed his 20-year-old brother after a breakfast table argument. He stabbed his father in the back once after his father had brutally beaten him. He stuck a knife into his mother when she refused to drive him to town. Other episodes were similar. All these stab wounds were superficial. When the mother went to the hospital 6 months before the boy was seen at the clinic, his father told him that he would not sleep with him because he felt that his son might kill him in his sleep. Several times when the boy had threatened his father with a knife, the father deliberately turned his back on the boy "to give him a better target if he wanted one."

To the patient, incest was a real possibility. The father agreed, too, that the boy could have intercourse with the mother because "he is physically able." He also said that he had thought that perhaps the boy might rape his mother, but he did not mention it to her because "It might scare her." He was aware that on this trip the boy and his mother were sharing the same hotel room.

The patient's father described his own father as sadistic and brutal and related how brutal beatings had had little effect on himself. He said that he had stopped beating the patient, his son, "Because I felt I might kill him." The patient's mother told how her own father was arrested for child neglect and how her mother had told her dying sister that she had been prenuptially conceived.

The patient had an I.Q. of 112. The Rorschach test showed marked impulsivity, with distortion of reality and poor insight; there were no indications of a schizophrenic process in the projective test results.

Comment on Case 7.   This family showed massive psychopathology. Since birth this adolescent boy had been infantilized
and feminized. The father's murderous outbursts toward the
boy were barely controlled and in his own violent aggression the
patient was identifying with his father. The patient showed no
guilt over his incest fantasies or murderous outbursts, which
were expected and condoned by both parents.

Comment on Cases 1 to 7 as a Group.   These 7 patients and
their families showed many of the factors described in other
series. Each of the 7 boys was emotionally closely tied to and
identified with the mother in a hostile fashion. The fathers in
these families were not available to their sons for healthy identification, through death of the father, brutal rejection of the son
by the father, or failure of the father to play a definite mascu-
line role in the family. Generally these boys had been maintained in a dependent relationship to their parents; lack of
privacy, physical overcloseness and, at times, the grossest seduction were repeatedly found. These boys were set the pattern
of physical violence either by parental example or parental approval. Most of these boys had collections of knives and guns;
these collections they were allowed to retain and, in some cases,
to augment, even after several episodes of extremely violent
and menacing behavior. In each case the child was repeatedly
given to realize that his parents expected him to be physically
violent and antisocially aggressive, even to the point of murder.

These children had the opportunity to commit murder and
yet did not actually kill. Several of the patients were stopped
in their violent behavior, yet they had so made their murderous
attacks in some public place that they could be stopped. Several
of these children made attacks that could have been fatal, yet
the knife wounds were superficial and the gun was aimed poorly
or not fired at all. During this investigation period we did make
a psychiatric evaluation of one child murderer and his family.
It is interesting and instructive how this patient, ostensibly from
a "normal" socially acceptable family, showed many of the
psychopathologic features described above.

Case 8.   "If only he had had a motive I could have understood it." Thus a 50-year-old Midwest lawyer summed up his feelings about the murder committed by his 10-year-old son. The boy shot his music teacher from his bedroom window. The teacher, a middle-aged spinster, was a close personal friend of the patient's mother. The boy made some attempt to conceal the body in the local woods, but freely confessed when questioned by the police. At the time of the psychiatric interviews the patient was under indictment.

The boy's mother said that this son was "never close to anyone"; "he has rejected us all along"; "he never was a cuddly baby"; "he seemed to like it when I would nibble his ear to tease him, but not in bed." At 10 years of age this boy was still bathed by his mother. He had been enuretic until age 7.

When he was 7 years old the patient set the family gasoline storage tank alight and was himself severely burned. Two years later he was caught stealing from his grandmother's purse. The same year he and his brother stole a gun from the local hardware store. He was not punished for any of these thefts. Both the boy and his 16-year-old brother had a collection of guns. They both had guns mounted above their beds. The patient stayed at home even after his confession of homicide and the guns remained in the bedrooms. On the day prior to the shooting, the patient had broken his bedroom window after an argument with his mother over his piano lessons. It was through this broken window that he fired at his victim.

When seen at the Mayo Clinic the patient was moderately depressed. Physical examination gave normal results, as did all the laboratory studies, roentgenograms of the skull, and electroencephalograms. His I.Q. was 110.

The boy's father, a moderately successful small-town lawyer, frankly expressed his dislike for his controlling domineering wife. On his many business trips away from home he was active sexually with prostitutes. The patient's mother described herself as "high strung." She said that she never expressed anger because "it was a waste of time." During each interview session she constantly bit her nails. She gave a past history of addiction to barbiturates. She had been very close to her own father. Her mother died when she was 14 years old. When her father remarried 2 years later, she felt greatly rejected by this father and resented the stepmother. "But after a year I decided she was wonderful for my father and my younger brother." This younger brother was the person after whom the patient was named. When the patient's father and the 2 boys went hunting, the mother went along; she was a better hunter than the father. She boxed with the boys and could beat them both. The mother could not in any way understand the boy's homicidal act.

Comment on Case 8. Many studies . . . give detailed histories of murder committed by "normal adolescents." The family in our Case 8 was intelligent and well motivated. The collaborative investigating psychiatrists were most interested in the psychodynamics of homicide. Nevertheless, even with intensive interviews with the patient and both parents for many hours, only vague hints as to the possible dynamic factors could be elicited. This may be due to the fact that the patient was under indictment at the time of the interviews. The murder was still recent and the family was numbed and bewildered by the shock of tragic events.

The mother's dissatisfaction in her female and maternal role was obvious. Physically, she was overclose to this preadolescent boy. The father, himself a legal man, showed obvious defects of conscience. The boy collected and gloried in guns. He was allowed to retain his gun collection even after murder had been committed. No constructive attempts had been made to deal with his previous delinquencies. To the father, murder was understandable if it had a motive; he was able to visualize his own son as a murderer.

Physical illness, be it a convulsive disorder or a physical deformity, sibling rivalry, parental seductiveness, or brutality—these factors and others may cause intrafamilial turmoil, but only where there is parental permission is a child's conflict acted out in lethal violence. In a normal home, murder would not be understandable or condoned, no matter what the motive. All these 8 boys acted violently with parental permission and approval. Only 1 boy proceeded to actual murder. Why only he and not the other 7 committed murder is not clear and requires further intensive study.

Murder and murderous violence committed by children and adolescents occur where there is parental fostering, albeit unconscious.

. . . Eight cases are presented, the oldest patient being 16 years of age. Seven of these patients made a murderous assault and 1 actually did commit murder. The background family psychopathology of these patients is varied both in its character and in its malignity but shows certain definite psychodynamic patterns. All cases demonstrate that one or both parents had fostered and had condoned murderous assault.

By means of the cases presented in the foregoing article, Easson and Steinhilber indicate that violent assault by children and adolescents occurs when parents provoke aggression and then permit it. The patients described are very much like the rest of us in seeking to overcome feelings of inferiority by achieving power and control. The crucial difference is that these children were allowed to pursue this goal in a violent and destructive way.

In the next reading, Blackman, Weiss, and Lamberti investigate aggression in terms of the sudden murderer. They present six representative case histories of sudden murderers which are not included in our excerpt but can be summarized as follows: three of these individuals were diagnosed "schizophrenic," two "schizoid personality," and one "passive aggressive personality." Altogether 43 sudden murderers were studied. The authors suggest a general description which fits most such persons. They see this kind of individual as being pulled by opposing forces. He feels inadequate yet wants to succeed; feels isolated yet strives toward conformity. He yearns to become close and intimate with others but fears being rejected, and this conflict creates self-doubt, tension, and rage. He is constantly preoccupied with curbing surges of anger. When he is at the point of an intimate personal interaction which he both desires and

fears, his emotional equilibrium is extremely precarious. At
such a time, an "insult" from the social environment (rejection,
disapproval, indifference, etc.) may lead to an explosion of
aggressive feelings and murder. Again, the outburst of aggression is viewed as a response to circumstances in a person made
vulnerable by life experiences.

The Sudden Murderer: III. Clues to Preventive Inter-action

*Nathan Blackman, M.D., James M. A. Weiss, M.D.,
and Joseph W. Lamberti, M.D.**

. . . Modern society has been increasingly concerned with the
discharge of hostile feelings through resort to violence, especially when such acting-out culminates in murder. Of particular
interest has been the "sudden murderer," the person who, without having been involved in any previous serious aggressive
antisocial acts, suddenly, unlawfully, and intentionally kills (or
makes a serious attempt to kill) another human being. . . .

In previous studies we have investigated the life histories and
offenses of 13 such "sudden murderers" and compared their
behavioral patterns to those of other "control groups" of offenders (specifically, one group of habitual criminal offenders,
and another of sexual deviates). Our concern was with persons
who had committed a murder which was "sudden" in the sense
that it appeared to be a single, isolated, unexpected episode of
violent impulsive acting-out behavior—behavior which was never
well thought out, behavior which had no obvious purpose nor
hope for personal advantage or profit foreseeable as a result.
We found that the sudden murderer did have a distinctive behavioral history, which contrasted quite strikingly to those of
the two control groups. Characteristically, the sudden murderer
came from a cohesive home where mother was a domineering,
overprotective figure who emphasized conformity to the rules
of the social system. Failing in his attempt to conform because

* *Ibid.*, Vol. 8, No. 3 (March 1963), pp. 289-291, 293-294.

of underlying feelings of inadequacy and hostility, the murderer-
to-be tended to blame other people, and to wander from place
to place looking for greater opportunities. As a result, he felt
quite consciously alone and isolated from other people.

Surprisingly, when such a person seemed to be getting along
quite well, when society apparently expected him to be even
more conforming and mature, and when he had no one to blame,
he would become more and more tense and angry. At such a
time, even a slight provocation would set off the violent surge
of rage which resulted in murder.

These 13 murderers were originally studied in the Social
Maladjustment Study Unit of the Malcolm Bliss Mental Health
Center in St. Louis between July 1, 1956, and Dec. 31, 1957.
Since that time, in the period from Jan. 1, 1958, to June 30,
1962, thirty additional murderers were referred to this Unit,
making a total group of 43 such offenders evaluated over a 6-
year period. Of these, 29 demonstrated behavioral patterns
similar to those we have defined. However, 5 of the 14 who
did *not* fit the pattern were suffering from clinically apparent
organic brain disorder, and 3 of them were mothers who had
killed their children. As Tuteur and Glotzer have pointed out,
such "murdering mothers" tend to be quite different from other
murderers, and their actions seem to be consistently related to
a primary depressive disorder. Even including such obviously
atypical cases as the 8 noted above, however, it may be seen
that more than two-thirds of the murderers seen at our Unit appeared to fit the described behavioral pattern of the "sudden
murderer."

In order to further test the validity of our description of these
behavioral patterns, six independent experienced professional
persons (three psychiatrists and three clinical psychologists)
were asked to evaluate six representative case records. Each
rater evaluated two such records. In general, there was good
agreement with our original ratings. There was particularly
good consensus of the raters characterizing the "sudden murderer" pattern in terms of the following points: that such a
murderer was likely to be a young male adult, with no history

of previous serious aggressive antisocial acts, who had been reared by a dominant natural mother in a family of origin that had been overtly cohesive during the patient's childhood, except that the father had been either hostile, rejecting, overstrict, or indifferent to the patient; that the offenders were generally in good physical health, with intelligence at least in the dull normal range, but with a record of poor work performance; that the patient maintained some ties with his family of origin; that his sexual activities were either markedly inhibited or markedly promiscuous, but that he had no record of homosexual activities. The offender himself was characterized by a tendency toward introversion, by feelings of inadequacy in interpersonal relationships, by feelings of isolation (of being different and apart from other people), by a strong sense of insecurity, by confusion about sexual identity, by some ability to get along with other people but with a tendency to blame other people for his troubles, and by the demonstration of underlying feelings of anger and resentment. It was also emphasized that the murderer had a period of overtly adequate social adjustment for at least one month preceding the offense, that the murderer then received some provocation or "insult" which precipitated the offense, that he then assured his own apprehension by the police, and that after apprehension the patient confessed his guilt and appeared bland, unconcerned, or "righteous."

If this is a consistent pattern, then, it might provide some means for recognizing those persons who are likely to become sudden murderers, and recognition of the pattern might have certain implications in terms of prevention of such violence. In fact, there was a definite record in the case histories of 21 sudden murderers in our total sample that they had been seen sometime prior to the crime by professional persons such as psychiatrists or social workers or by other medical or social agency personnel. The typical story, however, was one in which after a short period of evaluation and/or treatment, the patient was completely discharged from further care. It seems obvious, of course, that not *all* persons with behavioral patterns such as we have described end up as murderers; it appears likely that

in some cases—perhaps many cases—some intervening socializing factors provide such persons with ways of solving their
conflicts and assuaging their feelings of insecurity or aloneness,
so that the underlying hostility, rage, and tension do not build
up to the point of explosion. Whether such socializing forces
might include experience with formal social organizations, such
as church groups, scout activities, or educational agencies, or
whether these might involve more limited interpersonal experiences with perhaps an employer or a friend or even a spouse,
is not clear. . . .

The fact that many of these persons who later attempted or
committed murder were discharged from professional care
seemed to occur because part of the pattern of such offenders-to-
be was an attempt to conform and to maintain some surface
ability to get along with other people. The psychological (and
often social) "isolatedness" of these patients apparently prevented a truly therapeutic involvement with the professional
worker. At the same time, there was some suggestion that the
patients' continually denied and repressed anger is threatening
to the worker, perhaps in an almost unrecognized way. Yet the
dynamic pattern of the person who becomes a sudden murderer
clearly suggests that he has a strong need for recognition of his
dependency. It appears quite possible that even infrequent but
continued supportive contact with a member of the helping professions might have aided such patients in a socializing process
and thus have helped them to overcome some of their conflicts.
Essentially, the predominant feeling mode of these patients is
one of emotional confusion, and although the patient may be
difficult to deal with therapeutically because he tends to project
blame for his lack of success, he is basically looking for more
effective mechanisms of dealing with his emotional confusion,
and for recognition that other persons are concerned about his
feeling of inadequacy.

Such a patient is likely nevertheless to be very frustrating to
a professional worker. Although accepting discharge from professional care with superficial approbation (as a sign that he is
returning to a more successful life), the patient undoubtedly

feels that in some ways he is being rejected by a person who did not help him enough, and also that he is being returned from a comparatively sheltered situation to the continued frustration of trying to solve his conflicts in a difficult world. The offender is aware of his dependent needs, but he tries to deny them; the explosive reaction of rage becomes the ultimate, brutal denial. Although understanding and satisfaction of these dependent needs by the professional worker might have minimized the build-up of hostility and tension, the very denial of these needs makes it more difficult to establish a therapeutic relationship.

The period of overtly adequate adjustment immediately preceding the offense of murder becomes somewhat clearer in light of the cases cited in the present paper. In each case cited, the total effort toward becoming integrated and accepted as an adult (whether in social, economic, or emotional spheres) appears to be tenuous and precarious. The very effort to maintain a facade of competence and independence saps some of the strengths and weakens some of the defenses with which the patient wards off his more basic feelings of insecurity and inadequacy. Essentially schizoid, or on the verge of a schizophrenic break, or existing in a schizophrenic magic-like way, the murderer-to-be finds that trying to prove to himself and others that he might act like a mature person enhances his own doubts about his identity. Without any continued positive relationships to help him, the patient's struggle against dependent needs becomes exaggerated, the effort toward denial becomes accentuated, and the precariousness of the "good" adjustment is maintained only to build up to the explosion of violence. It seems likely that it is during this period, when the patient presents a superficial appearance of conformity and adequacy, that in reality he is more and more preoccupied with his feelings of helplessness and with the necessity to terminate his ever-increasing inner disequilibrium—it is during this period that the patient most needs professional help, and it is then that he is least likely to get it.

This study of 43 "sudden murderers" reveals that most such persons suffer from constant conflict between inner feelings of inadequacy and conscious needs to succeed, between an inner sense of psychological isolatedness and an outward drive toward conformity. Such persons maintain an extremely precarious emotional equilibrium; they are constantly preoccupied with the need to curb surges of angry affect, with a reluctance to reveal their feelings of hopelessness in ever becoming close and intimate with others, and with a desperate hope of overcoming this sense of crippling aloofness. It is just when this emotionally isolated person is at the threshold of an intimate personal inter-action, when his relationships with other persons (be they emotional, sexual, or social) are at the point of becoming real or meaningful—it is then that the conflict between his dependent needs and his fear of being again rejected creates an increasing sense of self-doubt, tension, and repressed rage. At that time even an insignificant "insult" from the social environment may lead to an explosion of aggressive feelings culminating in murder.

The importance of sustained professional contacts with such schizoid or schizophrenic persons even during periods of apparent conformity and adequacy is stressed as a means of helping the inadequate, oversensitive, and overdoubting individual to maintain at least one area of interpersonal relationship where there is sufficient freedom to express and share his doubts about his existence. Alertness to the behavioral patterns described might well strengthen the evaluative abilities of workers in psychiatric facilities or social agencies, so that professional contacts with patients demonstrating similar maladjustment will be maintained, so that the "mask of adequacy" presented by such persons will be recognized, their doubts about identity and dependency explored, their hostilities uncovered, and their isolatedness lessened. There is yet no evidence available to prove that such efforts will be truly preventive. However, the psychodynamic pattern of the kind of persons described in this study is such that—*without* such efforts—they are very likely to end as "sudden murderers."

In each of the two preceding selections, passing reference was made to the fact that a proportion of the perpetrators of violent assault under study had been found to have some organic brain disorder. In our next reading for this chapter, Dr. Vernon H. Mark, director of the Neurosurgical Service, Harvard Medical School, focuses our entire attention on the role of brain dysfunction in the perpetration of violence. He finds definite evidence for linking abnormal brain function with violent behavior, postulating that certain brain abnormalities prevent an individual from attaining adequate self-control over his impulses. As a result, the person has a low threshold for violence and loses control with insufficient provocation.

Freudians do not consider brain function as one of the factors related to aggressive behavior. For them, whether or not a person acts violently generally depends on the balance of forces among the id, ego, and superego.

The Neurology of Behavior: Its Application to Human Violence

Vernon H. Mark, M.D.*

That environment, past experience, and learning are powerful forces in modifying and producing abnormal human behavior has been accepted by physicians, scientists, and sociologists for many years. The role of brain dysfunction, however, has remained an open question. Aside from the obvious behavioral impairment in persons with dementia, hemiplegia, hemianopia, and epilepsy during a seizure, most patients' behavioral abnormalities are considered to have a psychological or environmental origin.

A strict dichotomy exists: abnormal human behavior is the result of *either* environmental and psychological factors *or* brain damage. This dichotomy, a heritage from Aristotle and Descartes, often separates neurologists and neurosurgeons from a proper assessment of environment, and psychiatrists, psychologists, and sociologists from a realistic evaluation of brain function. Such a division may have been helpful in the nineteenth

* *Medical Opinion & Review*, Vol. 4, No. 4 (April 1968), pp. 26-31.

century for the evolution of psychiatry and neurology as separate specialties. At the present time, however, it is a barrier to the development and proper understanding of the neurology of behavior, and it must be overcome.

One of the reasons for the perpetuation of this useless dichotomy is the nature of the organ under study, for the brain is unique. It has been described as the primary organ of behavior. Certainly, a tiny reticular lesion in the midbrain of the human being can put an end to all meaningful behavior even though every other organ system is functioning perfectly.

In a larger sense, however, the brain is the organ that links a person to his environment—including not only the perfection and maintenance of homeostatic mechanisms and internal body equilibrium but also the relation to the world outside the body. This relation, in fact, is crucial in establishing the special function of the brain, for the external environment, in the form of past experience (memory), is actually incorporated into brain structure. It is an important basis of the individual reaction to ongoing environmental stimuli and expectations for the future. This one fact helps to explain the frustrations suffered by neurologists hoping to interpret and influence brain function (while having only a minor consideration for environment) as well as the impotence of sociologists and public officials attempting to change human behavior while ignoring the brain.

This dichotomy, lack of cooperation, and failure to progress is nowhere more evident than in our efforts to deal with human violence. With rare exceptions, domestic violence has been considered a social problem; persons who commit homicide, manslaughter, rape, and aggravated assault are arrested and confined in penal institutions. At times, either before or after the trial, psychiatric consultation is obtained. The prisoner's competence to stand trial is then decided by a vague psychiatric-legal formula. The role of brain dysfunction, in truth, is so grossly discounted by some public officials and clinicians that the recent surprise finding of a malignant brain tumor in a man guilty of multiple murders was publicly reported to be unimportant and noncontributory to this man's unusual behavior.

In spite of assiduous and competent efforts by talented social scientists and public officials working through law enforcement and social welfare agencies, crime in general, and crimes of violence in particular, have increased in number. The urgent necessity to approach this problem in a more effective fashion is underlined by the new and horrible means of producing mass destruction. The recent rapid advances in all phases of technology now give a single abnormal person unprecedented opportunities to kill immense numbers of people.

If abnormal brain function is to be indicted as a factor in violent behavior, it is important to define the kinds of violent behavior that can be reasonably associated with abnormal brain function. Normal human beings may, of course, engage in acts of violence in appropriate circumstances or under sufficient provocation. Young children assault one another readily while at play and they may become quite uninhibited when sexually stimulated. Even children, however, rarely become violent enough to hurt one another intentionally. When they do injure a playmate seriously, it is usually an accident. The child who behaves viciously, at any age, often can be identified as brain-injured or seriously emotionally disturbed.

As children become adolescent they normally gain more control over their instinctual and libidinal impulses; assaultive and sexual feelings become increasingly conditioned by the moral and legal codes of the family and society. Deliberate acts of violence are then confined to socially sanctioned events, such as killing in war and capital punishment. In this discussion we are concerned with those persons who have never been able to attain the degree of self-control dictated by the demands of communal living and civilization or who periodically and with insufficient provocation lose this control.

An important aspect of the evidence linking abnormal brain function with violent behavior is disclosed by thorough study of patients who have certain brain abnormalities. We have been most interested in a group of patients with focal brain abnormalities and behavioral aberrations (often leading to aggressiveness and violence), including fifteen with epilepsy who have had electrodes surgically implanted in the medial temporal lobe.

Many of these patients suffered from temporal lobe seizures that could not be controlled by medication. Aggressive or assaultive behavior in the interictal period was often more disabling than the epileptic attack. Moreover, the correction of behavioral abnormalities by amygdala lesions was sometimes not accompanied by any change in the frequency or pattern of the patient's seizures. The net clinical improvement in job stability and successful social relations, moreover, further emphasized the importance of these behavioral symptoms and further differentiated the symptoms of aggressiveness and assaultiveness from the patient's typical form of seizure. There is a significant incidence of striking behavioral abnormalities associated with abnormal temporal lobe electroencephalographic patterns, often in the absence of a frank seizure disorder.

The frequent occurrence of four major symptoms in our patients has been grouped under the eponym, *dyscontrol syndrome.* This is used as a more comprehensive term than the "episodic dyscontrol" of Karl Menninger and Martin Mayman in their work at the Menninger Clinic and includes most of the symptoms listed by Menninger in his third order of dyscontrol. The symptoms of the dyscontrol syndrome are: wife and child beating, or other evidence of physical brutality (often without a motive); manic or assaultive behavior after a small alcoholic intake; sexual assault; and multiple, serious auto accidents.

Some of our patients with the dyscontrol syndrome would previously have been labeled "psychopathic deviate" or "sociopath." All, however, have at least a focal abnormality in the electroencephalogram or localized atrophy on the pneumoencephalogram. Many have the additional, often minimal, symptoms of other varieties of brain dysfunction. These include: difficulties in speech and reading; defects of the visual field; memory impairments; seizures (particularly of the temporal lobe variety); hallucinations or other secondary psychotic manifestations; gross sleep disturbances, somnambulism, or fugue states; and mood disturbance, particularly episodic depression or anxiety (including panic).

It is important to emphasize that these signs of brain dysfunction may occur in people who do not give indication of violent behavior or the dyscontrol syndrome. For example, the incidence of behavioral abnormalities in patients with parietal lobe seizures is no higher than the incidence in the general population, but behavioral abnormalities are definitely more frequent in patients who have grand mal and temporal lobe seizures.

The following three cases illustrate various manifestations of the dyscontrol syndrome.

Case 1. This history is of a man who had the striking symptom of pathological intoxication. He was a twenty-five-year-old skilled machinist committed to an institution for the criminally insane after assaulting his mistress and fracturing her facial bones. He had beaten his young wife many times, once with a lead pipe. He became especially violent after a small intake of alcohol and after such consumption broke out of all restraints during an electroencephalographic examination. This patient had also suffered a serious head injury while driving a vehicle involved in a near-fatal accident.

A neurological examination disclosed that he was quite unable to read and could write his name only with difficulty, although he was of good intelligence. On reviewing his brain wave examination, Janice Stevens found bilateral temporal lobe abnormalities. He is now being evaluated on anticonvulsant and ataractic medication.

Case 2. The case of patient L.K. clearly shows the traffic hazards generated by these patients. The man is a thirty-four-year-old engineer with several important patents to his credit. His history of violence extended over a ten-year period and included spells of rage with a number of serious assaults on his wife and children. He was repeatedly late for work even though he started at an appropriate time. This patient invariably became infuriated when any driver cut in front of him and would go miles out of his way in hot pursuit, endangering the lives of many drivers and pedestrians. If he avoided an accident, he would arrive late and disheveled at work.

Prolonged psychiatric treatment did not improve his behavior, and his psychiatrist decided that his periods of staring, automatism, and rage represented an unusual form of temporal lobe seizure. An electroencephalographic examination disclosed temporal lobe spikes more pronounced on the right and a pneumoencephalogram revealed a right ventricular dilatation.

After a futile attempt to control his seizures and violence with a wide range of pharmacological agents, temporal lobe electrodes were implanted in both amygdala. Over a period of weeks, repeated stimulation and recordings were carried out to find the optimal site for destructive lesions.

Stimulation in the medial portion of the left amygdala nucleus produced a feeling of "going wild" and "I'm losing control." On the other hand, stimulation in the lateral amygdala, three millimeters away, repeatedly produced a sensation of "hyperrelaxation," a feeling of "detachment," "just the antithesis of my spells." In his usual state, this patient was keenly aware of the slightest personal insult or threat, and his response was often sudden or violent. Under the effects of lateral amygdala stimulation, he showed bland acquiescence to the suggestion that the medial portion of his temporal lobe was to be destroyed. This suggestion, under ordinary circumstances, would provoke wild, disordered thinking.

Indeed, eight to ten hours after stimulation had been completed and coincident with the disappearance of his detached and hyperrelaxed feeling, he became wild and unmanageable and protested vigorously against any destructive lesions in his amygdala. It took many weeks of patient explanation, and a near social tragedy produced by his uncontrollable rage, before he accepted bilateral amygdala lesions. These were carried out sequentially, and he has not suffered an attack of generalized rage in the six months following his last amygdala lesion.

Case 3. Even in an era of rapidly changing social codes, the sexual activities of C. D. are sufficiently unusual to demonstrate a part of the symptom complex. She is a thirty-eight-year-old woman admitted to the psychiatric ward of a general hospital. She openly masturbated eighteen to twenty times a day and had a history of promiscuous relations with Lesbian prostitutes. She often took two or more men to bed with her and quickly exhausted them with her sexual demands. She once attacked her husband with the razor sharp edge of a broken bottle and attempted to emasculate him.

Prolonged psychiatric treatment was ineffective and an astute psychiatric resident requested a brain-wave examination. This disclosed a generalized pattern of pronounced abnormality. She was placed on anticonvulsant medication (diphenylhydantoin), which considerably reduced her sexual activity.

The medical literature is replete with examples of focal brain disease and abnormal behavior. Most recently this has been emphasized by Nathan Malamud, who has described the correlations between neoplasms involving the limbic system and gross behavioral abnormalities, including many examples of aggressive and assaultive behavior, in eighteen patients. Furthermore, the successful treatment of aggressive, hyperactive, and assaultive behavior in epileptic and nonepileptic patients with obvious brain damage has been recently described by R. R. Heimburger, H. Narabayashi and M. Uno, and B. Ramamurthi and V. Balasubramaniam. They used precise focal lesions in the amygdala to change the behavioral state of their patients, further stressing how important is the role played by limbic brain structures in uncontrolled violent behavior.

Is there a relation between these thoroughly studied patients with focal brain disease and the huge group of unstudied law violators guilty of assault, murder, manslaughter, rape, and arson?

Evidence on this score is suggestive but not conclusive. It relies heavily on the results of psychiatric and psychological testing and electroencephalographic recordings of selected prison inmates. Manfred Guttmacher found fifty-three psychotic and seventeen "deranged" prisoners in a group of one hundred and seventy-five accused of murder. Of the two cases presented by Guttmacher as murders committed by "normal" persons, one had a history resembling that of our patients with symptoms of dyscontrol syndrome.

Electroencephalographic examinations of ninety-seven French and twenty-two South Africans accused of murder disclosed six to nine times the frequency of abnormal brain waves as occurs in the population at large. D. Stafford-Clark and F. H. Taylor studied sixty-four English prisoners accused of murder. They divided these prisoners into five categories and found abnormal brain waves in only one of eleven guilty of killing in self-defense or killing during the commission of another crime. Four of sixteen murderers with a clear homicidal motive had electroencephalographic abnormalities; but, an abnormal pattern was present in eleven of fifteen prisoners who did not have a motive for committing murder.

From time to time, large-scale urban rioting has swept across the continental United States. At the height of these episodes, assault, arson, and murder were committed. It would be of more than passing interest to find what percentage of the attempted and completed murders were done without a motive.

As a microcosm of violent behavior, urban riots may present investigators with unique opportunities. For example, the interdependence and interrelation of the social and biological roots of violent behavior may well be clarified by a thorough study of these riots. The importance of poverty, unemployment, slum housing, and inadequate education in fashioning the background for social unrest is obvious. It is equally important, however, to remember that only a small number of those millions of individuals living in the competitive, adversary society of our urban slums actually took part in the riots and that only a small fraction of those who rioted indulged in arson, physical assault, or murder.

If slum conditions alone determine and initiate riots, why are a vast majority of our slum dwellers able to resist the temptations of unrestrained violence? An inevitable conclusion is that a thorough study of urban riots should include not only an indepth investigation of the social fabric of the riot-torn areas, but also a complete investigation of those rare individuals com-

mitting the violent acts. The goal of such a study would be to
determine whether or not it is feasible to pinpoint, diagnose, and
treat persons having low thresholds for violence before they
contribute to further serious tragedies.

Aggression reaches its ultimate extreme when it takes the
form of assassination of public figures. In this country, beginning in June 1963, a series of assassinations has taken place
which prompted historian Arthur Schlesinger, Jr. to brand the
American people as the "most frightening people on earth."

The horror of the murders of Medgar Evers, John F. Kennedy, Martin Luther King, Jr., Robert F. Kennedy, and others
has increasingly compelled Americans to face the fact that our
culture is permeated with violence. More than ever before, we
can recognize that we feed violence both to children and to
adults through television and comic strips. The glorification of
war through these media, as well as through motion pictures and
books, over the years has made Americans of all ages more
accepting of, and more casual about, the idea of one man killing
another. Millions of children have grown up with toys that are
replicas of weapons and machines of destruction, and the very
possession of such toys has shaped their play with peers into
imitations of aggression.

In the week following the death of Senator Robert Kennedy,
President Johnson reported that the homicides committed in
the United States in a recent year were two hundred times the
number committed in Great Britain. Many Americans felt
deeply guilty over what they considered to be our sick society,
while others insisted that 99 per cent of our people never engaged in violence and could not be blamed for the assassinations.
The head of the American Rifle Association stated that there
are 200 million guns owned by citizens, and only one of these
guns killed Senator Kennedy. Others suggested that there still
persisted a frontier mentality that was compatible with the
notion of settling disagreements by direct, violent action.

It appears that, in any given year, there are more homicides
in the United States than in all other countries combined. In

some countries, gun ownership laws are so strict that only a very small percentage of citizens possess guns, a situation entirely different from that prevailing here.

The editor takes the position that our culture accustoms and desensitizes both children and adults to the idea of killing. In addition, within our culture, a lethal weapon can be easily obtained. However, it is not the culture that is reponsible for the assassination of public figures but the sick individuals within the culture. Undoubtedly, there is a strong interplay between the culture and the assassin. Predisposed by his mental illness to violence as a way of relieving unbearable tensions, the assassin's distorted perception can find encouragement and little deterrent in the casual attitude of the various "entertainment" media toward killing. If he moves from thought to action, he will not have much difficulty in acquiring a gun.

Shortly after the death of Robert Kennedy, Charles Frankel [2] wrote:

> The violence in the air today increases the likelihood that violent people, who are around in the best of times and places, will be still further inflamed. Undoubtedly, too, the murder of John Kennedy increased the likelihood of an attempt against Robert Kennedy; as he himself knew, it was bound to put thoughts into suggestible minds. There are certain kinds of public figures—John Kennedy, Martin Luther King, Robert Kennedy—who are more probable targets than others for murderous feelings. They have a kind of inner invulnerability about them—something, whether it is their bearing or supreme good fortune or special lucidity, that gives the sense that they cannot really be pierced or hurt. Envy reaches out to pull them down. So there are causes, a pattern of explanation, that can be offered for Robert Kennedy's murder, and the violence in America is part of the story. But it is only a part, and we cannot even say that it was a necessary part. The murder itself might have happened anyway. For in the end, Robert Kennedy was killed, it appears, not by an American but

by a Jordanian, and not for what he stood for in this
country but for what he stood for, in one man's odd, un-
accountable mind, in the Middle East. The murder could
have happened in a tranquil America.*

Professor Frankel's comments point up the concept that perhaps assassination can be understood best in terms of the individuals who perpetrate it. In any consideration of the psychology of the assassin, it is suggested that the reader keep in mind
Dr. Mark's article on the neurology of violent behavior, immediately preceding, which asks us not to ignore the possible role
of brain damage in human violence.

Albert Ellis [3] believes that assassination is rarely the result
of a belief that killing a public figure will accomplish a particular
political purpose. He states that "contemporary assassins are
almost always exceptionally deranged individuals," and points
out what he thinks are some of the main psychological factors
that drive people to assassinate political figures.

The first factor is low self-esteem. Because of his low estima-
tion of himself, the assassin is a continual failure in his work,
social relations, and personal life. He cannot admit his inadequacy to himself and the necessity for hard work to change.
Instead, he builds up defensive hostility against others and
claims they are persecuting him, comes to hate all authority
figures, and insists that it is they who are keeping him down. He
often becomes insanely jealous of outstanding achievers and
resolves to drag them down from the heights they have attained.

Magical thinking is another factor mentioned by Ellis. Political assassins almost always seem to believe that they can get
away with their crimes, and that the public will rise up in their
favor and condemn those they have killed. Because of their
magical thinking, they fail to work out careful plans for escape,
and this is probably the reason why such a high percentage are
caught so quickly.

Extreme moralism and hostility is a third factor. The assassin

* Copyright *Saturday Review,* Inc. 1968.

demands that his own views be considered absolutely right and those of everyone else completely in error. He cannot tolerate disagreement. This grandiosity is a defense against tremendous feelings of inferiority. He fears others will discover his weaknesses and take advantage of him, imagines they are plotting against him, and feels impelled to kill them before they do him injury. Ellis comments that the political assassin tends to be either a paranoid schizophrenic or someone close to it who has led a highly disordered life since childhood. He considers Lee Harvey Oswald to have been seriously aberrated from his early years and to have become at least a borderline schizophrenic.

Like other non-Freudians, Ellis implies that Oswald's life experiences molded him into the kind of person who became a failure in all areas, was rebuffed on all sides, and desperately needed to perform a world-shaking deed that would even the score and give him the delusion of success and/or revenge. Even if we reject the idea that Oswald worked alone and believe, instead, that he was part of a conspiracy, the same psychological factors could have been operating.

Non-Freudian interpretations of Oswald are based on the totality of his life experiences, his goals, and the premise that the assassination was an attempt to cope with his overwhelming feelings of incompetence and isolation. This is in complete contrast to the approach of Joseph Katz, clinical psychologist and faculty member of the Training Institute of the National Psychological Association for Psychoanalysis. Dr. Katz sees the act of assassination as a consequence of unconscious forces related to a single aspect of Oswald's life: possible Oedipal inclinations and fantasies; hatred of a rejecting and untrustworthy mother displaced on to President Kennedy; and making President Kennedy the target for all his pent-up fury and libido, meant really for his mother. According to Katz,[4] Oswald did not kill his mother because to do so "was too much akin to penetrating her sexually and this he could not face at any cost."

In our final reading on aggression, Robinson reviews the history of presidential assassination in the United States. He ap-

pears to agree with Ellis that the assassin does not really expect
to effect a political change by the murder he commits. Rather,
the assassin has come to hate authority and develops a *personal*
antagonism against the national leader because that man is a
symbol of the authority he resents. Robinson's view supports
the non-Freudian contention that aggression is not innate, but
a product of one's perception of the external world. In the case
of the assassin, the individual is sick and his perception is
gravely distorted.

A Study of Political Assassinations

G. Wilse Robinson, M.D.*

We may consider that the first political assassination was the
murder of Abel by Cain. Cain was living in a theocracy, and his
God had shown a preference for Abel. Cain reasoned that if
Abel was destroyed he would succeed to this position of prece-
dence.

Perhaps the second most publicized assassination was that of
Julius Caesar. Ostensibly this action on the Ides of March, as
explained by Cassius to Brutus, was to prevent Julius from
becoming Emperor. Augustus, Julius' grandnephew, became
Emperor of Rome 21 years after the assassination which was
supposed to rid Rome of Emperors.

Cassius and most of the other conspirators were in fact not
primarily interested in preventing an autocracy in Rome; they
wished to revenge Pompeii's death. There were a few, like
Brutus, who had somewhat higher motives, if such can be said
of a murder. These felt that they were maintaining the Roman
Republic. This they did not do. Once more an assassination
with somewhat high motives failed to accomplish what the
perpetrators expected.

While murder for profit, for religious or political reasons, has

* *American Journal of Psychiatry*, Vol. 121, No. 11 (May 1965), pp.
1,060-1,064. Copyright 1965, The American Psychiatric Association.

been with us for centuries, it would seem that our word "assassination" comes from the name of a tribe in Asia Minor. . . .

This group was the first "murder incorporated." Most of their killings were to improve the power of the "Old Man of the Mountains," their leader, whoever that might be.

During the latter years of the Roman Empire, emperors were killed by the people, by the Legions, or by individuals, but nothing was changed except the name of the man who wore the purple. Rome deteriorated and was destroyed finally by the barbarians.

The cultural and scientific Renaissance did not lead to an improvement of morals. Political murder was almost a way of life. Slaves were forced to taste food before members of the oligarchy or of the aristocracy would eat it. No person of importance ever left his house without his hefty bodyguard, and there were many battles on the streets of Rome, Florence, Verona, Milan and Venice. These had political overtones.

Yet they changed nothing. The city-states continued along their diverse political ways and their cooperative activity in cultural and scientific progress. The man of the Renaissance grew and developed in spite of the political chaos around him.

During the French Revolution and the Reign of Terror, there were many assassinations, both officially by the Committee and the guillotine, and by direct action, as happened to Marat. These occur in every time of trouble and are different from the type of assassination we are considering. These were killings for power, the transfer of power from one group to another, or from one person to another. They are very similar to our gang killings, resulting from lawlessness and producing more lawlessness.

The same thing happened in the Russian Revolution and has happened many times in countries with unstable governments in this century. These are similar to the political murders during, before, and after the Renaissance in Italy and other parts of Europe.

There is another form of assassination where dedicated men seek to destroy a true tyrant. In this age of enlightenment and reason, we seem to end up with many dictators who keep their places through fear, their secret police, and their complete suppression of all civil liberties. Several plots were made on the life of Hitler, although only one reached to the point of action. It was unsuccessful.

The murder of Trujillo was perhaps the latest successful one in this category. For a while it seemed that democracy had returned to Santo Domingo, but it was not to be for long. The military took power and to all intents and purposes a dictatorship returned.

Political assassination had not changed for thousands of years from the time of Cain to the last of the Medicis, but as we move into our modern era, we find a subtle change in the character of the people involved.

Assassinations, both successful and attempted, can be grouped into three general classifications: conspiracy, person-to-person, and by a hired killer who has no personal involvement with his victim.

While the members of the tribe of Assassins were for hire (and many medieval murders were committed by hired killers), today these individuals want no part of assassination of prominent political leaders. It is too dangerous, and they can ply their trade on less prominent victims with almost complete safety.

The best known conspiracy is that developed by Shakespeare in his great classic, "Julius Caesar." It is the best known only because it is re-enacted frequently all over the world. The deed itself may have been almost forgotten before it was made the subject of the play.

The assassination of Franz Ferdinand, Archduke of Austria, and his wife on June 28, 1914 was carried out by a group of Slavic conspirators who sought to bring about freedom of the Slavic people held subject by the Hapsburgs. While this was one of the causes of World War I, it is doubtful that the conspirators expected the world cataclysm that they triggered.

Empires fell, dynasties were ended, and millions died and after it was all over Jugoslavia was established. But the irony of it all was that the Croats found themselves again a minority but in a different setting. They remained a restless group who were a constant threat to the authority of the Serbs.

Conspiracies in the last hundred years in this country resulted in the death of Lincoln and the attempt on the life of Harry Truman by a group of Puerto Rican nationalists.

The attempt on President Truman and the simultaneous shooting up of the Senate was hardly a conspiracy, even though it involved several people, but seemed to have been a disorganized emotional outburst of a group of individuals.

Lincoln's death resulted from a so-called conspiracy, one of the most stupid, futile and poorly conceived conspiracies in history.

How a group of people could believe that the killing of a few persons in Washington could make it possible for the South to rise again is beyond understanding. Lee had surrendered his barefoot army and all field pieces. Rifles and equipment were stacked and in the hands of Grant's veterans. Grant and Sherman between them had hundreds of thousands of well-trained, well-equipped, and well-fed veterans facing a few die-hard guerrillas who were armed only with sabres, rifles, and hand-guns, with perhaps a few rounds of ammunition apiece.

Such an unsuccessful attempt to overthrow the government could only have increased the desire of the radicals to destroy the culture of the South. Lincoln might have controlled them. Neither Johnson nor anyone else could. The crushing blow of reconstruction fell full force on the defeated Confederacy.

It would seem, from what we know of this tragic farce, that it was conceived by John Wilkes Booth, who retained for himself the most glamorous target.

If this is so, and all things point to this conclusion, then the murder of Lincoln follows the general pattern of most modern-day political assassinations: A single man with a desire that results from long brooding to destroy a leader who is antagonistic to some belief that the assassin considers to be important. It is very important to him. This is a very personal matter to the man, and is a kind of person-to-person action. The individual to be destroyed has become a personal enemy of the assassin and must be destroyed.

Such a person cannot be diagnosed or catalogued in psychiatric terms. He is undoubtedly sane under the M'Naghten Rule and might be under the Durham decision.

They are not average members of their society. Most of them are "loners," living very much to themselves. Their mental orientation is inward, not outward.

John Wilkes Booth was a fine actor, but all his life he was a rebel against authority. He was raised in a home of moderate luxury and attended private academies, but he was a disciplinary problem throughout his younger years. He was a practical joker of a sadistic type.

While he sat out the War between the States in the North he was a rather outspoken Southern partisan. He brooded a great deal as defeat after defeat wracked the Confederacy, and he began to develop a feeling that Lincoln was the cause of it. Thus he reasoned that if Lincoln and other top leaders were eliminated, the North would collapse and defeat would be turned into victory.

His sister wrote his story and left out very little of his early-day troubles, but insisted that he was not insane. Under the M'Naghten Rule, he certainly was not, but he was hardly an average member of his society.

He had poor judgment because by the time he decided to act, the cause of the Confederacy was completely lost. Even if all the people designated by the conspirators along with Grant and Sherman had died, nothing would have happened except some temporary high-level confusion, but the succession of government would have been as complete as it was in our day, 98 years later.

He was no student of history, although he was aware of the fate of the conspirators who killed Caesar, and the utter futility of their act. One might think that Lincoln had become a symbol to him, a symbol of authority. It must be remembered that the primary cause of the War of the 1860's was not slavery, but the authority of the Union versus States' Rights.

He also developed an obsession for fame. He did not seem to think that his acting fame, which was considerable, was enough. He had told his friends, "What a glorious opportunity for a man to immortalize himself by killing Abraham Lincoln." This concept may motivate more assassins than is now realized. It may have been a major motivation to Lee Oswald.

Charles Guiteau who murdered Garfield has been called a half-crazed, disappointed office seeker. Apparently, from what little is known about him he was not half-crazed but a fully developed acting-out schizophrenic, who killed his victim because he believed God had told him to. He was hardly a serious office seeker since he had no qualifications. He was not a typical political assassin and was not responsible for his act by any rule of law. Nevertheless, he was executed.

Leon Czolgosz who killed McKinley may have been more typical. However, some of the alienists of his day considered him to be a schizophrenic or suffering from dementia praecox although no one was permitted to examine him sufficiently to make a firm diagnosis after his arrest.

He was always strange, made no close friends. As a boy, he never associated with girls and preferred to play with younger children. While he read a good deal, he was a poor student. He was not an active disciplinary problem in school but was definitely a passive one, in that he was, to say the least, uncooperative. As was the practice in those days, he was considered lazy.

While he showed certain withdrawal characteristics, he never acted out except when he declared himself an anarchist. Those who belonged to this group never accepted him and considered him to be a spy.

Dr. Allen McLane Hamilton considered him to be a defective who had drifted into paranoia and had developed delusions of paranoia and grandeur.

But Czolgosz stated that he killed McKinley because he was an oppressor of the working man. These were the days when the working man was oppressed. Perhaps McKinley was partially responsible because his government was definitely anti-labor and pro big business. Again, though, McKinley could only be a symbol and not the cause of this situation. He could only have been a symbol to his murderer, a symbol of authority to a man who had resented authority all his life.

Perhaps we can say that we have three men who were very much alike in basic personality defects. Booth, in spite of his statements to his fellow conspirators, must have known that killing a president would not change anything except the name of the man who lived in the White House.

We must assume that they did not expect to change the basic political philosophy of the country as it was at the time. There must have been other motives. Two interlocking concepts seem probable. One, that they were seeking immortality and second, that they were destroying the symbol of the highest authority in this country. There was no personal animosity involved. Their victim was a symbol of their general basic anger against the social order. It was also their road to immortality.

Can assassination of our political leaders be prevented by arrest of potential killers? Absolutely not. Many people have commented upon the fact that the F.B.I. interviews individuals who are potential assassins but do not arrest them and that they have failed in their duty. This is very fuzzy thinking. We do not know of the purposes of these interviews.

The F.B.I. interviews hundreds of persons every year who have some connection, vague or more or less real, with some subversive group or party. Most of these persons have a history of rebellion against authority at some time in their lives. Many of them own some kind of firearm. Probably all of them want to change our form of government, or, at the very least, the person in office.

Which of them should be arrested? Obviously, none can be under our Constitution. One must have committed an overt act or be suspected of having committed one before one can be picked up for questioning. That is as it should be. Otherwise we would have a police state, and all of our martyrs would have died in vain.

Many persons, including some prominent news commentators, have stated that President Kennedy died because of the mass hate toward the Kennedys engendered by their fight against segregation. This we find very hard to accept. If the assassin was a sympathizer with Communist principles, then he should have approved integration and should not have been personally involved in that aspect of politics.

However, it is possible that inflammatory statements made in the press and over the airwaves may have stimulated a number of persons to think that someone ought to shoot "that man." Perhaps the assassin was infected with this deadly virus. Perhaps, though, he is like most other modern day assassins in that he approached that day with a purely personal desire to destroy the symbol of the form of government which he despised, democracy. We shall never have a factual answer to this question.

The successful assassin does not write threatening letters, come to Washington and state that he is going to kill the President, or in other ways tip his hand. Those who do are obviously ill. Those who succeed are ill only in the degree and type that are all murderers who plan their crime in advance.

We can state that political assassination does not change the flow of history in a nation or state. It does not change the character of the government of the state or nation.

Since most successful assassins are uneducated it is possible that they might think that the murder of "that man" would make it possible for the people to rise and set up a people's government.

It is more logical to assume that the assassin has developed a personal antagonism against "that man" not because that man is named Lincoln or McKinley or Kennedy but because that man is a symbol of the authority which the assassin resents.

So the symbol must be destroyed and "that man" dies.

REFERENCES

1. Lawrence Kolb, *Noyes' Modern Clinical Psychiatry,* 7th ed. (Philadelphia: W.B. Saunders, 1968), p. 134.
2. Charles Frankel, "The Meaning of Political Murder," *Saturday Review* (June 22, 1968), p. 18.

3. Albert Ellis, "The Psychology of Assassination," *The Independent,* No. 139 (November 1963), pp. 1, 4-5.
4. Joseph Katz, "President Kennedy's Assassination," *Psychoanalytic Review,* 51 (4), 1964, pp. 121-124.

7

Alternatives to Other
Freudian Interpretations

Posthypnotic Behavior

Dr. C. Knight Aldrich, in *An Introduction to Dynamic Psychiatry*,[1] discusses the idea that a part of man's psychologic function is out of his conscious control. He states:

> This conclusion is perhaps most dramatically demonstrated by the phenomenon of post-hypnotic suggestion. A hypnotist tells his subject that after he is awakened from his trance, he will respond to a given signal by carrying out a specific action without knowing why he does it. He might suggest that when the hypnotist snaps his fingers, the subject will whistle. He then induces amnesia (forgetfulness) for all that has gone on during the trance, "awakens" the subject, and snaps his fingers, whereupon the subject whistles, even though the whistling embarrasses him and he has not the slightest idea why he is doing it.

Aldrich restates the widespread belief (which began with Freud) that the phenomenon of posthypnotic suggestion supports the concept that one can be controlled by a force of which

215

he is completely unaware. This concept is, of course, the basic principle in psychoanalytic doctrine.

In a comprehensive review of experiments done by others and himself in the field of hypnosis, with 85 references to the literature, T. X. Barber examines the assumption that a post-hypnotic act is characterized by the absence of any demonstrable conscious awareness in the subject of the underlying cause for his act. Barber refers to R. W. White's contention that, prior to participation in hypnosis experiments, individuals subsequently found to be "good" hypnotic subjects appear to show a "need for deference," i.e., "a tendency to yield willingly, not to say eagerly, to the wishes of a superior person." He then offers experimental findings to show that subjects for whom amnesia was suggested by the hypnotist did indicate directly or indirectly in postexperimental interviews that they were aware they were responding to a suggestion they had received under hypnosis. If Barber's findings can be widely corroborated, posthypnotic behavior will have to be abandoned as a proof of the existence of an unconscious.

Toward a Theory of Hypnosis: Posthypnotic Behavior

*Theodore Xenophon Barber, Ph.D.**

Statements made by "amnesic" subjects in describing their inability to remember suggest the possibility that "posthypnotic amnesia" may refer to no more than an unwillingness on the part of the subject to verbalize the events when questioned by the hypnotist. White has noted that "amnesic" hypnotic subjects make such spontaneous remarks as: "I haven't any inclination to go back over it"; "My mind doesn't want to think"; "I do remember but I can't say, I can't think of the word . . . (Later) I could remember it without being able to say it. Something inside me said, 'You know what it is all the time', I partly knew and partly didn't." Blum has presented similar remarks

* *Archives of General Psychiatry,* Vol. 7, No. 5 (November 1962), pp. 338-339.

made by "amnesic" hypnotic subjects; e.g., ". . . I know it but I can't think about it—I know what it is but I just kind of stop myself before I think of it." Along similar lines, Pattie has noted that "the reports of subjects in referring to posthypnotic amnesia support, not a dissociation theory, but rather a motivational theory, a theory that such amnesia is due to an unwillingness to remember, an attempt to occupy oneself with other things than an effort to recall." After completing a series of intensive interviews with "amnesic" hypnotic subjects, Rosenberg arrived at a similar conclusion: ". . . Posthypnotic amnesia, whether of the spontaneous or suggested variety, is usually achieved through effortful, motivated inattention and deverbalization . . . these do not bespeak dissociation, nor even repression, so much as vigorous *suppression* of hypnotic content."

A series of experiments employing long-term posthypnotic suggestions appears to support the hypothesis that "amnesic" hypnotic subjects remember the "forgotten" events but are unwilling to verbalize them to the hypnotist until he gives them implicit or explicit permission to do so. In these studies "somnambulistic" hypnotic subjects were given posthypnotic suggestions to be executed after a period of weeks or months, and the "amnesic" subjects executed the suggestions at the appointed time. However, when the subjects were given permission, during the intervening period, to verbalize the "amnesic" suggestion, they not only verbalized it but also stated, in most instances, that they had been thinking continually about the "forgotten" suggestion. For example, Gurney instructed a "deep trance" subject, who invariably showed "amnesia" for trance events, that on the 123d day following the hypnotic session, he would place a blank sheet of paper in an envelope and mail it to a friend of the hypnotist. On the 23d day he was asked, during a second hypnotic session, if he remembered anything in connection with this gentleman. The subject at once replied that he did, verbalized the posthypnotic suggestion, and added, "This is the 23d day, a hundred more." In addition, he confided that: (a) he counted the number of days as they passed early in the morning when something said to him, "You've got to count";

(b) after making the computations, he did not think of them again during the remainder of the day, but (c) he was continuously aware that "it's got to be done." Mitchell found comparable results in a study employing a larger number of subjects. For instance, Mitchell instructed a "somnambulistic" subject who invariably showed posthypnotic amnesia that on the 39th day following the hypnotic session she would make a cross on a piece of paper. After 16 days had passed, the subject was asked under waking conditions if she had been doing any sums. She replied that she had "the feeling that she had been adding on one every day." Mitchell then said: "Sleep! How many days are gone?" She immediately gave the correct answer, related the contents of the posthypnotic suggestion, and indicated that she had been thinking about the "amnesic" suggestion. Bernheim presented similar findings and concluded that "the amnesic suggestion which is to be executed may be present in their minds a great part of the day; only the subject no longer knows this when we speak to him." Hooper also arrived at a similar conclusion from comparable findings. Bramwell, however, found conflicting results in an experiment with one "somnambulistic" hypnotic subject. Although this subject executed a series of long-term posthypnotic suggestions at the appointed time, she generally stated, when questioned under trance during the intervening period, that she did not remember the exact contents of the suggestions and never thought of them. In summary, with the exception of Bramwell's study with one subject, investigations concerned with long-term posthypnotic suggestions (Gurney, Mitchell, Bernheim, and Hooper) have yielded the following findings: (1) When questioned under waking conditions, during the interval between the reception and execution of a long-term posthypnotic suggestion, "amnesic" subjects either deny awareness of the suggestions or state that they are aware of only certain aspects of the suggestion. (2) However, when given explicit or implicit permission to verbalize the "amnesic" suggestion—by rehypnotizing the subject, by "giving a hint," or by other indirect means which are discussed above—"amnesic" subjects generally state that they have been *continually aware* of the "forgotten" suggestion, have been counting the days as they passed, and have been set to execute the suggestion at the appointed time.

The above findings suggest the possibility that "posthypnotic amnesia" may refer not to a forgetting of the trance events but to an unwillingness on the part of the subject to verbalize the events in order to comply with the wishes and expectations of the hypnotist who is usually a prestigeful person with whom the subject has a friendly or close relationship. This suggests an experiment as follows. "Amnesic" hypnotic subjects should be interviewed by a prestigeful person who is ostensibly not associated with the experiment but with whom the subjects have a friendly or close relationship. This person should inform the subjects that he would be highly displeased if they did not tell him what occurred under trance. It can be hypothesized, from the data presented in this review, that under these conditions "amnesic" hypnotic subjects will verbalize the "forgotten" material.

The Pavlovian View of Man

Earlier in this volume, we indicated our awareness of the fact that the physiology of an individual plays a part in all of his behavior. We noted also that generally Freudians are not interested in the physiological structure within which a psychological process takes place. While it is not necessary for non-medical professionals who help those in emotional distress to have a technical knowledge of the functioning of the cerebral cortex and nervous system, a general understanding of the mechanisms of conditioning enriches our concept of the nature of man and our therapeutic approach.

Using Pavlov's original theories about conditioning as a foundation, workers in the field of conditioned behavior have experimented extensively and learned much. They incorporated their findings into behavioral science, even while psychoanalytic doctrine was dominating the scene. The present chapter's survey of alternatives to Freudian interpretations would not be complete without some attention to the Pavlovian view of man, which, in relation to psychoanalysis, is located at the opposite end of a psychodynamic-physiological continuum. A brief summary of part of the material in two articles by Cammer [2,3] will now be presented, together with some comments, in the hope of interesting the reader to study more fully a theory which explains human thought, behavior, and emotional patterns in terms of cerebral cortex activity. There are many books available on the subject.

Cammer tells us that Pavlov's fundamental thesis was that psychology is incorporated into the study of higher nervous activity. Pavlov and his followers produced evidence that phenomena such as learning, memory, habit formation, thinking, emotions and ways of social interaction primarily result from intact cerebral cortex physiology.

Man's behavior is composed of unconditioned or inborn reflexes, sometimes called instincts, which do not depend on previous experience. Examples are the ability to breathe, salivate and blink. Man's behavior is also composed of response patterns acquired after birth and based on experience, known as conditioned or conditional reflexes. The formation of these conditioned reflexes depends upon an intact nervous system; surgical removal of the cerebral cortex abolishes conditioned reflexes while subcortical nervous centers continue to control the inborn reflexes needed to survive.

The basic concept of conditioned behavior is that any neutral environmental stimulus can come to affect the physical or mental functioning of the body if it is associated with a stimulus which already triggers either an inborn or conditioned reflex. The famous Pavlovian experiment in which a gong was sounded at the same time that food was offered to a dog is too familiar to require detailed description. Suffice it to say that the sound of a gong was originally a neutral stimulus. After repeated association with the presentation of food, which was the stimulus for the inborn reflex of salivation, the sounding of the gong was able to trigger salivation in the dog when the food was omitted.

This same kind of experiment can be used to condition or link all kinds of motor, glandular, cognitive, emotional and behavioral responses in human beings. In other words, a particular inborn or conditioned reflex to a particular stimulus can be made to occur in response to a different, entirely unrelated stimulus. Furthermore, outside the laboratory, life experiences can work in the same way. Through the intentional or accidental association of a new person, situation or object with another person, situation or object that already triggers a given response in an individual, the new person, situation or object can become the trigger of the same response. If the response that is transferred to a new stimulus is an inborn reflex, we call the process conditioning; if the response that is transferred to a new stimulus is a conditioned reflex, we call the process linking.

Conditioned responses can be positive (excitatory, stimulating) or negative (inhibitory). Examples of positive responses include muscle coordination that is developed in response to visual and auditory signals in the mastering of a musical instrument, or the fear, anger, or decision that comes into existence as a reaction to an environmental situation. Conditioned responses decay when they are not used, but retraining or reinforcement will establish them again.

Negative or inhibitory responses are characterized by the noncompletion of a reflex for any of the following reasons: the related stimulus is absent; the related stimulus is present but is not effective because it is too weak or infrequent; the related stimulus is present but is suddenly counterbalanced by an intercepting stimulus.

Cortical activity increases with positive responses and decreases with negative responses. It is possible to produce a positive response (excitation) by inhibiting an inhibitory response. This can be illustrated by a wife who takes her husband for granted and has become sexually indifferent until her inhibition is disinhibited by the husband's interest in another woman.

There is a total kind of response which is neither positive nor negative. It has been named the "what-is-it" reflex by Pavlov, the "investigatory response" by Gantt, and the "vigilance response" by Liddell. It is a total body reaction to a threatening situation, an orientating mechanism when environmental signals indicate something critical or unforeseen, when one cannot discriminate between signals, or when there are signals calling for positive and negative responses at the same time. What Cammer seems to be delineating here is a physiological representation of anxiety, very much akin to the concept offered by Sarbin that anxiety is the consequence of cognitive strain. (See Sarbin's article in Chapter 5.)

Cammer considers in detail how the cerebral cortex functions, and discusses phenomena that have been identified through experimentation: summation of responses, irradiation, negative and positive induction, schizokinesis, and many others. This brief summary will not attempt to go further into the complexities of conditioning, but in conclusion, rather it will try to suggest how the conditioning theory is used to explain human behavior.

Cammer [2] states: "The human being . . . responds directly only to stimuli similar to those which have conditioned him or which involve survival. Other stimuli remain neutral and have no direct meaning as motivation for behavior, thoughts, or feelings."

What Cammer is saying is that man lives by patterns he has learned. He responds to signals such as people, objects, situations, sounds, and smells, and to the spoken and written word—which is the signal of signals. However, for each individual, the specific stimuli within each category that will be significant or neutral are different. Also, each individual's perception of the same specific stimulus will be different. Therefore, the patterns will vary from person to person. While these patterns tend to remain once they are established, they can change in response to strong, new stimuli which appear either unplanned in living situations or by intent in therapeutic situations. In addition, responses decay if not repeated or reinforced; new reflexes are acquired in response to new experiences or to achieve certain rewards. As a result, to look at man from the viewpoint of conditioning theory is not to see behavior as mechanical and fixed, but as responsive to the circumstances of his life.

Emotional disturbances can be explained in terms of conditioning theory as follows: depression is a massive inhibition of all kinds of reflexes accompanied by a marked decrease in cortical activity; neurotic behavior is the result of a collision between excitatory and inhibitory processes; maladjustment in a new situation is the inability to unlearn old responses and acquire new reflexes that are more adaptive; and difficulty in sexual responsiveness is a culturally conditioned pattern of responding to a conflict between society's attitudes on sex and one's own sexual morality.

Dreams

One of Freud's major theoretical contributions was his interpretation of the nature of dreams. He saw dreams as the guardians of sleep; in his view the function of the dream—the dream work—was to keep the dreamer from awakening because of the appearance in his dream of disturbing content which had escaped from his unconscious. According to Freud, the dream content emanates from the unconscious, and its spatial and temporal distortions and lack of logic serve to preserve sleep by disguising anxiety-provoking material. He was convinced that the dream distorts its imagery so that repressed wishes, conflicts, fears and guilt temporarily released from the unconscious do not make themselves known to the dreamer and shock him into wakefulness.

Freud regarded dreaming as a purely mental process governed by the unconscious. Montague Ullman, a psychiatrist with a special interest in the subject, has suggested an alternative approach to the study of the dream process, in which this phenomenon is investigated in physiological terms first. The psychological aspects of dreaming are then fitted into place on a physiological framework, which Ullman constructs from the discoveries made by Pavlov about the cerebral cortex and its activity. Furthermore, Ullman regards the dream as a form of consciousness rather than the product of unconscious mechanisms.

Ullman's insistence on clarifying the physiology of dreaming, instead of regarding it purely as a mental process, is part of a growing trend to seek out more and more the organic basis of psychic phenomena. The great volume of physiologically-oriented research into schizophrenia is an outstanding example. Linus Pauling has predicted that the problem of schizophrenia will be solved by the biochemist. Any orientation in the direction of discovering the physiological structure within which a psychological process takes place represents an alternative to the almost exclusively psychodynamic approach to people that is practiced by Freudians.

In another work, the editor [4] has summarized some of Ullman's concepts about dreams as follows:

He believes that primarily we dream about problems or situations that we have not mastered in our waking existence. These unsolved problems and situations have been acting as stimuli to our cortical centers during the day and will not cease to do so until they have been mastered. When we are asleep at night, they continue to impinge on our consciousness, but those parts of the brain associated with the secondary signalling system are inactive and not available for selecting, organizing, and systematizing the imagery that is produced. It is for this reason that the dream content is often distorted, illogical, or contradictory. Dreaming occurs only in a transitional state between being awake and deeply asleep where there is partial inhibition of higher cortical activity. Falling into a deeper sleep is the result of the spread of inhibition over both signalling systems, in which circumstance dreaming cannot take place. Excitation of the primary signalling system beyond a certain point results in the activation of both signalling systems and waking up. The impact of the dream itself may set in motion the arousal process, or the ringing of the alarm-clock bell, or a need to go to the bathroom. In any case, it is not how well the dream masks repressed material that determines whether or not the sleeper awakes, but tissue needs. If the body's need for rest is stronger than the disturbing stimulus, he will not awake. If his body is well-rested, relatively weak stimuli will arouse him.

Ullman's ideas are presented in greater detail in the text below, excerpted from an article published in 1958. It is included here because the editor found no papers appearing in 1960 or later which stated this viewpoint so well.

The Dream Process

Montague Ullman, M.D. *

. . . The work of Pavlov and his successors has given us a starting point from which to begin to objectify both the study of conscious behavior and the dream process. Pavlov depicted three possible levels of organization of responses of the organism to the environment, namely: the reactions based on the unconditioned, inborn stimulus-response mechanism; these reactions modified by the formation of conditioned stimuli; and lastly, reactions of an infinitely more complex and qualitatively different character based on the development of abstract thought and language. This last level, the exclusive possession of man, was termed by Pavlov the secondary signalling system as contrasted with the preceding level or primary signalling system. The primary signalling system is concerned essentially with the modification of responses to sensory stimuli and in animals lower than man provides for a great deal more flexibility in response and therefore a greater adaptive potential. These responses occur in the form of more or less immediate reactions to sensations originating in either the external or internal environment of the organism. . . .

In man the activity of the brain in reflecting reality not only at the sensory level but also at the level of abstract thought and concept formation results in the specifically human form of consciousness differing qualitatively from all other forms of con-

* *American Journal of Psychotherapy,* Vol. 12, No. 4 (October 1958), pp. 672-677, 681-682, 684-687, 689-690.

sciousness. Responses are no longer at the immediate level of reactions to conditioning sensory stimuli. By virtue of the ability accurately to conceptualize the nature of the relations existing in the material world about him, including himself, man reacts in the specifically human way of consciously changing that environment and in the process changing his own consciousness. . . .

Sleep has been identified by Pavlov with a state of internal inhibition radiating over the cerebral hemispheres and dreams have been correlated with the heightened activity of the primary signalling system as the spread of the inhibitory wave alters the relations between the two systems. Theoretically, as both systems undergo total inhibition, there would perhaps be no manifestations of consciousness in any form. The two inferences here stated are (1) that dreams represent a phenomenon of the transitional state, the term transitional being used rather loosely to indicate the state between that of deep sleep and complete awakening, during which the higher centers are sufficiently activated for conscious reflection to occur, and (2) that dreams can be correlated with the activity of the higher nervous centers during the transitional state.

What this means as applied to the problem of dream consciousness is that whatever aspects of the individual's past social experience may be potentially available as a source of dream content during the transitional state, the form the actual presentation takes is determined by the physiological fact that the primary signalling system is in a state of relative dominance. In the process of falling asleep it assumes dominance over the secondary signalling system as the latter undergoes inhibition. In the process of awakening the procedure is reversed and an excitatory phase occurs in the primary system prior to its spread to the secondary system. This primary system is one which reacts to concrete stimuli and reacts to such stimuli at an involuntary level. Consciousness experienced under these conditions differs in two fundamental ways from the consciousness of the waking state. First, whatever conceptions gain expression in the dream do so in a concrete manner, generally in the form of visual imagery; secondly, whatever the actual nature of these conceptions, their presentation in the dream occurs as a completely determined experience; that is, they arise in an involuntary way and develop and recede independently of the will of the dreamer. We may appear to be free to say or do certain things in a dream, but in reality we have neither written the script nor chosen the role assigned to us.

Every sleeper has to awaken, and furthermore, even during the period of sleep there are variations in the depth of sleep, so that at times one may come close to awakening without doing so. If during sleep we are not conscious in the sense that we have considered the term, and if our waking state is characterized by consciousness, then somewhere in between there must be a transitional stage—a stage of becoming conscious—a stage characterized by the beginning awareness of the relations that obtained prior to sleep, and yet in a stage in which the full relations of the waking state are not yet grasped because the sensory and motor modalities for the expression of these relations have not yet been activated. Our consciousness during this transitional stage is experienced as dreams. . . .

The necessities which confront the human organism in connection with sleep are of a twofold nature. With the inception of the sleeping state there arises the need to effect a radical transformation in the activity of the individual. Social orientation and relatedness to the external environment give way to a form of activity governed primarily by physiological needs and hence occurring at an involuntary level. Similarly the transition from sleep to wakefulness in response to any stimulus of sufficient strength impinging upon the organism is characterized not simply by the process of awakening, but more significantly the resumption of consciousness of one's social existence. . . .

We have indicated that the sleep state involves a profound change in the nature of the individual's relatedness to his environment. Once sleep sets in there is no longer active involvement at a human level, that is, at the level of planned activity in a human society. The individual remains oriented to some extent to incoming sensory impressions. This does not imply consciousness, however, but rather an orientation towards self, one which we share in common with other members of the animal kingdom, but which in humans is simply a prerequisite to consciousness and is not to be confused with consciousness at any level. This state of affairs may be contrasted with the waking state, which may be considered as established when this self-orientation or consciousness potential is realized through an orientation to social reality. While asleep the individual is not faced with the primary problem of dealing with a changing external environment. The necessities he faces are of a different order. There is the physiological need for rest and tissue restitution, which in the absence of unusual stimuli regulates the duration and depth of sleep. There is in addition the unique necessity we have already alluded to, namely, that the human is faced not with the task of re-establishing a reflex relatedness to his environment at an animal level, but with the infinitely more complex task of restoring the state of conscious relatedness. He has to grasp in some manner the inordinately complex relations that determine the conscious state, and he has to do this not in a state of consciousness, but in a state of becoming conscious. We are then faced with the question of which relations seek and gain expression in the dream, how this is accomplished, and towards what end. . . .

We have regarded dream consciousness as analogous in a basic sense to waking consciousness and can now regard its function in an analogous fashion. Its function would therefore be to reflect the experience of the individual during the period of transitional activity and to facilitate the resolution of this activity in either of the two possible directions, namely, along the path of sleep should the stimuli be kept below a certain threshold or conversely toward the resumption of the conscious state should the necessity arise to awaken completely. In either event a transitional state comes into being characterized by the appearance of mental imagery. . . .

According to Freud, the dream is the expression of a wish. Disguise occurs when the wish is associated with unpleasant feelings. . . .

. . . The function we have postulated was that the dream served as an intermediate form of consciousness reflecting either the changes in activity that characterize the process of falling asleep or, once the sleep state has been established, reflecting the change in activity that occurs in response to any stimulus intense enough to initiate the waking state. The motivation, if one can properly speak of motivation, is implicit in the conditions given. Tissue needs assume a position of greater importance relative to social needs during sleep. Dream consciousness is dependent upon the balance that exists between tissue needs operating in the service of maintaining sleep and all other stimuli tending to reestablish the waking state. . . .

Waking consciousness is characterized by the effort to understand, plan, and control in relation to the environment. Analogously, dream consciousness is the effort to master the activity engaged in by the dreamer. In this case, the activity is real, but essentially involuntary and compulsory. The initiation of the transitional state is not controllable by the sleeper. At the same time, the only way the change can be depicted is through the imagery available to the individual, and the only imagery available is via his memory and the translation into imagery of immediate physiological stimuli. Just as waking consciousness reflects current reality in order to change it, so this imagery of the dream must reflect the rapid physiological changes occurring during the transitional state. The reflection must in some way both express the involuntary nature of this activity and at the same time change the activity.

The dream in its totality has been regarded as a complicated psychological event occurring in relation to other processes influencing the outcome of the transitional state. When the tissue needs for continued sleep prevail, the dream reflecting the disturbing influences facilitates the return to sleep. When the movement in the direction of awakening prevails, the developing content expressed in the dream and derived from past social experience is geared to bringing about the change from the sleeping organism to the conscious human being. In either event, the mode of expression employed in the dream is not integrated spatially and temporally in relation to the communicating function of speech and thought.

Owing to the compulsory nature of the activity involved, the necessity exists to employ imagery appropriate to this type of activity. This means that the role of consciousness under these specific conditions would be to utilize symbols to depict the forces acting on the individual. As a result, there arises the subjective sensation of being the involuntary participant in the dream. Imagery is evoked in the service of depicting an activity in which the physiological movement is the effective instigator of the situation to be comprehended and in relation to which the individual is a relatively ineffectual bystander. The most appropriate imagery is imagery of the sort that incorporates this element of independence from the will and control of the dreamer. This can be noted in the setting of any dream where the individual is never in the position of being a free agent, no matter how pleasant the dream. It also occurs more specifically in terms of the symbols themselves. They represent those elements of our lives which are actually involuntary. Freud's great contribution to dreams is in terms of therapy, because the dream by its very nature does of necessity deal with that which still besets the individual, the distillate of that part of his past experience which has never been mastered and which therefore still operates in an involuntary way.

The complexity and range of dreams vary to a considerable extent, but the common element in all dreams lies in the use of visual imagery to depict relations in which the individual is currently involved and which have not yet been mastered. The symbols of the dream serve a dual purpose; these unmastered relations are stated, a fact which in and of itself is an initial step towards mastery, but they are stated in the form of myth and fantasy because, being as yet unmastered, the real nature of these relations, though experienced, is not understood by the dreamer. The so-called disguise of the dream is not based on the conflict between the activity of an unconsciously operating and threatening instinctual impulse and the censor as representing the inhibiting influence of the ego all directed toward the function of preserving sleep. The dreamer neither consciously nor unconsciously recognizes the true nature of the influences at work and so is not in a position to depict their true nature accurately. A dream, no matter how thoroughly analysed, can never reveal a known instinctual impulse at work. All it can ever reveal is the effect of certain influences at work, but influences the true nature of which can never be stated in a dream, disguised or otherwise, because they do not exist for the individual in the dreaming state. Moreover, the change from waking to dream consciousness is a qualitative one and the former state of waking consciousness cannot be represented by the censor or any other postulate because the conditions for waking consciousness no longer exist in any form. The symbol is the resultant not of disguise but of the dual necessity of stating in the form of visual imagery a series of relations influencing the individual in an involuntary way precisely because they are unknown and unmastered and the necessity in so stating them of employing pseudo-explanatory devices, a recourse to which the human race has always had when confronted with the unknown. The myth, magic, and fantasy of the dream, the symbolic distortion, and the discrepancy between the manifest and latent content of the dream have to be understood not in terms of disguise, but rather as the statement of a problem the answer to which is not within the sleeper's awareness or potential awareness at the time. The dreamer is forced to do something with the problem. All that he can do is to state it in the form of visual imagery and then as the waking state approaches through the movement and interrelations of the symbols themselves, construct his own personal, although inaccurate, explanation.

The peculiar temporal and spatial relations depicted in dreams have been the starting point of many speculations concerning dreams. When we consider these apparently bizarre features of the dream in line with our effort to correlate the dream process with the activity of the dreamer, I think that an account can be rendered without recourse to the postulate of a timeless unconscious. The activity in which the dreamer is engaged is of a unitary character; that is, it is either movement toward deeper sleep or movement toward awakening. The brain in reflecting this activity is of necessity forced to reduce all stimuli to a concrete level. In addition to this general need, there is the specific need to deal with transitional states, the development of which is beyond the dreamer's control and which may vary from one of relatively long duration to one which may be almost instantaneous. The spatial and temporal distortion of dreams has to be understood in relation to both of these factors. The relations which are grasped by the dreamer are dealt with spatially and temporally in a manner appropriate to the nature and rapidity of the bodily processes at work. This involves a transformation or disregard of the real spatial and temporal relations of the symbols to conform with the immediate experience of the dreamer. What would be appropriate in terms of the meaning of the symbols in relation to waking activity would not be appropriate in terms of the meaning of the symbols for dream activity. Viewed from the waking state, there is temporal and spatial distortion. Temporally, dreams are characterized by a rapidity of changing scenes and an elusive furtiveness. Spatially, there are distortions by way of condensation, superimposition, and elimination of spatial barriers. In both instances the liberties the dreamer takes with the symbols are strictly determined—not by the operation of fantasy or a primitive unconscious, but by the necessity of dealing with the rapidly changing and uncontrollable physiological processes operating at the time. Once the balance of forces is such as to terminate the transitional state either in the direction of awakening or a return to sleep, the dream conciousness is of no further value, and in fact has a negative value, and there follows in the one instance a sharp transformation to waking consciousness and in the other to the dissolution of consciousness itself. It is significant that whereas the stage from sleeping to initiating the waking state may appear transitional and gradual, the step to actual awakening is sharp and definitive and the dream generally fades quite rapidly. The form and content of dream consciousness is totally inappropriate for the waking state. In the waking state the efforts at mastery involve motor activity and communication, two elements lacking under the conditions of sleep. . . .

The dream regarded by Freud as primitive is so in a very limited sense only. Whenever human beings are influenced by factors which they can neither know nor control, the efforts at mastery are limited to the projected use of fantasy. Human beings, while dreaming, are in such a situation in a total way; while awake, less so. Never is there complete freedom from such influence. In fact, there can only be freedom in the recognition and understanding of such influence.

The dream, then, can be regarded as one of the many roads toward an understanding of consciousness. Granted the conditions under which it operates, dream consciousness accurately reflects the reality of the individual in contrast with a waking consciousness which is often of limited value because of distortion, evasion, and myth. It is the limitation of our consciousness and not the disguise of our unconscious which accounts for the fact that dreams need to be interpreted in order to be understood.

Infantile Sexuality

Another of Freud's major theoretical contributions is the theory of infantile sexuality. This proposes that every child in his or her first five years lives a rich sexual life with drives, wishes, and conflicts of a genital nature which are comparable to adult sexuality. Freud contended that the memory of all this is repressed and forgotten by the young child, but in his adulthood his infantile memories can be recovered through psychoanalysis. Chodoff takes the view that the scientific validity of Freud's work on infantile sexuality and infantile amnesia has never been objectively assessed, and his own conclusion is that the validity of the Freudian theory thus far is still unproven.

Chodoff does not deny that the young infant engages in some sexual behavior of a genital nature. What he does take issue with is Freud's broadening of the term *sexuality* to also include many nongenital activities of the infant and then constructing a theory which maintains that all these activities have crucial sexual meaning and controlling influence on later personality development.

A Critique of Freud's Theory of Infantile Sexuality

Paul Chodoff, M.D.*

It is no longer news to most educated people that behavior occurs in childhood which is clearly sexual in the genital sense of the word. Too, there is no doubt about Freud's major role in bluntly bidding the world to use its eyes and pay attention to certain events which it had preferred to ignore during the then prevalent age of the "innocent child." Thus, in the strict sense, Freud's achievement was not a discovery but a disclosure, while what he discovered (or, in the minds of his opponents, invented) was the far more inclusive concept of infantile psychosexuality, of which infantile genital behavior is only one component, and which emphasizes the extremely broad range of childhood sexual activity, its nongenital elements, and the fantasies and other hidden mental activity accompanying it. It is these elaborations upon, and additions to, the incontestable facts of infantile and childhood genital behavior, not such behavior itself, which are in question, a point worth remembering when critics of Freud's position are themselves criticized as denying the very existence of any form of sexual life in infancy and childhood.

Infantile psychosexuality in the Freudian sense does not lend itself readily to a simple or clear-cut definition, since it includes a number of different observations, concepts, and constructs at varying levels of concreteness and abstraction. An essential feature of the Freudian theory is its broadening of the term *sexuality* to embrace the function of obtaining pleasure from the zones of the body rather than being limited to genital behavior alone. A second essential feature is the postulation of an

* *American Journal of Psychiatry*, Vol. 123, No. 5 (November 1966), pp. 508-517.

energic force, the libido, which progressively illuminates and activates the zonal areas, and which, through interaction with objects in the environment, is responsible for the child's sexual activities. However, the phenomena generated by this interaction of unfolding drive and phase-specific environment include not only observable behavior, but, more importantly, other activities which are to a much lesser degree, or not at all, accessible to ordinary observation, and which include a melange of fantasies, wishes, fears, fixations, identifications, etc., occurring in early life. Although subject to repression almost in statu nascendi, all of this churning mental activity of the first five years exerts a profound influence on later personality development and later psychopathology. . . .

To begin the examination of . . . evidence, a distinction worth considering can be made between sexuality of the preoedipal (oral and anal), and of the oedipal-phallic stages. Although these are all described as successive stages of libido concentration in the course of psychosexual development, yet the postulated mental activities of the phallic era, such as penis envy, fantasies about birth, the primal scene and castration, oedipal fantasies associated with masturbation, and sexual sibling rivalry, have a much more direct connection with sexuality in the ordinarily accepted sense of the term than do the oral and anal activities of the preceding stages.

That psychoanalysts find it necessary repeatedly to explain that by sexuality they mean the function of obtaining pleasure from the zones of the body, rather than genital stimulation leading toward orgasm, is testimony to the confusion this concept has engendered. Psychoanalysis has always had to assume the burden of proof in establishing a real rather than simply a semantic connection between sexuality in the special sense in which it is applied to the oral and anal activities of babies, and sexuality in the genital-reproductive sense in which it is generally understood. Experimental attempts to establish this connection have had equivocal results, but it is worth mentioning at this point that Freud's linking of thumb-sucking and masturbation has been called into question by Peter Wolff who, as a result of direct observation of infants, challenges the interpretation of stereotyped rhythmic activities in infancy as "autoerotic," maintaining that they bear only a superficial relation to later masturbation.

Freud and Freudian theorists in their efforts to establish a relationship between sexuality on the one hand and oral and anal activities on the other have laid great stress on the fact that adults engage in behavior which is clearly sexual involving oral and anal areas, either in the perversions or in normal foreplay. There is no doubt that such behavior in an adult is sexual, but it seems something of a logical discontinuity to assume that a man or woman who feels sexual pleasure in fellatio or intercourse per anum is regressing to a stage in which his pleasurable sensations are analogous to an infant's sucking on his mother's breast or expelling a stool. The oral and anal mucous membranes are capable of being stimulated pleasurably by a number of different stimuli and in many different settings, and the "presumption that all contacts with, or stimulation of, the end organs of the infant have either a protosexual or completely sexual meaning" has been criticized as an overgeneralization. Furthermore, Rado has demonstrated that the same data may be ordered equally plausibly if one postulates a superordinate pleasure organization with contributions from genital, alimentary, tactile, etc., systems rather than considering all pleasure functions as sexual. . . .

The occurrence of penile erections in male infants and children has always, so far as I know, been accepted unequivocally as a manifestation of sexual behavior. However, the recent confirmation by Fisher and associates of a very high correlation between REM sleep and penile erection suggests another possible interpretation of at least some of the erections occurring in infants and children. It is now well established that REM, or dreaming sleep, is associated with a metabolic state which differs materially from the metabolic state of either wakefulness or nondreaming sleep, and which is manifested by alteration of a number of body functions. Thus, the occurrence of penile erection during REM sleep may represent simply another of the nonspecific expressions of this altered metabolic state. It may have no more specific sexual significance than, say, the hypotonia which also occurs in connection with REM sleep.

Since REM sleep is present during a considerably higher percentage of the sleeping time of infants and children than of adults, and since, of course, infants and children sleep more than adults, the interesting speculation arises that at least some of the erections observed in infants and children, even up to as late as puberty, may not be a manifestation of a primary sexual drive or may not be a primarily sexual phenomenon at all. If confirmed, this finding would require revision of current ideas about infantile sexuality based on the observation of penile erections and associated activities.

There is good reason to hope that the increasingly precise and sophisticated experiments of the neurophysiologists will soon add a stabilizing ingredient to much psychological theorizing about sexuality in general. Already MacLean has demonstrated that stimulation of the amygdala of the squirrel monkey, a region involved in oral mechanisms, produces chewing and salivation, with partial erection occurring after many seconds of stimulation, presumably as a result of spillover of the stimulation to the septal area which is concerned with genital function. This close neural relationship between areas responsible for oral and sexual behavior may be thought of as providing physiological support for the Freudian concept of oral sexuality, although it is also possible to explain this relationship in terms of Rado's hypothesis that the oral and sexual centers in the brain are closely connected because they both subsume pleasure while they are nevertheless motivationally distinct. . . .

Let us now turn from the nonanalytic evidence to the method of testing the theories of infantile sexuality which, unlike experimental methods, has Freud's imprimatur: the study of the data derived from the psychoanalytic treatment of patients. Here one is confronted with a voluminous mass of more or less detailed case reports and theoretical articles with case illustrations. It is primarily on this corpus of clinical material that psychoanalysts base their confident assertions about the secure position of the theories of infantile sexuality. No observer can fail to be impressed by the sheer bulk of this evidence and by the consistency of its conclusions, all confirmatory, with minor changes and extensions, of the formulations Freud made many years ago. But, in spite of the undoubted brilliance of some of these case reports and papers, and the intuitive flashes which hit one with a shock of recognition, certain doubts and reservations are not entirely dispelled.

. . . psychoanalysis operates within a closed system, so that it is impossible to avoid the possibility (which is, in fact, supported by certain evidence) that the analyst's preconceptions are influencing what his patient produces, and are thus providing a "proof" of psychoanalytic theory which is essentially a form of petitio principii.

The dangers inherent in this absence of an extra-analytically produced baseline against which to measure psychoanalytic findings I take to be the gravamen of the important statement made by Rapaport that "the extensive clinical evidence, which would seem conclusive in terms of the system's internal consistency, fails to be conclusive in terms of the usual criteria of science, because there is no established canon for the interpretation of clinical observation."

In the absence of such a "canon of interpretation," the case material on which the doctrine of infantile psychosexuality is based can be only heuristically rather than veridically convincing, except in those rare cases in which some external evidence can corroborate an event which has been reconstructed through psychoanalysis.

From the standpoint of their power to persuade and convince the reader, there is a great deal of variation in the quality of the case reports in the psychoanalytic literature concerning or utilizing genetic reconstructions in the field of infantile sexuality. Even though all case reports are subject to the criticism that there has been selection of the material to be presented, some of these reports supply ample samplings of what the patient said. They keep as close as possible to this data and make in-

terpretive conclusions which appear reasonable and appropriate
on the basis of the observations made.

Other case studies, however, do not share these virtues. They
simply reiterate largely preformed conclusions on the basis of
observational data, either insufficient for conviction or requiring
a kind of "leap of faith" to arrive at the conclusions reached.
These case reports convey a strong impression that the analyst
already "knows," and has safely pigeonholed the meanings of
his patient's productions, even before they are made. To quote
Hartman, Kris, and Loewenstein:

> In many instances . . . it is extremely difficult to dis-
> tinguish at which point theory ceases and observation be-
> gins. The extreme in one direction can be found in those
> case histories in which "theory" is reported as observation.
> This circumstance arises when the assumption from which
> the clinician starts is so firmly rooted in his mind that
> minimal and finally no observation of clues suggested to
> him what he expected to find from the very beginning.

The psychoanalytic literature contains repeated assertions
that the theories of infantile psychosexuality were worked out
primarily through the analysis of adult neurotics, and only later
were said to be confirmed by direct observation of children and
infants. Whether material derived from individuals whose psychopathology is sufficiently severe to bring them to the analyst's
couch can and should serve as a basis for theories applied universally to all individuals, sick or healthy, affords room for doubt.
However, assuming that this objection is not a serious one, or
that it has been overcome by the very widespread variety of
reasons for which people have subjected themselves to analysis
in recent years, it is clear that the psychoanalytic answer to the
question of how this feat was accomplished would be through
the overcoming of the infantile amnesia, the lifting of the veils
of repression which have barred adult individuals from conscious access to the feelings and fantasies of their infancies and
childhoods.

At first, it was stated definitely and unequivocally by Freud that the object of a well-conducted analysis was to overcome the infantile amnesia so that the individual being analyzed could recover the lost memories of this early and crucial stage of his life, and that therapeutic effect depended on such a recovery. But the belief that adequate analysis meant the recovery of childhood memories, and that therapeutic efficacy depended on such a recovery, did not survive the accumulated experience of psychoanalysts, including Freud, as the method grew in popularity and as more and more people undertook analysis.

It is interesting to follow, in Freud's writings, how his changing attitude reflects an increasing caution about the possibility of recovering infantile memories, so that in 1938, in modest contrast to his previous assertions, Freud says:

> Quite often we do not succeed in bringing the patient to recollect what has been repressed. Instead of that, if the analysis is carried out correctly, we produce in him an assured conviction of the truth of the construction which achieves the same therapeutic result as a recaptured memory.

In effect, what has happened by 1938 is the end of the era in psychoanalysis when the recovery of infantile memories was the therapeutic goal, an era which survives only in Hollywood movies and in the disappointed expectations of patients entering analysis even today. However, the method of reconstruction, the "this is what must have happened to you" approach, appears to have undergone rather significant modification since Freud made the statements quoted above. The belief in its importance is not today maintained by all psychoanalysts with the unshakable conviction expressed in Kurt Eissler's pronouncement that, "In whatever way psychoanalytic technique may have changed since, the reconstruction of the first quinquennium remains the fountainhead of analysis." This is not the position of Ernst Kris, or of Ekstein and Rangell, whose papers indicate the limitations and qualifications as well as the value of re-constructive methods.

It appears that this gradual retreat from confidence in the analyst's ability to find out "what really happened" in his patient's infancy and childhood should raise questions about the reliability of theories of infantile sexuality which were worked out in the analysis of adult neurotics through methods which have now been questioned. For, if we can no longer regularly recover memories of their infancy and childhood from patients in analysis, and if we can no longer be so certain about our ability to reconstruct the past of these patients, why should these tasks have been easier or more effectively carried out in the earlier, more unsophisticated days of psychoanalysis? One explanation of this inconsistency is that in the early days Freud and his first disciples were still insufficiently aware of the ubiquitous power of the transference, and of the tendency of patients in the rather authoritarian setting of the early analyses to please their analysts by providing them with the kind of material which the latter seemed to want to hear.

The preceding discussion of the validity of genetic interpretations concerning infantile psychosexuality has not as yet questioned the actual regular occurrence of the infantile amnesia. The psychoanalytic theory of the infantile amnesia makes several assumptions: that physiologically, the ability of the child, aged two to five, to remember is as adequate as at any other time during his life; that forgetting is independent of any direct relationship to time since the repressed memory traces suffer no changes even over the longest periods; that "all impressions are retained in the same form as they were received . . . every former state of the memory content could be thus restored even though all original relations have long been replaced by newer ones"; that the massive repression occurring at age five to six with the resolution of the Oedipus complex constitutes a countercathexis barring direct activation of these memory traces into consciousness. Thus, the concept of the infantile amnesia is an integral component of the theory of infantile sexuality, since its presence accounts for the unavaila-

bility of childhood memories without psychoanalytic dere-
pression.

The evidence for its regular occurrence stems entirely from
the findings of psychoanalytic treatment, and thus is subject
to the same disabilities discussed previously in connection with
other items of theory which depend entirely for their proof on
psychoanalytic methods and techniques. There is no question
about the scantiness of the memories available to adults deriving from the early period of life covered by the presumed infantile amnesia. However, this phenomenon is susceptible to
other explanations besides that offered by psychoanalysis. It
may be that in the case of childhood memory, we are dealing
simply with an as yet immature function in the exercise of
which the growing child gradually develops increasing skill as
he does with many other functions dependent on the level of
central nervous system maturation. If this is so, one would
expect studies of the remembering abilities of children to show
a gradual and smooth increase with advancing age, and, in
fact, this is what is found in such studies as those of David
Wechsler and Woodworth. Analyses of memory in terms of
information theory by George Miller emphasize the intimate
relationship between memory and both the ability to reason and
the previous store of information. Thus a child, whose reasoning
powers are not yet developed and who has little background of
information to form a mosaic against which to pin and fix new
items, will not be able to remember as well as the adult who is
better able to reason and who is in possession of much more information as an available background.

Aristotle's statement that "only those animals which perceive
time remember" reminds us that the world of infancy and childhood, that "blooming, buzzing confusion," is infinitely less time-
bound and time-structured than is that of adults. And it is not
only in regard to time that children structure the world differently than grownups. Both Kurt Goldstein and, more recently, Ernest Schachtel have criticized the psychoanalytic concept of a specific infantile amnesia due to repression on the
grounds of the gulf which exists between children and adults

in their categories of experiencing and conceptualizing, so that the adult is unable to remember how he felt and how the world appeared to him as a child because his present ways of cataloguing experiences are so different. An important element in this difference is the existence of verbal methods for tying down and delimiting experience in the adult, and their absence or incomplete development in the preverbal and early verbal child.

A discussion of the psychoanalytic evidence for the theories of infantile psychosexuality should include at least some mention of the special contribution to the subject deriving from the psychoanalysis of children. Certain advantages come immediately to mind which make this area one of great hopefulness as far as theory validation is concerned. Young children are actually within or at least certainly very much closer chronologically to the period of purported infantile sexual behavior, so that their activities and fantasy life should be more readily available for analytic uncovering. Parents or parental figures and siblings, whose relationships with the child form much of the material of analysis, are present and accessible for the checking of data acquired from the child. Although counter-cathectic barriers presumably would be less firmly entrenched at this early stage of their development and thus more easily breached, on the other hand the rigidity and uncompromising nature of the archaic superego of the child may be a negative counterbalancing force.

Other practical and theoretical difficulties also limit the value of child psychoanalysis for the purpose of confirmation of theories. Clearly, communication with young children for the purpose of consensual validation is more difficult than with many adults. There are two overlapping reasons for this. First, the child's incomplete mastery of language, and his idiosyncratic use of it, require that verbal communciation be supplemented to a very considerable degree by play therapy, which must be translated back into verbal terms before it can be utilized for interpretation by the therapist. Second, as has already been pointed out, the fact that the categories of experience of small children are quite different from those of adults interposes another barrier to adult understanding of childhood productions.

It is not a simple matter to judge whether and to what extent the adult therapist unconsciously influences the responses of his child patient. Here it is not so much a matter of the child's falling easy prey to the adult's conscious or unconscious suggestions. Many children, especially among those in therapy, are relatively unsusceptible to direct adult influence; in fact, much less so than many of the psychoanalytically "hip" adult patients one sees today who are so eager to accept the analyst's symbolic interpretive suggestions. Rather, the communicative difficulties between child and adult make it more difficult even than with adult patients for the therapist to know whether the child is, in fact, really accepting his interpretations in a meaningful way. As an example, a reading of Melanie Klein's *Narrative of a Child Analysis* does not remove doubts that she has avoided this danger.

As a further possible illustration of the difficulty in knowing whether the child and analyst are operating on the same wave length, one could wonder why "Little Hans" * had absolutely no recollection of his infantile phobia or of his analytic treatment when he visited Freud more than ten years later. Rather than looking for reasons why the amnesia had been reimposed after having been dissolved, one might wonder whether the analytic experience was simply not very comprehensible to the child.

A perusal of some analytic case histories of children leaves the impression that the behavior of the child, verbal and otherwise, provides a very thin and precarious underpinning for the heavy weight of complicated theoretical inferences it often must support and suggests that there may be simpler and less ornate behavior in relationship to his parents and analyst. Thus, as an example, the inhibiting effects of having a child in analysis on the limit-setting role of parents, especially on the kind who choose psychoanalytic treatment for their emotionally

* See Chapter 4 for a brief description of the case of "Little Hans."

disturbed offspring, may also be playing a role in producing the fantasies of omnipotence in the child patient reported by Berta Bornstein which were interpreted as a reaction formation against intense passive sexual desires.

For most psychoanalysts, the validity of the main conclusions reached by Sigmund Freud about the nature, meaning, significance, and effect of what he regarded as the sexual life of infants and children has become obvious, not requiring further substantial proof or support. However, the evidence here reviewed does not justify such a degree of certainty and it appears that Freud's theories of infantile psychosexuality deserve at most the Scotch verdict: not proven. It is suggested that these theories were arrived at by Freud and presented by him in a world which was emotionally polarized into dogmatic opponents and excited adherents, a climate of opinion which made calm assessment of these important matters difficult, and which resulted in a premature closing out of investigation and discovery. . . .

I submit that the psychoanalytic contention that the theories of infantile psychosexuality were accurately deduced from the analyses of adult neurotics and later confirmed by direct observation of children can not be accepted at face value and that unanswered questions remain which are sufficiently serious to justify a fresh look at infantile and childhood sexuality and its psychic concomitants. An example of such an approach is the thesis of Frieda Fromm-Reichman that the entire Freudian psychosexual sequence is not a regularly occurring and normal development but constitutes, rather, a pathologic formation symptomatic of serious disturbances and hypersexualization of intrafamily relationships.

Oedipus Complex

Freud considered the Oedipus complex to be the central complex of the neuroses in general and his greatest discovery. He named it after the legendary king of Thebes whose tragedy was dramatized by Sophocles in "Oedipus Rex." Freud claimed that the young male child universally directs his first sexual impulses toward his mother, and his first impulses of hatred and violence toward his father. To the extent that he does not withdraw his sexual impulses from his mother and overcome his jealousy of his father, he will develop neurotic problems later in life. Freud maintained that the Oedipus legend had its source in dreams of mother-son incest dating back to the beginning of man: the appeal of Sophocles' play to us is that we identify with Oedipus' incestuous relationship to his mother, since falling in love with the opposite parent is a basic psychic impulse in everyone's early childhood. Freud therefore chose Oedipus to symbolize the wish that every young male child inevitably comes to have. He saw the story of "Oedipus Rex" as primarily sexual, the fulfillment of every adult's primitive childhood wish, now repressed. The sexual attraction of the young girl to her father was called the Electra complex.

In the next article, Frances Atkins examines the myth and the play about Oedipus and finds not the slightest hint of a sexual attraction of the son toward the mother as a motivating force. She concludes that, if the story of Oedipus is studied for its social meaning, the real crime of Oedipus turns out to be not his unwitting incest, but his persistence in acting for his own personal satisfaction in defiance of the rules of society. Her paper represents a highly original and carefully thought out alternative to Freud's interpretation of the Oedipus myth.

The Social Meaning of the Oedipus Myth

Frances Atkins *

The Oedipus complex, which Freud considered to be his greatest discovery, is an outstanding example of the way in which our thoughts were imprisoned by his boldly imaginative terminology. Because he saw the parent-child relationship as a sexual one, he titled it after the incestuous marriage of Oedipus and Jocasta in the Sophocles play, "Oedipus Rex," and he con-

* *Journal of Individual Psychology,* Vol. 22, No. 2 (November 1966), pp. 173-184.

sidered the statement in the play, that such a marriage was or-
dained for Oedipus at birth, to be symbolic of the biological
origin and universal occurrence of an incestuous urge. With
the wide acceptance of Freudian theory, the phrase "Oedipal
situation" has, in broad professional circles, become the lan-
guage-term for the entire relationship between parents and their
children.

Adler, Jung, Horney, Sullivan, Fromm, and others who have
quarreled with Freud's interpretation in this area, have, for
the most part, agreed on the crucial importance of early family
relationships in the formation of personality. But they have
vigorously denied the concept that there is a universal, biologically determined, *sexual* attachment between child and parent.
In spite of their dissent, it is only quite recently that social
scientists in general have begun to free their minds from the
boundaries of Freudian phraseology, and to be able to view
human behavior from fresh vantage points. Many of them are
abandoning the term "Oedipal situation" because of its implicit incestuous content, and are inclined to consider the
emotional tie between parent and child to be a function of
family-group dynamics, rather than a predetermined, immut-
able process.

Adler was probably the first critic of this presentation of
Freud's. In his experience, sexual desires of a child toward a
parent were rare, and he attributed any too-strong attachment
to overindulgence by either parent. If a boy wants his father
to go away, Adler said, it is because he does not want to share
his mother's attentions, and not because he has an unconscious
desire to kill his father. Adler explained any serious rivalry between the child and the father as a neurotic form of the life
process of striving to grow from weakness and inferiority to
strength and superiority.

While the word "Oedipus" immediately evokes thoughts of
mother-son incest, there is evidence that incest was not the main
theme of the Oedipus story, and that its symbolic meaning may
have been quite different from the one attributed to it by Freud.
I propose here to examine the play and the myth from which

it was derived, in a search for the true key to Oedipus' inexorable journey on the road to disaster.

In the play as we know it, Oedipus tells the story of his life in flashback style. He had been brought up, he says, as the son of Polybus and Meripe, king and queen of Corinth, but when he was 18 years old, a drunken man taunted him with the statement that he was not their son. Greatly disturbed, Oedipus questioned his parents, who, to spare his feelings, gave him an evasive reply. Dissatisfied, he consulted the oracle at Delphi, where he did not get a direct answer to his question, but was warned that he was fated to kill his father and marry his mother. His horror at this prophecy caused him to leave his parents' home, and to set out to seek his fortune elsewhere.

On the road to Thebes, he met an older man with his party, who arrogantly ordered Oedipus out of the way. A violent quarrel followed, in which Oedipus killed the man and all of his party except one, who escaped.

When Oedipus arrived in Thebes, he found the city terrorized by the Sphinx, a monster with a woman's face; the breast, feet and tail of a lion; and wings of a bird. The Sphinx carried off young men and women and strangled them when they could not solve her riddle. Oedipus freed Thebes of the Sphinx by solving the riddle and was rewarded with the throne and the widowed Queen Jocasta for his wife.

He ruled peacefully and benevolently for 16 years and had four children. Then a severe blight struck the city and Oedipus was instructed by the oracle to investigate the death of the previous king, Laius.

His investigation, carried on against the advice of Apollo's prophet Teiresias, and later of Jocasta, revealed that Laius was the man he had killed 16 years before; and that Laius and Jocasta were his true parents. Jocasta then committed suicide, and Oedipus blinded himself and left Thebes.

Traditionally, myths are considered to have a symbolic significance that goes beyond the manifest story content, and every myth has been interpreted in many different ways. Adler once commented on the multiple meanings of the Oedipus story, referring to the fact that Socrates had used it in an effort to abolish the cruel custom of abandoning crippled children, and to instill a respect for human life.

Freud adopted the Oedipus story as a frame of reference for his theory regarding the son's sexual desire for the mother. But Erich Fromm points out that the Sophocles version contains no indication that Oedipus is sexually attracted to Jocasta; she merely "goes with the throne." In Fromm's opinion, the Oedipus myth is not a symbol of an incestuous tie between mother and son, or of sexual rivalry with the father, but of competition between father and son for power and authority. The marriage with Jocasta, he believes, is one of the symbols of the son's victory, as he takes over the father's place with all its privileges. Fromm asks us to consider the whole Sophocles trilogy, not only "Oedipus Rex." While in "Oedipus Rex" the father-son conflict is symbolized by the killing of Laius, in "Oedipus at Colonus" the struggle for power is between Oedipus and his two sons; and in "Antigone," it is between Creon, Jocasta's brother, and his son Haemon. There is no reference to incestuous desires between Oedipus' sons and their mother, or between Haemon and his mother. Of all the many older versions of the Oedipus myth, according to Fromm, there is only one in which Oedipus marries his mother.

From a broad view of Greek mythology, it would appear that the Oedipus story is only an incident taken from the larger myth of the Curse of the House of Cadmus, and in some versions of this myth, Oedipus is not even mentioned. This story, which might be considered a parallel to that of Adam and Eve, begins with the first marriage on earth, between Cadmus and Harmonia. At a great wedding ceremony, attended by all the gods, Cadmus was made the founder of the city of Thebes.

A daughter, Semele, born of this marriage, was later loved by Zeus and by him became the mother of the god Dionysos. Hera, wife of Zeus and goddess of marriage and married love, enraged by Zeus' infidelity, cursed the House of Cadmus and vowed that it would eventually destroy itself. The lives of Cadmus and

Harmonia were then beset by an endless succession of evils, as were those of their two succeeding generations.

Then we come to Laius, the father of Oedipus. Euripides refers to him as the originator of homosexual eroticism, and the story goes that he fell in love with a handsome boy named Chrysippos and kidnapped him. The boy's father, Pelops, put a curse on Laius which stated that Laius must never beget a son, for if he did, that son would kill him. Pelops' curse was confirmed by Apollo, protector of boys and youth, and by Hera, angered at Laius' blasphemy of the marriage bed in replacing his wife with a boy. Hera, indeed, sent the Sphinx to terrorize the Thebans because they tolerated their king's passion for Chrysippos.

One night, under the influence of wine and lust, Laius did conceive a child with Jocasta. When a son was born, Laius consulted the oracle and was informed that Pelops' curse was still in effect, that the child was indeed fated to be his father's slayer.

The Sophocles play relates that Laius then ordered Jocasta to put a spike through the infant's ankles, tie his feet together and leave him to die on a mountainside. But he was saved by a kindly shepherd and taken to Corinth, where the childless king and queen accepted him and brought him up as their own son.

The other two plays of the Sophocles trilogy, as mentioned above, relate the struggles over the throne of Thebes. Finally, in Aeschylus' tragedy, "The Seven Against Thebes," the city of Thebes is destroyed and the Curse of the House of Cadmus is completed.

It appears, then, that Freud derived the inspiration for the labeling of the Oedipus complex from one version of a small segment of a Greek myth, taken out of context, and dramatized by Sophocles as part of a series of events. Obviously, if we are to understand what Sophocles tried to tell us through the character of Oedipus, the play must be examined against the whole background of Greek thought.

Aristotle considered Greek drama to be a means of catharsis for the people, and in "The Poetics," "Oedipus Rex" was used as a model to illustrate the ideal tragedy for this important purpose. Oedipus was presented as the better-than-ordinary good man, the innocent victim of fate, and his useless struggle against overwhelmingly powerful forces evoked intense emotions of fear and pity in the audience.

However, we should recognize that by the time that Aristotle (384-322 B.C.), Socrates, and Plato had become influential, Greek drama had become separated from religion, of which it had been an integral part. Men no longer accepted the old polytheistic faith, whose myths and legends had become merely a source of ideas for the imaginative creations of poets.

But in the Athens of Sophocles' day (496-406 B.C.), a theatrical performance was a religious ritual. Aeschylus and Sophocles were orthodox theologians, and the purpose of their plays was to portray the power and influence of the Greek gods over every facet of human life and behavior, "to show a moral principle upheld by divine power."

In order to serve this moral purpose, certain conventions were followed. In every Greek tragedy, the hero must contain the tragic flaw, or guilt (comparable, perhaps, to the Christian concept of "original sin"), called *hamartia*. He struggles against his fate, but because of his guilt, he is doomed to die. Each play is a dramatized aspect of ". . . the old myth of man's effort to circumvent the divine will . . .", which must forever end in tragedy.

For us, as in Aristotle's day, the emotional power of "Oedipus Rex" lies in the acceptance of the popular interpretation that Oedipus is the *innocent* victim of powerful forces beyond his control. But, as both Reinert and Vellacott have noted, such an interpretation is morally ambiguous. "Oedipus has committed the worst imaginable of human crimes: he has killed his father and slept with his mother. But since he is obviously innocent of evil intent, can the god be called just who exacts such suffering for crimes thus committed?" "What is the moral and religious value of this play?" asks Vellacott. "If Oedipus sinned in innocence, if the gods deliberately contrived parricide and incest, is there any meaning in goodness?"

If we accept the common interpretation, we would have to believe that the Greek religion was based on gross injustice and irrational fear, and that the great principle of "the justice of the gods and the heroism of man" was a lie. If it was not a lie, then Oedipus must have been guilty; but if so, what was he guilty of?

Reinert suggests that the tragic flaw, *hamartia,* of Oedipus was *hubris,* translated as "overconfidence," or "arrogance," and inquires, "Is his crime, then, not the parricide and the incest, but his attempts to outwit the god?", and Vellacott, a classicist, in his analysis of the play uncovers some discrepancies which imply that this was indeed Sophocles' intent.

For example, there is the scene in which Oedipus tells Jocasta of the events that drove him from Corinth. He was so frightened, he says, of the oracle's "shameful prophecy," that he left Corinth in order to prevent its fulfillment. Vellacott is skeptical that Oedipus, whom Sophocles had invested with unusual intelligence and reasoning ability, could at this point have completely forgotten the question about his parentage. On the contrary, it would be this very question that made the prophecy so frightening. He must have known that to leave Corinth was no precaution, since there was no telling where he might encounter his real parents.

"What thoughts would Sophocles imagine to be in Oedipus' mind as he left Delphi?" Vellacott asks, and concludes that the overriding question would be, "How can I avoid killing my father and marrying my mother?" The only possible answer would be "two unbreakable rules: 'I will never kill a man much older than myself; I will never marry a woman much older than myself'."

When, only a few hours after leaving Delphi, Oedipus breaks the first of these rules, he is already guilty, in Vellacott's judgment. He must now relate his every action to the prophecy: the choice of behavior is his own, he can no longer claim to be "the innocent victim of malevolent powers."

Another discrepancy revealed by Vellacott is that 16 years after his accession to the throne, Oedipus learns for the *first time* that the man he killed was Laius, the king of Thebes.

Vellacott believes that when Oedipus entered Thebes, he could not have avoided hearing about the king's death, and could not fail to connect it with the incident in which he himself had killed an apparently important Theban traveler. Yet, he immediately seeks out the Sphinx, solves the Riddle of Man with his superior intellect, and takes as reward the throne of Thebes and a wife who is old enough to be his mother.

There are many more seeming discrepancies in "Oedipus Rex," but these are enough to indicate that Sophocles did not mean to portray Oedipus as being led blindly along his path of self-destruction, innocent and powerless against a malevolent force. And yet, nowhere in the play or in any version of the myth is there the slightest hint of a sexual attraction of the son toward the mother as a motivating force. As we look elsewhere for an explanation of the guilt and punishment of Oedipus, I think we will find that it was indeed *hubris,* a supreme arrogance, which caused him to bring disaster upon himself.

Adler's concept of the superiority complex seems to be the key to this ancient puzzle. The individual with a superiority complex is characterized by such qualities, among others, as ". . . disdain, . . . arrogance, . . . boastfulness, a tyrannical nature, . . . [and] heightened affects like anger [and] desire for revenge. . . ." The superiority complex is one expression of lack of social interest, social interest meaning to relate to other humans in a generally useful, cooperative way. To act contrary to social interest is to be antisocial. Social interest was Adler's criterion for mental health.

Adler stated that the superiority complex is rooted in increased hidden feelings of inferiority:

> A superiority complex is a second phase. It is a compensation for the inferiority (feeling) complex. . . . Behind everyone who behaves as if he were superior to others, we can suspect a feeling of inferiority which calls for very special efforts of concealment. It is as if a man feared that he was too small and walked on his toes to make himself seem taller.

Sophocles makes it quite clear that his tragic hero suffered from deep inferiority feelings. The name Oedipus means "swollen-footed," and Oedipus' bitter, life-long awareness of his crippled feet is shown in the scene with the shepherd-messenger who had rescued him as an infant:

Oedipus: What ailed me when you took me in your arms?
Messenger: In that your ankles should be witnesses.
Oedipus: Why do you speak of that old pain?
Messenger: I loosed you; the tendons of your feet were pierced and fettered,—
Oedipus: My swaddling clothes brought me a rare disgrace.

Oedipus' consideration that such treatment is a "rare disgrace" rather than cruelty, leads Vellacott to surmise that "the scars of pierced feet would be known as the mark of a foundling child. . . ." This possibility is strengthened by Aristotle's indication in "The Politics" that exposure of infants had once been a common method of birth control, but that the practice had since been forbidden by custom, except for infants who were deformed.

Sofie Lazarsfeld, in her analysis of Oedipus' personality, describes some further indications of Oedipus' inferiority feelings. These feelings, she says, "produce neurotic symptoms: a malbalanced mind, extreme sensitiveness of prestige, reactions out of proportion to even small incidents, the tendency to fly into violent rages, lack of capacity 'to take it,' to give in, the tendency for revenge, and . . . an extreme will for power, for supremacy. . . ." To illustrate these symptoms, Lazarsfeld cites Oedipus' encounter with Laius at the crossroads, where, for the comparatively trivial insult of being pushed off the road and struck with a staff, Oedipus flew into such a towering rage that he killed five men in revenge.

"That power means a great deal to Oedipus," Lazarsfeld continues, "is clearly seen when Teresias accuses him to be Laius' murderer. Oedipus quickly concludes that Teresias is hired to rob him of his power with his accusation—ready to assume just those motives which he nursed within himself." Even his high intelligence is seen by Lazarsfeld as a "significant symptom of non-neurotic, productive compensation. Training himself to become wiser than others, Oedipus develops his wits to such an extent that he alone of all people is able to solve the riddle of the Sphinx."

It is now becoming apparent that Oedipus' *hubris* consisted of an irresistible drive for power, and Fromm's suggestion that this is the theme of the Oedipus story is supported—though not restricted—to a father-son conflict, as Fromm believed. The very title of the play is significant: "Oedipus Rex," which translates to "The Swollen-Footed King," or ruler. Adler referred to the power-striving individual as "the ruling type," which

> . . . has . . . not enough social interest. Therefore, if confronted strongly by a situation which he feels to be . . . a test of his social value, a judgment upon his social usefulness, a person of this type acts in an unsocial way. The more active of this type attack others directly. They become delinquents, tyrants, sadists. It is as if they said, with Richard III, "And therefore, since I cannot prove a lover . . . I am determined to prove a villain."

Fromm has noted that in Greek tragedy it is the powerful and strong who are suddenly struck by disaster, and Reinert warns us that "In the Prologue, we feel he is too much the 'I, Oedipus, who bears the famous name' not to come to a tragic end."

Now I am going to paraphrase Vellacott, and with the foregoing evidence in mind, try to imagine what thoughts and feelings Sophocles would have given to Oedipus as he traveled on the road to Thebes.

The feeling of deep shame about his crippled feet which Oedipus had carried all his life would have made especially poignant the taunt that he was not the son of the only parents he had known. Deeply hurt by his parents' deception, and filled with rage and doubt, he consults the oracle, only to be confounded by the enigmatic reply that he would kill his father and marry his mother. It would be safe to assume that in his highly emotional state, Oedipus' vaunted reasoning powers were not operating at full capacity. His deep resentment might cause him to distort the message, to prevent him from suspecting that it could be a reference to his real parents rather than his foster parents. He rushes away from Corinth, sick with shame, anger and confusion, determined to strike out into the world and prove his superiority, despite his clouded origin.

His first encounter, on the road to Thebes, is with an older man who rudely orders him off the road so that he and his party can pass. Oedipus is oversensitive, quick to anger. How dare this stranger try to push *him* around! The old man strikes him, and in his fury and youthful strength, Oedipus sets about him and ends up with the man and four of his servants lying dead in the road.

The popular interpretation is that the killing of the man who turned out to be his father was the first step in the fulfillment of the prophecy: in Freudian terms, a symbol of the biologically determined urge toward parricide. But he had been warned by the oracle. Was not this the first sign of *hamartia,* the tragic flaw? Was it not *hubris,* his arrogance, which made him ignore the warning of the gods?

Now he is not the cool, rational young man whom Vellacott sees entering the city of Thebes. Inevitably, Oedipus hears about the murder of King Laius. He is frightened; he hides the fact that he, himself, might be the murderer, although it might not yet occur to him that the killing was related to the prophecy. But the news of the depredations of the Sphinx would excite him. Here was his first chance to display his superiority, to prove that he was "somebody."

He volunteers to pit his clever mind against the monster, and, amid a great public hubbub over the brave young stranger, he goes out to confront the Sphinx. To her famous riddle, "What creature walks on four feet in the morning, two feet at noon, and three feet at night?" he answers, "Man." He has demonstrated his extraordinary intelligence and clarity of insight. Oedipus, the foundling child, has saved the city of Thebes. He is acclaimed as a hero and offered the highest reward the city could give: the throne and its widowed queen for a wife.

Can we believe that our clever young riddle-solver would not hark back, at this point, to his own riddle, the meaning of the prophecy about his fate? He has killed a man old enough to be his father, and now he is being offered in marriage a woman who could have been that man's wife. The memory of the oracle's words must be deeply disturbing to him but he refuses to think about it, he wipes it from his mind. He, the swollen-footed child, rejected by unknown parents, has been "offered a city, a home, and a throne: [is] that shout of 'Bastard' to rob him of all three?" Is he to refuse them because of the doubtful validity of a garbled message from an unknown source? No, he is within reach of his goal of power and dominance and he will not let the remote possibility of incest prevent him from taking his just prize. As Mullahy synthesizes Adler's position: "The neurotic person uses sex, like everything else, as a means toward the one all-inclusive end."

We need no longer find it puzzling that when Jocasta tells Oedipus that her newborn son had had his feet pierced and had been left to die, Oedipus apparently does not think of his own scarred feet. Obviously, it is because he does not *want* to think of them. When Teiresias tells him repeatedly that he, Oedipus, killed Laius; that he is not the son of Polybus; that he killed his father and is married to his mother, we can understand why Oedipus does not seem to hear Teiresias' words. He retaliates with angry and unjust attacks on Teiresias and Creon, incongruous with his benevolent and exalted role of king and saviour of Thebes, but which we can now recognize as defensive reactions against unbearable threats to his self-image. Even on the precipice of his tragic doom, he is driven by what Adler called the "predestination complex," the conviction that ". . . he can accomplish the most unusual achievements, that nothing can happen to him, that he will prevail somehow." He boasts of his superiority and continues his arrogant disregard of the warnings of Jocasta and Teiresias not to uncover the past:

> Break out what will! I at least shall be
> Willing to see my ancestry, though humble.
> Perhaps she is ashamed of my low birth,
> For she has all a woman's high-flown pride.
> But I account myself a child of Fortune . . .
> And I shall not be dishonoured . . .
> . . . Such is my breeding,
> And I shall never prove false to it,
> As not to find the secret of my birth.

After this examination of the mythological background of the Sophocles drama, as well as the play itself, it seems unlikely that it could have been intended as a symbol of fatally inevitable incestuous desires. As Lazarsfeld showed us, Freud, in his narrow concentration on the sexual relationship, blinded himself to the complexity of the Oedipus character, which Sophocles had so painstakingly and purposefully created. What, then, was Sophocles' purpose in portraying this intricate and tragic personality?

The importance to us of the ancient Greeks lies in the great questions they raised and tried to answer. "What is Man?" they inquired. "What is his relationship to the cosmos? To other men? To himself?" Even the riddle of the Sphinx was a phrasing of this question. Writes Fromm, "He who knows that the most important answer . . . to the most difficult question . . . is *man himself,* can save mankind."

The religion of the Greeks, as expressed in their mythology, was a structure of rules by which men would be able to live together. Their gods were personifications of human attributes in idealized form; the "will of the gods" was the system of rules which forbade socially destructive acts; the wrathful punishment, *nemesis,* was the social chaos which resulted from breaking these rules.

Here is what Adler wrote about religion:

> We recognize religion as an expression of (the) coercion
> toward communal life, although not yet in a form under-

stood as such. In religion, the sanctification of social forms takes the place of insight into their true significance and serves as a bond between members of the community. If the conditions of life are determined in the first instance by cosmic influences, they are in the second instance determined socially. They are determined by the fact that men live together and by the rules and regularities which spontaneously arise in consequence of this. The demands of society have regulated human relations which had already existed from the beginning as self-understood, as an absolute truth.

We understand now that all the rules of the game—such as education, superstition, totem and tabu, and law—which were necessary to secure the existence of the human race, had first of all to do justice to the idea of a community.

If we look back at the myth of the Curse of the House of Cadmus, we will see that the *hubris* for which each generation was punished consisted of a lack of social interest; each arrogantly persisted in committing acts for his own personal satisfaction, without regard to the damage which might result to the community. The marriage of Cadmus and Harmonia symbolized the beginning of the patriarchal family, the basic unit of Greek society, while the city of Thebes represented the whole of that society. Incest is only one of the indiscriminate sexual acts of which man is biologically capable when his social interest, his responsibility to society, has not been developed. Adultery, homosexuality (especially the corruption of children), parricide and incest are all destructive of family life; but the striving for power is the most destructive of all, because, by ruthlessly using any and all antisocial behavior, it destroys society itself. The moral and religious message we have been seeking in "Oedipus Rex" is clearly not that man is endowed with an ontological drive toward incest, but that arrogant and persistent defiance of the will of the gods—the rules of society—can only end in tragedy.

That Oedipus' blind pursuit of power was his crime, and the parricide and incest, with their social consequences, his punishment, is evident at the end of the play, after he has put out his eyes. He recognizes that, by his antisocial conduct, he has destroyed not only himself, but those he held most dear:

> Now I am godless and child of impurity . . .
> Madness and stabbing pain and memory of evil deeds
> I have done!
> What can I see to love?
> What greeting can touch my ears with joy?

In summary, we find Oedipus, as portrayed by Sophocles, to be a power-striving individual with a superiority complex, who goes to the most extreme lengths to prove his superiority, despite solemn warnings from Heaven itself. The handicap and shame of his swollen feet, his unknown origin, and abandonment at birth were conducive to intensified inferiority feelings which became the basis for his power striving. In his supreme defiance, he performed the most abominable acts, violated the blackest taboos known to the ancient Greeks, and thus brought upon himself the most awful nemesis.

REFERENCES

1. C. Knight Aldrich, *An Introduction to Dynamic Psychiatry* (New York: McGraw-Hill, 1966), pp. 30-31.
2. Leonard Cammer, "Conditioning and Psychiatric Theory," *American Journal of Orthopsychiatry*, Vol. 31, No. 4 (October 1961), pp. 810-819.
3. ———. "Conditioning, Learning and Psychopathology," *Conditional Reflex*, Vol. 2, No. 4 (October-December, 1967), pp. 294-301.
4. Harold Werner, *A Rational Approach to Social Casework* (New York: Association Press, 1965), pp. 117-118.

8

Practical Applications of
Our New Understandings

In referring to practical applications of our new understandings, we mean the transformation of theoretical ideas about the nature of man and his mental functioning into techniques of counseling or treating people who seek help for emotional distress. A professional's particular theories about human behavior strongly influence his treatment approach: theory guides his actions and molds his style. New concepts concerning behavior must inevitably result in new ways of treatment. Bear in mind we are concerned here only with functional psychotherapy of personal problems which are not based on organic injury or defect in the brain or nervous system.

The readings in this volume all converge toward the concept that man's emotions and behavior are consequences of his perceptions of reality or of his entrenched habits. He can push out of immediate awareness, or forget, unpleasant or unimportant material, but this material exerts no control over him while out of awareness. He does have conflicts, but he knows what they are.

Our new understandings of human behavior suggest that Freud's formulations about mental mechanisms were too narrow and need to be broadened. In essence, where Freud insisted that

261

displacement or sublimation, for example, took place unconsciously and always concerned either sexuality or aggression, the newer thinking can see these mechanisms as consciously recognizable and concerned with many different aspects of personality, of which sexuality and aggression are only two. While Freud viewed problematic behavior as stemming from internal conflict unrelated to the individual's immediate real-life situation, the newer thinking emphasizes the "embeddedness" of the person in his society.

Most current theories about the nature of man and his mental functioning fall into one of three categories. These approaches to the understanding of human behavior are as follows:

1. *Freudian* or *Psychoanalytic:* The principal sources of emotions and behavior are in the unconscious.

2. *Phenomenological* or *Cognitive:* The principal sources of emotions and behavior are in consciousness, in the way a person perceives himself and the external world.

3. *Behavioral:* The principal sources of emotions and behavior are stimulus-response pathways established in the nervous system by experience, training and/or repetition.

Since the purpose of this book is to illuminate non-Freudian theory and practice, this chapter will focus on the treatment techniques which logically flow out of cognitive and behavioral theory. Most of the ideas presented in the foregoing chapters are aspects of the cognitive approach; the remainder are based on learning, conditioning and behavior theory. We shall proceed now to formulate a brief summary of each of the books discussed and each of the articles presented in chapters 1, 2, 3, and 4. Each summarizing paragraph will be followed by a very brief discussion of the treatment technique which the theoretical concept implies.

Cognitive Theory (Books)

Alfred Adler

In his writing, Adler sees man as best understood in terms of his life goals, under whose influence the individual develops a style of living, modifies biological drives, and strives for a sense of completion.

The function of treatment is not to make a person aware of his drives, but to help him acquire a constructive goal in life. Adler says we should probe the person's past to piece together his style of living and discover his goals. We should note things which have made him feel inferior in the past, as goals are often formulated to compensate for past feelings of inferiority. When a person tries to overcome imagined or actual inferiority by personal success on the destructive side of life, he runs into obstacles, resistances, and pressures from society which cause him to suffer. All such failures are due to insufficient "social interest." The work of the professional is to redirect the client or patient to a constructive goal of his own choosing which will give him a sense of success and yet be on the useful side of life, compatible with his society.

Van Kaam

Van Kaam, representing the existential view of man, which is one of the phenomenological approaches, indicates that emotional well-being is related to the degree of readiness which an individual has developed to be open to whatever he finds in himself or in his environment.

The treatment techniques that proceed naturally out of the existential view of man stress that counseling should be an authentic human encounter. The worker should be totally present to the client, fully with him, and a participant in his personal existence. Counseling can only become authentic when the client freely participates in the process, doing nothing except out of his own choice, never to imitate or please another. The existential counselor fosters in the client an openness to all the important aspects of his existence. He helps the client to become aware of how he lives his daily life, of the implications of such living, and of what he really is. The counselor should accept all aspects of the client's existence; to praise or show interest in one aspect may encourage him to concentrate on this at the expense of not being open to other aspects. Scientific and psychological explanations which may obscure real meanings are avoided, since each person is regarded as unique and best understood in his own terms. The ultimate aim of existential psychotherapy is to enable the client to uncover what he really is and commit himself to fulfilling his potential. In the process, the client is helped to acquire the freedom to let others see that he is not perfect.

Pervin [1] has commented that the technique of existential psychotherapy has not been defined very specifically. He states: "The belief is that a flexible approach is necessary to understand the person-in-his-world. Technique is varied from patient to patient and from one phase of treatment to another: 'What will best reveal the existence of this particular patient at this moment in history?' "

Smalley

Smalley reaffirms the Rankian viewpoint: an innate push toward growth is primary in human beings; individuals reveal in their present functioning their entire past reaction patterns; the most important part of a person is his consciousness, of which a significant component is the will. People continually must choose between dependence on others and independence, between accepting limits and challenging limits.

In its practical application, Rankian theory implies a way of working with people in which the center for change is seen to exist not in the worker but in the client. The worker's task is *not* to decide in what way the client should change and then help him move in that direction. On the contrary, the worker's technique should consist of engaging in the kind of relationship which releases the client's own power for choice and growth. Rankians impose limits on their clients by actions such as fixing a time for ending the helping process, setting up rules for children's play interviews, and strictly confining the service given to the stated functions of the organization for which they work. They hope these restrictions will challenge the client to exert his will against them. They believe that, in the struggle against limits, the client will experience what it means to challenge and to accept the will of others, and will find for himself a proper combination of the two.

Anita J. Faatz [2] insists on the importance of the helper's capacity to work with pure psychological movement and emotion almost without content. This means that the emphasis should be on the fear and guilt generated by the limits imposed by the worker and agency; these "pure" emotions within the interview are considered to be the crucial ones with which to deal. Emotions arising out of daily life situations are considered of secondary importance; what Faatz calls the "will-impulse-feeling interaction" between worker and client is regarded as the essence of an authentic helping situation.

In social work, Rankian theory is applied mostly to casework which takes place in agencies that offer concrete services, such as financial help or child placement. The basic aim is to help a person use a social service or program, both in his own and in society's interest.

Ellis

Albert Ellis believes that emotions and behavior stem from the sentences we say to ourselves when we reflect upon our daily experiences. Inappropriate emotions and behavior result from inaccurate perceptions of reality, from blaming ourselves too severely for the human faults we have, and from excessive expectations or resentments of the external world.

Ellis calls his treatment technique rational-emotive psychotherapy. It consists of a direct attack on the false notions which the patient has picked up from his parents and his culture. Ellis pounds away time and again at the illogical ideas which underlie the person's fears, encouraging and at times commanding him to partake of some kind of activity which itself will disprove the nonsense he believes. The objective of Ellis' treatment is to get the patient to internalize a rational philosophy of living, just as he originally learned and internalized illogical propaganda and superstitions. Ellis insists that people must not only gain insight into what nonsense they are telling themselves, but must also act in counter-propagandizing ways. Therefore, he frequently gives them actual homework assignments, such as dating a girl whom the patient is afraid to ask for a date, looking for a job, or experimentally returning to live with a husband with whom one has previously quarreled continuously.

Glasser

William Glasser believes that people's basic needs are to give and receive love, and to behave so as to feel worthwhile to themselves and others. Those who do not fulfill these needs are, in Glasser's special definition, irresponsible, and may develop a degree of emotional distress which causes them to seek professional help.

In carrying out his own particular treatment technique, which he refers to as "reality therapy," Glasser is not interested in the patient's past history or why he developed his current behavior pattern. He feels these have no relevance toward helping him to change his conduct. The patient's recital of his past failures reinforces his sense of weakness and degrades him before the therapist. The reality therapist confronts the patient with reality, forces the patient to judge his own behavior as good or bad, and then educates the patient to behave better and take responsibility for fulfilling the aforementioned basic needs.

Glasser contends that behavior is much more important than feelings. Emphasis should be on what the patient is currently doing and what are his future plans. Emphasis should *not* be on his attitudes or feelings. Change in attitudes and feelings comes with change in behavior, not from a discussion of the feelings themselves. If the therapist concentrates on his patient's feelings, he gives the patient a chance to excuse his behavior by claiming he is emotionally upset or has had a hard life. Patients know that a therapist—or parent—cares about them when he insists

on a high standard of behavior and does not drop his demand
for responsibility on their part, no matter what their excuse.

Glasser has applied his reality therapy to the hospital treatment of chronic psychotic patients, forcing them to accept responsibility for work and self-care if they want privileges they
previously got automatically. He reports marked success at a
neuropsychiatric hospital in California.

Werner

The editor, in his previous book, has offered a "rational approach" which includes the following concepts: man can be
understood without assuming the existence of an "unconscious";
human problems are the result of either inaccurate thinking or
the inability—because of conditioning—to behave in a way consistent with a realistic perception; emotions and motives are
exclusively conscious phenomena; neurosis and anxiety reflect
problems of living rather than unconscious conflict.

Flowing out of these concepts is a counseling technique in
which I ask my client to pinpoint his problems and goals. Then
I work with him to accomplish the changes he chooses. I show
him when his behavior defeats his own stated purposes. I
try to help him reach the point where he can see things as they
really are and act on the basis of his correct understanding.
The focus is on the present and on what the client himself can
do to overcome his difficulties. When he is a prisoner of strongly
entrenched thinking or behavior which is inappropriate, I teach
him to weaken the old patterns by disuse and replace them with
new patterns which he must reinforce by practice. I encourage
him to put into words what he has been saying to himself about
crucial matters, and his unrealistic ideas are directly challenged.
I never assume my client's problem is entirely emotional; it
may have a physiological aspect that needs to be checked out
medically. Since I insist that the client himself determine the
goals of treatment, I feel justified in pointing out to him what
type of action will help him to reach these goals. I do not make
decisions for clients, but feel obligated to see that they have all
the information they need to reach a realistic conclusion.

Termination of counseling is encouraged, as soon as my client can handle the presenting problem on his own, with the understanding that he can always return should this or other problems arise in the future. When counselor and client successfully work together on problems of living, personality reorganization is likely to occur, although that was not the focus. I try to develop a warm, accepting relationship with the client so that he will be willing to struggle toward change. However, I do not allow him to become dependent on this relationship or encourage an intense attachment on his part.

Most people have untapped strength and courage which they should be helped to discover and use in confronting what they fear. There is an obligation for the professional to relieve the client's anxiety and tension as soon as possible, for humanitarian reasons and to improve his functioning in school or work, home and community. This can be often done by helping the client to assert himself in situations where he previously felt helpless. I do not spend much time on tracing the origin of currently distorted thought, emotion or behavior; I emphasize the client's taking action to alter them. I use what the client himself tells me of his accomplishments to foster a sense of worth, and try to suggest specific experiences which will alter his distorted thinking about himself and others. Finally, my client is held responsible for his acts in school, home and community, regardless of what other factors are contributory.

Support for this kind of "rational approach" has recently begun to appear in social work literature. Gottlieb and Stanley [3] affirm that "the value and success of social casework treatment is dependent upon the establishment of mutually acceptable goals between the caseworker and the client and that such goals determine the focus of the treatment." Hallowitz, Bierman, Harrison, and Stulberg [4] encourage the use of an "assertive counseling component" in therapy. This includes confronting the client with differences between his behavior and his goals and between his perception and reality. As another aspect of the "assertive counseling component," they state: "When necessary, the therapist straightforwardly expresses his understanding of the problem as he begins to see it, and he proposes the direction and the steps that he thinks are necessary to change the client's maladaptive functioning."

Cognitive Theory (Articles)

Ichheiser

In his article on Freud's "blind spots", Ichheiser makes the point that Freud, in his preoccupation with establishing the unconscious as the basis of mental life, always assumed that human irrationality has its roots mainly in the area of the unconscious; Ichheiser maintains that there are such factors as genuine false perception and genuine error of judgment which often arise out of peculiarities and defects in our conscious intellectual operations.

The implication of Ichheiser's position for treatment is that we should not assume all distortions of social perception are due to the operation of unconscious mechanisms. Furthermore, instead of probing an individual's past for clues to such unconscious mechanisms, it is equally valid to consider his intelligence, cultural background, upbringing, and social situation as possible distorting influences that need to be taken into account in the process of re-educating him to an accurate awareness of reality.

Papageorgis

In his paper concerning repression of painful material into the unconscious, Papageorgis attempts to reformulate this Freudian concept in terms of consciousness. He sees the distortion of experiences and their meaning, or the failure to recall childhood experiences, as a result of the following: unavailability of verbal labels, doubt about which verbal label applies, the failure of events to register their full impact or meaning at the time of occurrence, incomplete cognitive development in childhood, low intelligence, lack of education, limitations in available information, cultural patterns of reasoning, or intentional self-deception.

In concluding with the contention that the "psychopathology of everyday life" (memory blocks, slips of the tongue and pen, etc.) can be accounted for physiologically, Papageorgis completes the presentation of a viewpoint which, he says, grants support to treatment methods such as Adler's Individual Psychology, Wolpe's behavior therapy, or Ellis' rational-emotive therapy. All these treatment methods are discussed elsewhere in this chapter.

Robbins

In his critique of the concept of repression, Robbins concentrates on what he calls the myth of latent emotion. He denies that, when an individual exhibits inappropriate emotion, this is because the appropriate emotion has been repressed into the unconscious; he claims instead that inappropriate emotion is the result of inaccurate perception.

For Robbins, emotions are consistent with our perceptions; if an emotion appears irrational, it is because our evaluation of ourselves, others, or the external world is distorted. Therefore, treatment of an individual with inappropriate emotional responses (and consequently inappropriate behavior) consists of changing his consciousness so that it comes to reflect reality accurately. This approach is the essence of all treatment methods which are based on cognitive or phenomenological theory.

Salzman

In his paper on the paranoid state, Salzman considers its primary origin to be in a person's extremely poor self-image, whose source can be either sexual or non-sexual. The individual tries to overcome his anxiety-generating feeling of worthlessness by grandiose behavior which antagonizes the environment, and when other people rebuff him, he erects a delusional system to account for the rejection in terms that he can tolerate.

In the therapy of paranoid states, Salzman believes it is essential to instill some doubt about the delusional structure. (In paranoid schizophrenia, first there must be sufficient resolution of the schizophrenic process before the therapist can tackle the paranoid distortions rationally.) The paranoid's view of the world is questioned and he is helped to consider alternate explanations of his perceptions. Salzman states that it is extremely difficult to work with paranoid individuals; their defenses are tenacious because they are covering up enormous feelings of worthlessness. If, through trust in the therapist, the patient can begin to let go of some of his delusions, the way is open to investigate with him why he needed to develop them in the first place. However, great care must be taken not to activate the feelings of shame and humiliation which underlie the paranoid state. Concommitantly, the therapist should steer the patient into everyday tasks which will result in real achievements and a sense of success in order to combat his previous low self-esteem. It is Salzman's conclusion that in therapy delusional states which are misinterpretations of conscious experiences must be dealt with in conscious, rational terms.

We also summarized briefly, without reproducing any of the text, an article by Salzman that deals with obsessive-compulsive reactions. He believes these develop out of excessive feelings of insecurity that require absolute guarantees before action is pursued. In treating obsessive-compulsive disorders, Salzman urges a here-and-now approach which includes the following:

1. Discover and elucidate the basis for the excessive feelings of insecurity.
2. Demonstrate by repeated interpretation and encouragement to action that absolute guarantees against error are not necessary and in fact interfere with living.
3. Enhance the patient's sense of security and assist him to take risks and try new adventures.
4. Help the patient to reach the point where he can acknowledge that anxiety is universal and omnipresent and cannot be permanently eliminated from life, which means he must abandon his attempts at perfection and superman performance and accept the limitations of his humanness.

LaBarba

In his paper on the psychopath (sociopath), LaBarba considers the psychoanalytic theory which maintains that this type of individual has a developmental defect of the superego that renders him incapable of feeling any anxiety. LaBarba disagrees and suggests that, while the psychopath feels no guilt or anxiety about his ruthless and selfish antisocial acts, this is only because success in carrying out asocial behavior is his defense against the anxiety he does feel about his poor self-image.

Treatment is based on the premise that the psychopath's tremendous sense of inferiority arises from his inability to find success in cooperative living. In order to rebuild and preserve his self-esteem, he rules out all socially oriented behavior and turns to sociopathic acts as an overcompensatory defense. The more such acts enhance his feelings of self-worth and superiority, the less overt anxiety he will exhibit about them. LaBarba recommends a therapeutic approach that will evoke anxiety in the individual; when this happens, more traditional treatment methods can then be utilized. Group therapy is the treatment of choice, since the group members can contribute to the interpretation of his behavior and, with their help, the therapist can expose his behavior patterns and provoke anxiety with the implication that they will not be successful in the future.

Markowitz

Markowitz makes the point that emotional difficulties of adolescents are directly related to certain characteristics of the society in which they live. Their distrust of society is not surprising in view of the fact that the hypocrisy of so many adults justifies this distrust. Society only grudgingly tolerates adolescents and pressures them to grow as rapidly as possible, so that they often seek acceptance as adults through the short-cut of shallow adult-pleasing achievements of questionable value. Societal attitudes encourage self-effacement, conformity and opportunism as the most effective way to make good; at the same time, society does little to find a place for the adolescents who want to participate in the many opportunities for living more fully.

If we wish to decrease the emotional problems of our adolescents, Markowitz recommends that we concentrate on remedying the social injustices which heighten their sense of futility and cynicism. Parents have been relinquishing to society's organizations the role of guiding the growth of teenagers, and should become re-involved with them. Through closer relationships with their adolescents, and by a willingness to be self-critical, parents may be able to convince them that diligence and honesty can bring rewards, and that one does not have to trick or defeat society in order to survive.

Gordon, Singer and Gordon

These investigators postulate that the emotional disorders of people are related to socio-economic conditions in their communities and to the total number of background stresses they have experienced in their lives: death of a parent; parental separation; severe personal physical illness; previous personal emotional disturbance; family history of alcoholism or mental illness; personal failure to complete their educations; and lack of sources of security such as spouse, children, work abilities, outside interests, family ties or adequate parental guidance.

Treatment should consist of pharmacotherapy and psychotherapy. The patients—studied by Singer and the Gordons—who responded best to treatment were those with the most modifiable social environments. Improvability of the environment, with consequent decrease in total numbers of stresses seemed to be the important factor. Also significant were constitutional endowment, ability to tolerate hardships, and capacity to learn from experience. The authors believe that the quantitative overloading of stress which they studied might have parallels in neuroendocrine processes.

The therapist can help to reduce crucial stresses by recommending: regular medical and psychiatric checkups for preventive purposes; continuation of education; remaining at one's job even when upset; long engagements for teenagers instead of quick marriages; immediate training in job skills with a future for individuals in declining industries; cultivation of hobbies and community interests, so that self-respect does not entirely depend on job success; caution about assuming too many new responsibilities or making too many changes in one's life situation; avoidance of getting into financial debt in order to live beyond one's means; and less overprotection combined with more toughening of children to prepare them for the rigors of life.

Improving the environment would also seem to imply community or social action to establish or expand agencies which can provide the recommended periodic medical and psychiatric checkups, educational opportunities, job training, recreation, leisure-time community involvement, and family life seminars for parents. In this connection, it is of interest to note a recent annual conference of Psychiatric Outpatient Centers of America (POCA). This is a national organization of psychiatric clinics whose annual meeting in 1967 considered the theme of serving low-income populations. An article in the organization's journal, entitled "Social Action is a Form of Treatment," [5] reports: "Speaker after speaker made the point that so-called psychological problems are often internalizations of social problems such as poverty, discrimination, slum housing, second-rate education, neglect by society, limited job opportunities, absence of medical and social services, and a feeling of hopelessness. Therefore, what is called for in such cases is cooperative action on the part of clinic staff with the patients to organize the entire community for a frontal assault on these destructive conditions." One of the speakers, Dr. Mamie Phipps Clark, declared that, for many low-income families, mental health *is* the alleviation of psychosocial stress through mutual community action.

Occupational Stresses

The unsigned article on this subject discusses work situations that may precipitate emotional disorders. Essentially, such situations are those which confront the employee with changes or pressures which undermine his self-esteem or security or evoke fears of discharge or demotion. In regard to business executives, they, too, can suffer emotional distress from feelings of inadequacy, frustration, and summit loneliness.

The point is made that it is not always advisable to give an overly anxious and depressed employee a few days off to help him "snap out of it." Many people depend on their job for a feeling of belonging and accomplishment. Telling an employee he cannot work for a while may make him feel he must be sick, increase his sense of unworthiness and helplessness, and aggravate his upset.

We may wonder what is being done now about emotional disorders precipitated by work situations, which the article claims is "industry's top medical problem." Apparently, not very much. In this country, there is just a small number of psychiatrists and psychologists, hired by a few business corporations, who counsel emotionally disturbed employees where they work. These professionals sometimes recommend job changes within the company that will benefit both the worker and the employer. In some cases, they recommend changes in the work setup or plant administration that will reduce stress. In other instances, the employee is referred to a private therapist or mental health center in the community. For most working people, however, occupational stresses are a problem they have to solve for themselves by discussing it with the boss on their own initiative, seeking other employment, obtaining counseling in the community, or bringing the matter up with their union representative for advice or action.

Even the limited amount of in-house counseling of employees within a company has had a shaky course, because management people often feel their authority is undermined when a professional recommends a change in job, procedure, or relationships between boss and subordinate. Dr. Donald G. Livingston, a social psychologist working in industry, believes that business corporations are concerned about the matter and will soon begin to deal with occupational strain on a large scale. However, for reasons of economics and competence, industry will not focus on the individual worker, but on improving the social environment of the total plant. In a personal communication with the editor, Livingston predicts that industry in general will soon begin to make extensive use of organizational consultants for the following purposes:

1. To help management and supervisory personnel understand the concept of industry as a sub-culture.
2. To sensitize management and supervisory personnel to the possible motivational consequences of the work situations in their plants.
3. To teach the importance of interpersonal relationships of employees for the efficiency, quality, and success of the business enterprise.
4. To help the company examine those characteristics of its operations which create conflict or strain for the employee.
5. To help the company establish the conditions for positive motivation of the total employee group.
6. To assist in the development of an adult, democratic, and cooperative society in the industrial setting, examining both the structure and processes of management as contributors—or obstacles—to attaining these desiderata.

Livingston himself takes the position that difficulties on the job should be interpreted very infrequently on the medical model as an illness; they should be viewed primarily as a learning and motivational problem.

Recent accounts of mental health services in the Soviet Union inform us that occupational stresses can be handled differently in that country. Their medical program, free to everyone, is government-operated. According to Aronson and Field,[6] the keystone of the Soviet psychiatric arch is the psychoneurological clinic, a comprehensive mental health center geared to keeping the patient within the community and gainfully employed whenever possible. One of the clinic's functions is to provide assistance to the patient in his working conditions. It does this by arranging or changing job placements in terms of the patient's mental health needs. Clinic personnel are expected to know the occupational resources of the territory they serve. Job placements, considered medical prescriptions, are not too difficult to accomplish because of a manpower shortage and the fact that all economic organizations are owned and operated by the state.

Leifer

In his article on phobias, Leifer offers an alternative to the psychoanalytic theory that their function is to change an *internal* danger into an external one, that is, to provide an external symbol for repressed inner drives of a sexual or aggressive nature. Leifer agrees that man has the ability to symbolize by employing one stimulus to represent another, but contends that the phobic person uses avoidable external objects to represent unavoidable *external* threats.

The three basic threats to human existence are physical harm, disapproval by society, and loss of control over the environment. If an individual can avoid phobic objects which represent these threats, he achieves a sense of mastery over the dangers of life, even though the phobias themselves may disrupt a satisfactory way of living. The implication for therapy seems to be that, in the long run, the reduction of disabling phobias (or the necessity for them in the first place) will depend on social engineering, on the improvement of society so that basic threats to existence are greatly decreased. In a portion of his article not reproduced in this volume, Leifer acknowledges that behavior therapy (to be discussed later in this chapter) can reduce human suffering by deconditioning phobic responses. However, he sees behavior therapy as manipulating people on an animal level of response and calls for an additional therapeutic goal: educating every person to understand the cultural meanings attached to things in his society. What Leifer appears to be suggesting is that such understanding will enable an individual to handle conflicts with society directly, as well as the threat of losing control of his environment. Presumably, he would no longer need to create phobic objects to represent these threats.

Beck

Beck's thesis is that, during depression, a person's interpretations of his experiences become increasingly dominated by concepts of personal deficiency, self-blame, and negative expectations; this maintains the typical depressive feelings of sadness, guilt, anxiety, agitation, loneliness and pessimism, and leads to the distortion of thought processes involved in attaining self-objectivity and accurate perceptions of reality.

This formulation of a cognitive-affective model of depression, when applied in the psychotherapy of neurotic depressive reactions, calls for discussing with the patient his distortions of reality and illogical conclusions. Since Beck's thesis is that the affective response is determined by the way an individual structures his experience, his method of reducing depression involves careful examination of the patient's entire cognitive system: the nature of his observations and logical operations, his constellations of premises and assumptions. The therapist then corrects the underlying misconceptions, biased assumptions, and faulty reasoning of the patient. He trains the patient to apply the rules of evidence and logic to his cognitions so that his judgments will be more objective.

Kurt Adler

In this paper Kurt Adler utilizes his father's theory of personality to explain depression as a safeguarding device, adopted by individuals who feel incapable of achieving superiority or success by clashing with reality. Such a person depreciates himself and is full of self-blame but simultaneously forces his family to pity him, wait on him, make him the center of attention, and relieve him of any obligation to go out and face life. Feeling extremely inferior, he compensates by frustrating all efforts to help him and thus achieves a sense of superiority. He proves he is really ill by neglecting his health and outward appearance and presenting a pitiable condition which certifies his sickness. Finally, if he has not acquired sufficient control over a person close to him, he may threaten or attempt suicide to secure compliance, or he may actually kill himself to get "revenge."

The final section of this paper (not reproduced) deals with therapy. Kurt Adler's psychotherapeutic approach to the depressed patient includes the following:

1. Help in acquiring a more realistic and less frightening view of society.
2. Making no demands on the patient, but indicating that the therapist is powerless without the patient's help.
3. Convincing him that his pessimism serves the purpose of avoiding responsibilities and a cooperative way of living, which he regards as threats.
4. Interpreting guilt feelings as a cheap device for putting an undeserved halo upon one's head.
5. Uncovering the patient's underlying rage against certain people in his environment as proof that the motives for his actions are not noble.
6. Stressing that suicide is a vengeful device, filled with rage, about which nobody will feel guilty.
7. Acceptance of the patient, despite his shabby devices, and giving him hope that he can become a social human being, in order to eliminate his fear of being humiliated if he cooperates.

Salzman

In his second article, Salzman takes the view that masochistic behavior, although it tends to belittle or harm the self, may still be an attempt to solve certain personal and social problems. Rather than postulate a need to fail, a destructive instinct, or "unconscious guilt seeking for punishment," we should regard the masochist as someone who is trying to gain rewards through suffering because he has no hopes of fulfilling his goals in any other way.

Treatment is based upon the premise that the masochist's self-defeating behavior is personally adaptive, although culturally maladaptive. He feels powerless and worthless, cheated and abused, and attempts to obtain compensation for his claims by depending on his weakness and suffering to stimulate others to benevolent action. Therapy, according to Salzman, depends on recognizing the behavior not as a "search for punishment" but as an appeal by the masochist for recognition of his hopelessness. It seems logical for us to infer that the treatment process should consist of helping the individual to discover within himself the strength and courage to strive for his goals through direct action instead of through suffering.

Learning, Conditioning, and Behavior Theory

In Chapter 1, we referred to the book by Wolpe and Lazarus, entitled *Behavior Therapy Techniques: A Guide to the Treatment of Neuroses*. It is a basic premise of these authors that neuroses are persistent, inappropriate learned habits of reaction characterized by anxiety. Since phobias and other neuroses are conditioned responses which operate through reflex pathways established in the nervous system, they cannot be overcome by logical arguments; rather, they require counterconditioning techniques based on the concept that neurotic reactions are physiological phenomena.

Wolpe and Lazarus are behaviorists who regard most human reactions and conduct as learned habits. They believe that human functioning can be understood in terms of learning, conditioning and behavior theory, and they practice a form of treatment known as behavior therapy. The aim of behavior therapy is to change habits that are judged to be undesirable, whether these be neurotic anxiety-response habits such as phobias, or motor or thinking patterns of which anxiety is not a constituent.

Wolpe and Lazarus state that the elimination of anxiety-response habits seems to require the inhibition of anxiety by a competing response, by counterconditioning. For example, if an individual becomes anxious and cannot function effectively in the presence of certain persons, therapy consists of helping him to begin to respond to these people with acts of assertion instead of with blocking. (Assertion is a response which usually inhibits anxiety; others include deep muscle relaxation, eating and sexual arousal.) Each act of assertion inhibits the situational anxiety a little, slightly weakens the anxiety-response habit, reinforces the new assertive pattern, and is conducive to further acts of self-assertion. Thus change can begin and anxiety can gradually decrease. The principle involved is Wolpe's "reciprocal inhibition principle."

This principle is also applied in a systematic desensitization process by which individuals are helped to overcome severe phobias. Often in such cases, the response which the patient is taught for inhibiting anxiety is deep muscle relaxation, based on the work of Dr. Edmund Jacobson. When the patient has learned to completely relax all parts of his body at the start of each interview, he is presented with items of his anxiety hierarchy. This is a listing of several variations of his particular phobia. The patient starts with the least upsetting item, imagining a clear picture of it in his mind. When this image is called up at the direction of the therapist and after a few times no longer provokes anxiety, the therapist asks the patient to imagine the next most upsetting item in the hierarchy. At the start of subsequent interviews, the therapist and patient continue up the list at the point where they left off the previous time, until the most anxiety-provoking item no longer upsets the patient. Disappearance of phobias achieved in this way is claimed to be permanent by behaviorists, with no other phobias being substituted. What happens in systematic desensitization is that the phobia is broken down piecemeal while employing a physiological state (relaxation) which is incompatible with anxiety.

Sometimes the therapist shows the patient photographs of the phobic object or brings him into physical contact with it. At first, the content of the photograph or the closeness to the actual object is such as to evoke only a minimal amount of anxiety. However, based on the patient's own anxiety hierarchy, each succeeding photograph or confrontation is a little more anxiety-arousing than its predecessor. The treatment procedure is thus analogous to that followed when the patient is asked to *imagine* the items in his hierarchy.

An example of systematic desensitization *in vivo,* through actual confrontation, is reported by Garvey and Hegrenes.[7] They describe a ten-year-old boy who had an intense fear that he would lose his mother if he were separated from her. He developed a school phobia and refused to attend school. Over a period of twenty consecutive days, including Saturdays and Sundays, his therapist accompanied him to the school premises each morning. They began by just getting out of the car and approaching the curb. Later, they reached the sidewalk, then the school stairs, and then the school door. The final steps consisted of entering the school; then the classroom; being present in the classroom with the teacher; next, with the teacher and one or two classmates; finally, being present in the classroom with a full class. By the twentieth day, the therapist was able to withdraw from the situation, and a two-year follow-up indicated that the boy had remained in school ever since. As with a patient who is instructed to imagine phobic situations, the child was not asked to attempt the next step in his hierarchy until the one before no longer produced anxiety. He was praised each day for whatever he did accomplish. For this boy, the counterconditioning force which inhibited anxiety was the presence of the therapist whom he liked. The school cooperated fully in all the arrangements.

Another type of behavior therapy was originally propounded by B. F. Skinner and is known as "operant conditioning." This is used mainly for psychotic, autistic, delinquent, or retarded behaviors. While Wolpe's systematic desensitization procedure applies to already existing responses, Skinner's operant conditioning tries to create or shape behavior formerly absent from the individual's repertoire. This is done by rewarding desirable behavior and penalizing undesirable behavior.

In the classroom situation, operant conditioning goes on all the time, rewards taking the form of extra attention and approval by the teacher. The teacher's lack of interest or censure serve as penalties. Unknowingly, teachers often reward a child for lack of participation or timidity by giving the child much attention for his "problem" out of sympathy. They actually are reinforcing this pattern, when they might bring it to an end more quickly by penalizing it through lack of attention and giving the child strong approval when he struggles to rejoin the group.

The case of two day schools for emotionally disturbed children illustrates another aspect of operant conditioning. One school had trouble with its community relations: its children were encouraged to act out their negative feelings, and in so doing they upset the neighborhood. The other school utilized operant conditioning, rewarding self-control with wooden tokens which were exchangeable for various treats, and it had no problems with its neighbors.

Bachrach [8] describes a series of experiments involving operant conditioning which were conducted by Ayllon and Haughton in a hospital setting. They found that half of the schizophrenic patients on a hospital ward presented food problems. Spoonfeeding, tube-feeding, intravenous feeding and electroshock had been tried and had been unsuccessful in improving the situation. The problem was that they refused to eat. It was decided to try operant conditioning. All aids to feeding the patients were discontinued; they were left alone at mealtimes, and had to go into the dining room to eat. However, patients could not eat unless they appeared in the dining room within thirty minutes after a nurse called "Dinner!" The doors would then be locked and the patients would miss that particular meal. Successful establishment of self-feeding in the social dining room situation was achieved. The patients were next required to drop a penny into the slot of a collection can to gain entrance to the dining room, and pennies would only be given to those patients who congregated outside the dining room within five minutes from the time of meal call. All the schizophrenic patients learned the procedure for getting into the dining room and this new shaping was completely successful.

The experimenters concluded that the control of psychotic behavior largely depends on the use of strong reinforcers. They believe that the schizophrenic out of touch with reality can be controlled behaviorally when environmental conditions and manipulations are properly established. Difficult behavior among psychotic patients is not necessarily due to their underlying intellectual, perceptual, or sensory deficits, but may be the result of the hospital setup.

Behavior therapy has many other forms and can be applied to many other human problems. These are discussed in detail by Grossberg[9] in a very extensive review of behavior therapy literature. Among other conditioning procedures he mentions are:

1. Aversion therapy: Punishment in the form of a nauseant drug or electric shock is given every time an undesirable response is forthcoming, as the taking of a drink by an alcoholic.
2. Reinforcement withdrawal: Reinforcing stimuli are withdrawn following an undesirable response, such as attention to a child who throws a tantrum.
3. Negative practice: An undesirable response is purposely encouraged over and over by the therapist until it is extinguished by a reactive inhibition, e.g., stuttering, tics, compulsive handwashing.

For an explanation of the cerebral cortex and nervous system activity which these procedures set in motion, one must go to the conditioning theories developed by Pavlov and his present-day successors. A very general introduction to these theories was presented in Chapter 7.

Conclusion

As we have seen, the behaviorists base their understanding and treatment of human problems on the concept that behavior disorders are maladaptive habits, formed through a physiological process of conditioning, and capable of being extinguished through systematic techniques. The Freudian assumption that behavior disorders reflect unconscious conflicts, repressed drives, or underlying disease processes is discounted. There is no attempt to make the patient's unconscious conscious. There is no effort to help him develop insight, because his unpleasant reactions are regarded as emotional habits that he cannot help. For the behaviorist, there is no sickness; treatment is directed entirely to the symptom, i.e., the undesirable behavior.

Those who study man and the alleviation of his disturbances from the viewpoint of cognitive theory see inappropriate behavior as the result of inaccurate perceptions. For them, the therapeutic task is to help the individual arrive at a realistic understanding of himself, other people, and the external world. The Freudian hypothesis that man's behavior is controlled by unconscious forces of which he is unaware is replaced by an emphasis on man's consciousness. The belief is that, with the principal exception of phobias, man's behavior is usually based on what he thinks; the intensity of his acts depends on the strength of his will. The adherents of cognitive theory do help their patients to achieve insight, not into their unconscious but into the inaccuracies of their thinking.

Behavior theory and cognitive theory, while both non-Freudian, differ very much from each other. By offering us two alternatives to Freudian ideas, they greatly enlarge the arsenal of weapons available to counselors and therapists who seek to help people combat their personal suffering.

REFERENCES

1. Lawrence Pervin, "Existentialism, Psychology, and Psychotherapy," *The American Psychologist,* Vol. 15, No. 5 (May 1960), p. 307.
2. Anita Faatz, *The Nature of Choice in Casework Process* (Chapel Hill: University of North Carolina Press, 1953).
3. Werner Gottlieb and Joe Stanley, "Mutual Goals and Goal-Setting in Casework," *Social Casework,* Vol. 48, No. 8 (October 1967), p. 476.
4. David Hallowitz, Ralph Bierman, Grace Harrison and Burton Stulberg, "The Assertive Counseling Component of Therapy," *Social Casework,* Vol. 48, No. 9 (November 1967), p. 547.
5. "Social Action is a Form of Treatment," *Poca Press,* Vol. 5, No. 1, (Fall 1967), p. 4.

6. Jason Aronson and Mark Field, "Mental Health Programming in the Soviet Union," *American Journal of Orthopsychiatry*, Vol. 34, No. 5, (October 1964), pp. 913-924.
7. William Garvey and Jack Hegrenes, "Desensitization Techniques in the Treatment of School Phobia," *American Journal of Orthopsychiatry*, Vol. 36, No. 1 (January 1966), pp. 147-152.
8. Arthur Bachrach, "Some Applications of Operant Conditioning to Behavior Therapy," *The Conditioning Therapies: the Challenge in Psychotherapy* (New York: Holt, Rinehart and Winston, 1964), pp. 73-74.
9. John Grossberg, "Behavior Therapy: a Review," *Psychological Bulletin*, Vol. 62, No. 2 (August 1964), pp. 73-88.